Nothing would be more tiresome than eating and drinking if God had not made them a pleasure as well as a necessity.

—VOLTAIRE

illustrated by Serge Bloch

technical illustrations by Barbara Smullen

foreword by **Mario Batali**

Dad's
own
cook-
book by **Bob Sloan**

Workman Publishing, New York

Library of Congress Cataloguing-in-Publication Data is available.
ISBN-13: 978-0-7611-4214-0

Designed by Paul Hanson and Beverly McClain

Workman Books are available at special discounts when purchased
in bulk for premiums and sales promotions as well as for fund-raising
or educational use. Special editions or book excerpts also can be
created to specification. For details, contact the Special Sales
Director at the address below.

Workman Publishing Company, Inc.
225 Varick Street
New York, NY 10014-4381

Manufactured in the United States of America
First printing March 2007
10 9 8 7 6 5 4 3 2

Acknowledgments

Cooking is ephemeral. You eat dinner—it's gone. Ruth Sullivan, my editor at Workman Publishing, has played a big part in helping me create something that, hopefully, will last a long time. I am very grateful to her. Special thanks go to Paul Hanson who brought me into this project and has created a handsomely designed book. Karen Watts played a crucial role throughout this process, and our friendship is the first positive result of the book. Though it's been many years since I've worked with them, I still consider Mary Cleaver of the Cleaver Company and the late Fred Rothberg to be my first and best teachers. And Carmine Cincotta is still my first and only produce man. I have also learned a great deal about food and cooking from David Sanfield of the Pitfire Pizza Restaurants. From Mario Batali I have learned not just about food, but about larger, more ontological concerns, like how to keep from slicing my drives. And listening to Jim Harrison describe a great meal is as sublime an experience as having actually eaten it.

Now that my catering business has taken a backseat to writing about food, I have to keep my skills sharp by cooking for friends. It seems curious to be thanking them for coming to dinner, but I do.

Phil and Sally Sanfield have continued to be incredibly supportive of all my ventures, as have Alice Jarcho and Tommy Gallagher, Pat and Ron Nicholson, and Paul and Karen Izenberg.

My brother Larry didn't help much with this project, but I love and miss him a lot. My kids, Nate and Leo, have eaten almost a decade's worth of meals, many of them cooked from this book. They haven't complained, so I guess the recipes still work.

Above all, I thank my wife, Randi. None of this would have happened without her.

> *This book is dedicated to my wife, my kids, my mom, and especially, my dad, Big Irv.*

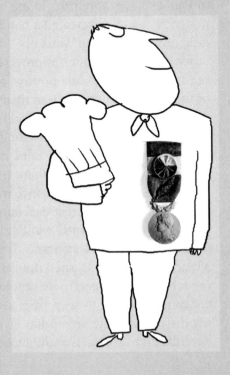

Contents

CONTENTS

CONTENTS

Two Fancy Dinners 143

Salads *159*

Pasta *177*

CONTENTS

Cooking for a Crowd *255*

How to Throw Your Own Cocktail Party *267*

CONTENTS

Foreword
by Mario Batali

Bob Sloan is the quintessential dad/chef and this dual expertise is what makes this both a fun and a practical cookbook. My family and I have had many meals at the Sloan home and Bob's cooking is seemingly effortless, fun, kid friendly, and most importantly, delicious. That kind of cavalier approach to food is reflected in these recipes. They work. They're easy to prepare. They have abundant flavor. My kids like them. So will yours.

Like his cooking, his approach in the book is straightforward. But the information, though casually presented, is comprehensive and will sneak a lot of worthwhile knowledge into an unsuspecting dad's head while he thought he was just making a school-night dinner.

He challenges you to make some things you never thought you could, leading you through the recipe like the best kind of cooking coach, leaving nothing to the imagination but never making you feel dumb for not knowing it in the first place. The book is organized in a way that both dads with no confidence or no experience in the kitchen as well as dads who can cook will appreciate and, more importantly, use. (If Ronald Reagan had read some of the vegetable recipes, ketchup would never have been considered

FOREWORD

one of the major food groups on the school lunch lines.) The primer information, cooking techniques, and useful charts of this book could easily stretch into another tome altogether as they are filled with tons of useful and relevant info. But what is most important is the simplicity and ease that Bob brings to all kitchen tasks—everything from cutting an onion (for the kitchen stooge) to making stocks from scratch ("for the truly committed"). He demystifies the kitchen and yet makes cooking intuitive to the novice. His spirit of camaraderie and cooking skills serve to augment his obvious joy in and love for everything about preparing food, something all dads (and moms) can really catch on to.

Bob is intensely aware of his kids at all times. He is also intensely aware of everybody else's kids. And if I go to someone's house and they offer special hospitality not only to me, but to my kids, they are anointed as heroes. Bob is such a hero. As my kids always say after dinner at the Sloan house: "That Bob is a good cooker!" Use this book enough, and you will become a good cooker, too.

Introduction

re you, or is someone you know, culinarily challenged? Do you, or does someone you know, lose the use of major muscle groups when it's time to cook? Do you have a fear of frying? Imagine this scenario—for a whole week your wife or girlfriend is away, too busy, or just doesn't want to cook. She says, "You deal with feeding the kids." She says, "You make dinner." So, all right. The first night you order in—you and the kids sit by the TV, eat pizza, and watch *Jeopardy*. The second night it's Chinese. Then, something hits you— you should be able to *cook* something. *Some*thing. You've certainly eaten enough. You've watched enough people cook. There must be *some* meal you could make, one dish you could serve for dinner besides tunafish salad or frozen entrées, something to keep your family from starving. But nothing comes to mind.

Sound familiar? Well, the reason you're stumped is that no one has ever taken the time to write a cookbook just for you. Other books intimidate you, or leave too much to your imagination. They figure you already *know* how to grease a pan,

INTRODUCTION

preheat an oven, separate an egg. This is where *Dad's Own Cookbook* comes in. It assumes that you know what you like to eat, but don't know how to make it. That you may have been brilliant at the operating table that morning, but are basically a dolt around the stove at dinnertime. *Dad's Own* leaves nothing to your imagination. Steps are explained. Its primers, timetables, and tips are all designed to keep you on track. I may treat you like an idiot, but I don't make you feel like one.

Many recipes here are familiar. They are the favorite foods of your childhood, so they're bound to be hits with your kids. Some are slightly adventurous. A few are daring. There are meals for every occasion—Friday night pizza, an elegant dinner for two, a Thanksgiving feast. I'll tell what cans to stock in your cupboard, the pots that should fill your shelves, the necessary ingredients to keep in your fridge. I'll clue you in to cooking techniques, shortcuts, kitchen tips that have been kept from you (deliberately, I might add) for too long. I'll teach you how to shop, read a label, buy the prime cuts, the freshest produce. I'll be your friend on the inside; the guy in the know; your uncle with a hot tip on the first race. I'll hold your hand while you stir the soup. And *what* soup! Dad's Own

Chicken Soup. Dad's Apple Pie. Dad's Meat Loaf! The kids will hope *you've* been busy in the kitchen when they come home from school.

This book will also wise you up to the latest health tips. While it's not necessarily a low-fat cookbook, I'm keen on helping Dad keep his cholesterol, salt, and fat intake in check. Options are given for low-fat variations, and salt, butter, and eggs are kept to a minimum throughout. There are even tips on how to get your kids to like vegetables.

Look, few of us want to rush into the kitchen after a hard day of work and start whipping up dinner. But more and more Dad is being called on to do his share of cooking. You've taken the right first step by starting with this book. Soon you'll be tearing up the kitchen, effortlessly throwing together simple, tasty, and healthful meals. And one night, when your kid has a friend over for dinner, after they've tasted the perfectly roasted chicken, savored the oven-roasted rosemary potatoes, crunched into steamed al dente green beans, the friend will say, "Hey, this is, like, really good." And your child will beam and respond, "Yeah, I know. My dad made it."

Getting Started

Cooking is like changing your spark plugs. At first it seems a job for the experts. Then someone hands you the proper tools, points you in the right direction under the hood, and you soon realize it's easy to change your own plugs.

Having the proper tools is crucial to success in the kitchen. This is not to say that you can't cook well if you don't have expensive, shiny pots hanging over your stove. But you do need heavy-duty pots, sturdy pans, and good, sharp knives. Check the equipment you already have against the list in this chapter. Get acquainted with your food processor and microwave; they can be your third hand in the kitchen.

Though good, fresh ingredients alone don't assure a good meal, they increase your chances of success about 100 percent. Locate reliable sources for everything—meat, fish, produce, and staples—then follow the suggestions below about smart shopping.

Shopping

Becoming a smart shopper is easy if you follow one important rule: Buy food in the supermarket, but do your shopping at home. This means you make your shopping decisions at the kitchen table, where your primary tool is the shopping list.

To prepare the list, first plan what you are making for dinner in the upcoming days. Check the ingredients in the recipes against what you have in the cupboard and write down what you need. Be meticulous. Some recipes hinge on one simple ingredient. Next, check the staples in the house: milk, juice, eggs, butter or margarine, oil, peanut butter, and so on.

For fresh fruits and vegetables, wait until you get to the store to see what looks best and is plentiful, but make a few notes on what vegetables would be appropriate for the entrées you are planning.

Try to do your shopping during off-hours—early in the morning or late at night. Once in the store, buy only those items on your list. Let yourself drift through the aisles and you'll wind up with a wagonful of food but nothing to eat. Beware: Supermarkets are carefully organized to separate you from your money. For example, the meat and dairy sections are deviously situated in the back, forcing you to wend your way through much of the store before you find what you're looking for.

To combat this trickery, you must move quickly through the aisles, list in hand, checking off items as you place them in the wagon. Remember, life's too short to spend time ruminating over chunk light versus solid white tuna. If you're on line at the check out counter (thumbing through the *National Enquirer*) within 15 minutes or less, you know you've done some professional-quality shopping.

Buying Fresh Food

Using the freshest possible ingredients helps ensure that the food you cook will taste best and that it has the optimum number of nutrients.

Frequent markets where the meat and produce are really fresh and appealing, even if you have to go out of your way to get there. Here are some tips to help you choose the freshest ingredients:

■ **Check dates.** Even canned and frozen foods don't last forever. Find dairy products with the latest date (they are often located in the back of the dairy case).

■ **Buy meat, fish, and poultry from stores you trust.** Locate a good butcher and fishmonger whose fare is fresher and of higher quality than a supermarket's. For detailed information about choosing cuts and judging freshness, see individual entries in the Dinner chapter.

■ **Don't be afraid to pick over piles of fruits and vegetables to find the choice one.** Examine your selections carefully for bumps, bruises, and other defects. For detailed information about choosing vegetables and fruits, see individual entries in the Vegetable and Dessert chapters. Wash all fruits and vegetables thoroughly before eating them as most have been sprayed with pesticides and other chemicals.

Health Food

You can buy just about anything in the health food store these days. And with something like Whole Foods' success, more mainstream supermarkets are expanding their selections of health foods and organic products and produce. These foods are prepared with few additives, are minimally processed, and are, in some cases, organic (cultivated and processed without any chemicals or artificial ingredients).

Your health food shopping list should include macaroni and cheese, vegetarian chili, brown rice in various flavors, freeze-dried soups, tofu burger mix, and whole-wheat pancake and muffin mixes.

Labels

Labels and ingredient lists on prepared foods can be deceiving. Food companies cannot lie on their labels, so if a product says it's "nonfat" or "low-sodium," it has to live up to that claim. Often, however, companies will boast in big letters about some singularly healthful feature of their product merely as a distraction. For instance, a potato chip bag claims "no cholesterol." But a quick scan of the label reveals very high fat, calorie, and sodium counts, and reminds you of what *is* there. "Lite" can have a variety of meanings, so read the small print carefully. Also check "serving size." For instance, a bottle of iced tea may not list a large amount of sugar, but when you multiply that by 3 (the number of servings in the bottle), it becomes excessive.

Ingredients

Everyone is much more health conscious these days, and as a result the information and ingredients list are much more comprehensive. The amounts of saturated fats and trans fats are clearly identified so you can keep the saturated fats to a minimum and avoid trans fats altogether. Also look for whole grains and organic whenever possible. Whole grains have much greater health benefits than white or processed flour. If organic products are available and the price is about the same, why not use them? Buying organic usually means you are getting something that is minimally processed, with a truer flavor, no antibiotics or hormones added, and with a better chance of being grown locally. The only downside is that in places where "organic" hasn't caught on, the produce may have sat around a little longer. So make sure it's really fresh.

1. Ingredient list

The product recipe lists ingredients *in order of quantity,* so look carefully to see where such items as fats and sweeteners fall on the list. For example, on a pretzel package the largest single ingredient is flour (probably white, if not specified), there is more salt than sweetener, and maybe a few artificial ingredients.

2. Special handling instructions and dating

Follow directions and use dates for safe storing of products.

Herb & Spice Primer

All cooks should know the importance of seasoning—balancing sweet tastes with savory, bringing out the flavors of meats and fish with complementary herbs, and adding character to salads and vegetables. Your spice shelf does not need to be packed with exotic dried herbs and spices that are used only once a year. (In fact, herbs and spices lose their pungency in about six to nine months.) So stock up only a dozen or so essential herb and spices like the ones listed here.

Always use herbs and spices judiciously. Remember, you can add more seasonings, but you can't take them away.

Dad's Handy Guide to Seasoning

If a spice is listed in the ingredients in a recipe, that's easy. But what do you do when you want to enhance the flavor of a basic fish or simple dish, but are fearful of creating some volatile combination or culinary mutant? Here's a handy reference guide to what seasonings to use when, and on what. Do not mix seasonings indiscriminately. Consult the list below and the charts on page 27.

Egg Dishes Fresh dill; tarragon; fresh or dried basil; oregano; parsley

Fatty Fish Fresh dill; fresh or dried rosemary; thyme; garlic

Lean White-Fleshed Fish Fresh or dried ginger; basil or oregano; fresh tarragon

Roast Chicken Dried basil, oregano, and/or thyme; fresh or dried rosemary; paprika

Sautéed Chicken Dried basil, oregano, and/or thyme; fresh or dried rosemary; paprika

Roast Beef Dried basil, oregano, and/or thyme; garlic

Roast Lamb or Lamb Chops Fresh or dried rosemary and garlic; thyme

Salad Dressings Basil; thyme; garlic

Tomato-Based Sauces and Stews Fresh or dried basil; oregano, thyme, and/or rosemary; bay leaf; garlic for sauces

Tuna Fish Salad Fresh or dried dill; fresh or dried basil

Fresh vs. Dried

As fresh herbs have become more widely available, dried herbs have gotten a bad rap. The truth is that dried herbs are perfectly fine for dishes that cook for a long time, such as pasta sauces, stews, chili, and soups, as well as marinades and salad dressings. They can also be used when fresh herbs are unavailable; for each tablespoon of a fresh herb called for in a recipe, substitute 1 teaspoon dried.

Fresh herbs impart their flavor quickly and are best when added toward the end of cooking. Pinch or strip the leaves from the stem, then chop them coarsely (or as directed in your recipe) before combining with other ingredients. One exception to this rule is basil, which is very delicate and should be torn into pieces rather than chopped with a knife. Buy only as large a quantity of fresh herbs as you can use within 2 or 3 days as they do not last long. Fresh herbs are available in some specialty shops and better supermarkets throughout the year.

A Well-Seasoned Trio

These three spices work well together, allowing their flavors to balance out. Use equal amounts of basil and oregano and half as much thyme.

Herb/Spice	Fresh	Dried	Use with
Basil	*	*	Pasta; tomatoes; eggs; chicken; fish; salad dressing; essential to Italian foods
Oregano	*	*	Fish; meat; poultry; beans; eggs; soups; tomatoes; eggplant
Thyme	*	*	Fish and shellfish; poultry; vegetables; fish chowder; stuffing

Solo Fliers

These herbs have strong, distinct flavors that will overwhelm other herbs or spices. As a rule, use them alone and sparingly.

Herb/Spice	Fresh	Dried	Use with
Dill	*	*	Baked fatty fish; chicken salad; salad dressing; cooked carrots and potatoes
Ginger	*	*	Use fresh in Asian dishes; marinades; white-fleshed fish; poultry; dried in vegetables and baked goods
Rosemary	*	*	Roasted lamb, beef, pork, veal, poultry; grilled fish and meats; roasted potatoes
Sage		*	Baked or broiled white-fleshed fish; inside whole fish; poultry stuffing; chicken
Tarragon	*	*	Baked or sautéed white-fleshed fish; chicken; eggs; salad dressings

Finishing Touch

Add sparkle to your meal by sprinkling on one of these just before serving.

Herb/Spice	Fresh	Dried	Use with
Chives	*	*	Fish or shellfish; fresh tomatoes; roasted potatoes; egg dishes; any cream sauce or soup; cheese; pasta
Paprika	*	*	White-fleshed fish; roasted chicken; cream sauces; potato and egg salads; dips; goulash; roasted potatoes and home fries
Parsley	*		Steaks; roasted meat and poultry; all fish; tomato sauces; egg dishes; salads and salad dressings; all vegetables; potatoes and rice

Salt & Pepper

Salt adds its own distinctive flavor to foods and also brings out the flavor of other ingredients. Too much salt, however, can easily overpower the flavor of a dish, so always add a little at a time, then stir and taste after each addition.

Tips

■ The flavor of salt will develop and intensify during cooking. Salt should be added to any dish with a long cooking time such as stew, soup, or chili toward the end of the cooking.
■ Stir the salt into whatever you are cooking and give it a few seconds for the flavor to develop before tasting.
■ Salt can draw the juices from meat while it is roasting, so do not salt meat until after it is cooked.

Black pepper perks up everything from a garden salad to roast beef. Freshly ground peppercorns are always preferable to preground black pepper because their flavor is much fresher and more pungent.

Tips

■ Pepper takes a minute or so for its flavor to be incorporated into the dish, so wait a bit before tasting.
■ Peppercorns do vary from brand to brand. If you're feeling adventuresome, buy peppercorns in small quantities and experiment with them until you find the ones you like best.
■ Keep a pepper grinder on the table so family and guests can pepper their food as they wish.

Dad's Basic Kitchen Equipment

High-quality pans and utensils make a big difference when you're cooking and will last a lifetime if cared for properly. The following equipment is all you'll need to prepare the recipes in this book.

Knives

Your knives should be made from high-carbon stainless steel and should feel comfortable in your hand. Unlike free agents in baseball, usually the more money you pay for a knife, the better it is. You can count on the quality of German knives made by Wüsthof and Henckels as well as the French Sabatiers and the American Gerbers. The following knives will cover your basic needs:

Chef's knife *(8 or 10 inches)*
For most cutting and chopping. A cook's primary knife.

Boning knife *(5 inches)*
For boning chicken and fish, trimming fat, and cutting meat into chunks.

Paring knife *(3 to 4 inches)*
For peeling fruits and vegetables.

Caring for Your Knives

■ Knives should be washed by hand after each use and drained immediately. Water droplets left sitting too long on a knife can discolor even stainless steel. Never wash your knives in the dishwasher, even if the handles are dishwasher-safe. It will dull the edges.

■ Store your knives on a magnetized bar or in a wooden knife block. Don't lay them loosely in a drawer. The banging together will dull and chip the edges.

■ The sharpening steel does not actually sharpen your knife, it only restores a fine edge to an already sharpened knife. But if you use the steel regularly, your knives should need professional sharpening only once a year.

■ Don't use your kitchen knives for anything but food-related activities. Never pry anything open with the tip of your knife. It will snap off.

How to Use a Sharpening Steel

■ Hold the steel upright. Place the blade edge of the knife (nearest the handle) at a 20° angle to the steel, near its tip. Draw the blade down toward you and across the steel until the knife tip almost reaches the handle of the steel. Repeat five times on each side. For proper maintenance, use the steel every time you use the knife.

Serrated bread knife *(9 inches)*
For cutting breads and cakes or very ripe tomatoes.

Carving knife *(8 or 10 inches)*
For carving roasted meats and fowl.

Sharpening steel *(10 inches)*

For maintaining a sharp edge on your knives. Sharp knives are safer than dull knives and are essential for efficient "prep" work.

Kitchen shears

For a variety of kitchen uses, especially cutting up cooked chicken

Cutting board *(11 x 17 inches)*

A high-density plastic cutting board at least ¼ inch thick is best. Wooden boards look better, but don't last as long and harbor bacteria more easily. Thin plastic boards, which warp easily, and glass boards, which are fine for slicing but useless for chopping, should be avoided. *Always* wash your cutting board after each use with ample soap and extremely hot water. Be especially diligent after cutting raw chicken and meats.

Pots & Pans

When choosing pots and pans, look for heavy-grade stainless steel, unless you're buying a pasta pot, which doesn't have to be made of such a heavy material, or a frying pan, which can be cast-iron.

Heavy-grade sauté pan *(10–12 inches)*

with lid and heatproof handle. Since this will be the pan you use the most, shell out a couple of bucks and get yourself a good brand, such as Cuisinart or All-Clad.

Nonstick sauté pan *(8 inches)*

with heatproof handle. Essential for cooking eggs and omelets. Use only wooden or plastic utensils with this

pan to guard against scratching the surface. For cleaning, use a plastic scrubbing pad. Eggs can be wiped off with a paper towel. Don't be tempted to use this pan for heavy frying or for browning meats. It's really meant for lighter work.

2½-quart saucepan

with lid. For cooking vegetables and grains, and for reheating.

4½-quart saucepan

with lid. For making soups and tomato sauce. Make sure it has a nonreactive surface, either enamel or stainless steel, and a heavy bottom for sautéing vegetables.

6-quart Dutch oven or casserole

with lid. Great for chili, stews, soups, and casseroles. Can be used in the oven as well as on top of the stove. Le Creuset probably makes the best pot in this size.

8-quart stockpot

with lid. For boiling pasta and making stock.

Roasting pan *(11½ x 16 x 5 inches)*

with rack. For roasting chicken or baking whole fish. It should be made of heavy-grade aluminum, stainless steel, glass, or enamel.

Shallow roasting pan *(10 x 15 x 2 inches)*

For baking such dishes as chicken breasts, fish steaks, and small casseroles.

Seasoning a Pan

When you first buy a cast-iron pan it must be pretreated or "seasoned" with oil to keep food from sticking while you cook. Preheat the oven to 200°F. Scour the pan, dry it very well, then rub the inside with vegetable oil. Add enough oil to fill the pan to about 1/2 inch, then set the pan inside the hot oven for 3 hours. Remove the pan from the oven and let the oil cool before pouring it out. Finish seasoning the pan by wiping the inside with a paper towel.

Microwave-safe casserole
(9 x 9 inches)

This is the most versatile pan for cooking and reheating. As you experiment with the microwave, you will want to acquire more microwave-safe pans.

Assorted microwave-safe plastic containers

Make it easy to transfer food directly from the refrigerator or freezer into the microwave.

Note

All pots and pans should be cleaned with minimal soap and low-abrasion scrubbers, and should be dried thoroughly after each use.

Bowls

You can't have too many of these. A set of four nested stainless-steel mixing bowls will get you started; they are durable, store easily, and won't react with acidic foods. You're likely to want an extra medium-size bowl also.

Baking Pans

2 heavy-grade stainless-steel or aluminum baking sheets
(11 x 17 inches)

Lightweight pans warp easily in a hot oven.

2 loaf pans *(5 x 9 inches)*

You never make one loaf of bread at a time.

2 or 3 round cake pans *(9 inches)*

For making layer cakes.

Springform pan *(9 inches)*

lets you remove your cake easily after baking.

2 heavy aluminum or glass pie pans *(9 inches)*

Muffin tin

For muffins, of course.

until the food softens and can be broken up, if necessary.
4. The food may now be reheated as for refrigerated food.

Note

Some foods, such as vegetables and soup can be defrosted and reheated in one step on high setting. Eight ounces of frozen soup, for instance, can be defrosted and reheated on high for 4–6 minutes. Stir the soup three or four times during the process.

Defrosting Uncooked Food

1. Place the frozen food in the microwave.
2. Microwave on the *defrost* setting for 6–10 minutes. Let the food sit for 7–10 minutes before continuing with cooking. For example, defrost two 8-ounce frozen steaks for 6–8 minutes, turning two or three times. They should then sit for 10 minutes before you continue with the cooking.

Stirring & Standing

Stirring is very important in microwave cooking. Since microwaves do not evenly heat all areas of the food in a container, stirring during the course of cooking or reheating helps ensure an all-over doneness.

After the prescribed cooking time in the microwave, there will usually be a short standing time. This allows the heat to be fully absorbed into the food. Most often the food should remain covered and can "stand" in the oven or on a heatproof counter.

Warnings

■ Never heat a baby's milk bottle in the microwave, as it will heat unevenly. Some of the milk might be very hot without your being able to detect it and could burn the baby's mouth.
■ Don't use a microwave when the food you are making is meant to have a crispy exterior.
■ Microwave dishes and bowls can be deceptively hot. Always use pot holders and be careful of steam as you lift up the plastic wrap or cover.
■ Chicken defrosted in the microwave should be cooked immediately after defrosting—whether you continue cooking it in the microwave or cook it conventionally.

Equipment

■ If you have the space for it, get a full-power oven that uses 650 to 700 watts of energy. It is more efficient than the smaller, low-power ovens and can accommodate large dishes for heavy-duty cooking. A small low-power model that uses 400 to 650 watts is fine for reheating, defrosting, and cooking vegetables.
■ 2 microwave-safe glass or ceramic casseroles, 1-quart and 2-quart, with covers, for things like rice, stews, soups, casseroles, and vegetables.
■ 1 microwave-safe glass or ceramic rectangular baking dish, 8 x 12 inches, for cooking chicken parts, fish, or pasta.
■ Several heavy microwave-safe plastic containers with lids, for freezing and reheating.
■ 4–6 glass or ceramic cereal bowls, for small portions.
■ Paper towels and paper plates. These can be used with foods that cook quickly, such as bacon.

Food Safety & Storage

In addition to the labor involved in shopping, cooking, and getting the kids to eat their food, there is another area of kitchen management that requires Dad's attention—food safety. Food must be bought, handled, and stored properly in order to prevent contamination. To avoid problems, follow these basic food-safety tips:

■ Wash your hands before and during cooking.

■ Defrost frozen food in the refrigerator, or in the microwave when appropriate.

■ Keep cold foods cold and hot foods hot. Bacteria thrive between 40°F and 140°F.

■ Never leave cooked food sitting at room temperature for more than two hours.

■ Keep raw meat and poultry well wrapped in the refrigerator. Meat and poultry drippings can transfer bacteria to other foods.

■ Always rinse your meat and poultry well in cold water before cutting and cooking, as this helps reduce bacteria, though it by no means eliminates them.

■ Wash cutting boards and knives with soap and hot water immediately after cutting any raw poultry or meat.

■ Always cook poultry to 170°F and pork to 160°F to kill bacteria.

■ Cook meat, poultry, and fish within 24 hours of defrosting and never refreeze it once it has been defrosted. Freezing slows the growth of bacteria, but it doesn't kill them. Ice crystals formed during freezing break down cell walls, making defrosted food very susceptible to contamination.

Freezing

Freezing is the best way to manage leftovers and to avoid wasting food. If properly wrapped, labeled, and frozen, many foods will last 6–9 months, some even longer. Freezing also enables you to have an arsenal of ingredients or prepared foods at your fingertips.

Rules for Freezing

Wrap tightly

Air affects food. Choose a container that you can fill almost to the top, leaving ½ inch of open space to accommodate expansion during freezing. With meat and poultry, wrap each piece individually, first in plastic, then in aluminum foil, pressing out as much air as possible. This way all you need to do is remove the foil to defrost the meat or poultry in the microwave.

Freeze quickly

The fresher something is, the better it will survive its stay in the freezer. Set your freezer at or below 0°F, then use a standard weather thermometer to check its temperature. Frozen casseroles, stews, and vegetables can be moved directly from the freezer to the microwave, stovetop, or oven. Keep the flame low when reheating to avoid scorching and changing consistency.

Label correctly

There's no point in freezing food if you don't label it. Frozen foods wrapped in aluminum foil become indistinguishable lumps of something cold. Write the name of the food and the date on freezer tape or masking tape.

How Long Will It Last?

Product	Refrigerator (40°F)	Freezer (0°F)
Eggs		
Fresh, in shell	3 weeks	Don't freeze
Raw yolks, whites	2–4 days	1 year
Hardcooked	1 week	Don't freeze well
Mayonnaise, commercial		
Refrigerate after opening	2 months	Don't freeze
TV Dinners, Frozen Casseroles		
Keep frozen until ready to serve		3–4 months
Deli & Vacuum-Packed Products		
Store-prepared (or homemade) egg,		Do not freeze any of
chicken, tuna, ham, macaroni salads	3–5 days	these products.
Pre-stuffed pork & lamb chops,		
chicken breasts stuffed with dressing	1 day	
Store-cooked convenience meals	1–2 days	
Commercial brand vacuum-packed dinners	2 weeks, unopened	
Soups & Stews		
Vegetable or meat-added	3–4 days	2–3 months
Hamburger, Ground & Stew Meats		
Hamburger & stew meats, ground turkey, veal	1–2 days	3–4 months
Hot Dogs & Lunch Meats		
Hot dogs, opened package	1 week	
unopened package	2 weeks	In freezer wrap,
Lunch meats, opened	3–5 days	1–2 months
unopened	2 weeks	
Bacon & Sausage		
Bacon	7 days	1 month
Sausage, raw from pork, beef, turkey	1–2 days	1–2 months
Smoked breakfast links, patties	7 days	1–2 months
Hard sausage—pepperoni, jerky sticks	2–3 weeks	1–2 months
Ham, Corned Beef		
Corned beef		Drained, wrapped,
in pouch with pickling juices	5–7 days	1 month
Ham, canned, label says keep refrigerated	6–9 months	Don't freeze
Ham, fully cooked—whole	7 days	1–2 months
Ham, fully cooked—half or slices	3–5 days	1–2 months
Fresh Meat		
Steaks, beef	3–5 days	6–12 months
Chops, pork	3–5 days	4–6 months
Chops, lamb	3–5 days	6–9 months
Roasts, beef	3–5 days	6–12 months
Roasts, lamb	3–5 days	6–9 months
Roasts, pork & veal	3–5 days	4–6 months
Meat Leftovers		
Cooked meat and meat dishes	3–4 days	2–3 months
Gravy and meat broth	1–2 days	2–3 months
Fresh Poultry		
Chicken or turkey, whole	1–2 days	1 year
Chicken or turkey pieces	1–2 days	9 months
Cooked Poultry, Leftovers		
Fried chicken or cooked poultry dishes	3–4 days	4 months
Pieces covered with broth, gravy	1–2 days	6 months

Reprinted from U.S. Department of Agriculture and Food Safety and Inspection Service

Real Men Do Measure

You've probably heard descriptions of your grandmother cooking without measuring, instead throwing in a fistful of this and a pinch of that, and the whole family sitting down for a delicious meal. But grandmothers usually have years of experience and a limited repertoire. No beginning cook should ever be cavalier about measuring.

Proper measuring is most crucial when you are baking. There, the balance of flour, leaveners, shortening, and liquids must be precise. Recipes are designed to have the proper balance of flavors, so follow the prescribed amounts of seasonings exactly. Improvising with the spices can make the final product overbearing or inedible.

As you begin to absorb the fundamentals of cooking, you'll feel freer about measuring some ingredients. You'll throw in those extra mushrooms, omit the cilantro, or splash a little more wine into the stew. But give it time. You're never too cool to measure.

Measures

Dash/Pinch	2 to 3 drops (liquid) or less than $\frac{1}{8}$ teaspoon (dry)
1 tablespoon	3 teaspoons or $\frac{1}{2}$ ounce
2 tablespoons	1 ounce
$\frac{1}{4}$ cup	4 tablespoons or 2 ounces
$\frac{1}{3}$ cup	5 tablespoons plus 1 teaspoon
$\frac{1}{2}$ cup	8 tablespoons or 4 ounces
1 cup	16 tablespoons or 8 ounces
1 pint	2 cups or 16 ounces or 1 pound

Measures *(cont.)*

1 quart	4 cups or 2 pints
1 gallon	4 quarts
1 pound	16 ounces

Some Useful Food Equivalents

Apples *1 pound*	3 medium (3 cups sliced)
Bananas *1 pound*	3 medium ($1\frac{1}{3}$ cups mashed)
Berries *1 pint*	$1\frac{3}{4}$ cups
Butter or margarine *1 stick*	$\frac{1}{2}$ cup
Cheese *$\frac{1}{4}$ pound*	1 cup shredded
Chocolate, unsweetened *1 ounce*	1 square
Chocolate, semisweet pieces *one 6-ounce package*	1 cup
Flour *1 pound* *all-purpose*	about $3\frac{1}{2}$ cups
Lemon *1 medium*	3 tablespoons juice 1 tablespoon grated peel
Onion *1 large*	$\frac{3}{4}$ to 1 cup chopped
Orange *1 medium*	$\frac{1}{3}$ to $\frac{1}{2}$ cup juice 2 tablespoons grated peel
Raisins *1 pound*	3 cups, loosely packed
Rice, regular long-grain *1 cup*	3 cups cooked
Salad oil *16 ounces*	2 cups
Sugar *1 pound* *granulated* *brown* *confectioners'*	$2\frac{1}{4}$ to $2\frac{1}{2}$ cups $2\frac{1}{4}$ cups packed 4 to $4\frac{1}{2}$ cups
Tomatoes *1 pound*	3 medium

How to Read a Recipe

This book, like most cookbooks, is filled with recipes. In general, *Dad's Own* tries to explain all unfamiliar terms as we go. But learning how to decipher a recipe takes practice. Here are some decoding tips.

1. Read the whole recipe first.

This way you'll know in advance what ingredients you'll need, how much preparation and cooking time is required, and what the cooking methods will be (baking, sautéing, broiling, etc.). While reading, walk through the steps in your head, estimating how long each one will take. Note words like "beaten," "chopped," and "sliced" in the ingredient list and allow enough time for this "prep" work. Your ability to predict how long a recipe will take will get better and better.

2. Make a shopping list.

Go over the list of ingredients and see what you have in stock in the pantry and refrigerator. Make a shopping list of the ingredients you need.

3. Get your equipment ready.

Dad's Own recipes include a list of the equipment you'll need to prepare each dish. Get the bowls, pots, pans, gadgets, and machinery ready and assembled before you start work so that you won't be interrupted while you're cooking.

4. Preheat the oven and prepare the pans.

There's nothing more annoying than charging through a recipe only to be stalled by a cold oven. And when you're baking, remember to butter and flour the pans before making the batter. It's easy to forget at the last minute when the batter is ready to be poured into the pans.

5. Do all the prep work.

Cooking *anything* is a snap once your ingredients are ready. Look at the ingredient list and the recipe instructions to see how things need to be measured and sliced or chopped. Assemble the prepared ingredients in bowls and arrange them neatly on the counter before you actually start to cook.

6. Once you start, don't stop.

Cooking demands attention. Prop some books in front of the kids and let the answering machine take care of the phone. Dad's in the kitchen! Keep the recipe near your work area so you can refer to it easily, but not so close to the action that it will get splattered with food.

Demystifying the Sauté Pan

More happens in your sauté (or frying) pan than in any other place in the kitchen. It's where many sauces are made, where meat, chicken, and vegetables are sautéed, fish can be poached, and pancakes and French toast are grilled to golden perfection. I like to use a heavy cast-iron skillet (shown here). Or invest in a 10– or 12– inch, high-grade stainless-steel pan with a long handle and cover. (Cuisinart and All-Clad are both good brands.)

The Right Heat

Always heat the pan (about 45 seconds) before you start to cook. The hot pan will keep the food from sticking and will help seal in the juices of meats by searing the outside quickly. You know the pan has reached the right heat to start cooking when the butter stops sizzling or the oil moves easily over the surface. Flick a drop of water in the pan; if it sizzles, the pan is ready for action.

Poaching

To poach fish or chicken, add about ½ inch of water or stock to the sauté pan and bring it to a simmer over *high* heat. As soon as the liquid is bubbling, add the food to be poached. When the liquid returns to a boil, reduce the heat immediately and cover the pan. The liquid should be barely simmering. If you don't have a tight-fitting cover for your pan, lay a piece of lightly greased foil on top of the food.

Sautéing

To sauté is to cook something quickly—often in a matter of minutes—over relatively *high* heat in a minimal amount of oil or butter. Pat dry whatever you are sautéing before adding it to the pan, as excess liquid lowers the temperature and impedes browning. Pieces of food to be sautéed should be relatively thin or small. Otherwise, the outside will burn before the inside is fully cooked.

Reducing Sauces

Pasta sauces, simple sauces made with stock, complex sauces made with cream—all originate in your sauté pan. Because of its large cooking surface, a sauté pan is the

About Deglazing

Deglazing is the process of scraping up the flavorful bits of meat left on the bottom of the sauté pan after browning or frying. After removing the large pieces of meat, add the deglazing liquid (usually wine or chicken stock) to the hot pan. It will steam and sizzle. Working quickly, use a spatula or wooden spoon to scrape the bottom of the pan, incorporating the bits of meat into the liquid. Remove this liquid from the pan just as soon as it has reduced a bit and use as a sauce.

Butter & Oil

Sautéing requires just enough butter or oil to cover the bottom of the pan; usually 1 to 2 tablespoons is enough. Sautéing differs in this way from frying, where a greater amount of oil is used. Using a combination of butter and oil prevents the butter from getting brown (butter that has turned brown will wreak havoc on the flavors of the food in your pan). Make a small pool of oil (a scant tablespoon) in the center of the pan and place a teaspoon of butter in the center of the oil, then swirl to coat the entire surface.

best place to reduce a sauce. Reducing is the process of cooking a sauce so that some of the liquid evaporates, allowing the sauce to thicken and the flavors to intensify. Most cream sauces require reducing. Use *medium-high* heat and stir the sauce regularly so it reduces evenly. A cream sauce is ready when it coats the back of a spoon. Simpler sauces (called "short sauces"), are made by deglazing the pan with wine or stock after the food has been cooked (see box above).

Cleanup

The cardinal rule is *clean as you go.* Here are a few tips to help you along the way:

■ Wash and put away your pots, pans, bowls, food processor, measuring cups, and other cooking equipment as soon as you are done using them. Getting them out of the way will keep the sink and counters free, and you won't have to spend two hours cleaning up after everyone has finished eating. The only exception to this rule is pans and food stuck to them; fill them with warm water and a little bit of dishwashing liquid and let them soak overnight.

■ Re-use bowls and pans rather than taking out every piece of cooking equipment in the house. A quick rinse and a wipe will ready a cup or bowl for another use. The exception to this is bowls, boards, or utensils that have come into contact with raw eggs, poultry, or meat. These should be washed carefully before re-using them.

■ Keep the counters cleaned and wiped, so ingredients won't contaminate each other and the dessert won't taste of onion. Keep a garbage can or bag close by so you can sweep scraps directly off the counter and into it. Put away ingredients and equipment as soon as you have finished using them; clear surfaces give you room to maneuver.

■ Wash your hands often. Besides being sanitary, it keeps food from being smudged on your clothes, the refrigerator door, and every pot handle you touch.

Breakfast

Breakfast has traditionally been Dad's domain. When I was growing up, my dad would get up early on Sunday mornings and whip up a batch of pancakes, French toast, or a monster omelet. He did this partly to give Mom some extra time to sleep and partly to show her that cooking ain't so tough after all.

But preparing breakfast on a daily basis is another matter. It's wonderful to start the day with a bowl of hot cereal or a warm muffin or scone with jam, but most of us don't have time to eat breakfast, never mind make it. Nevertheless, breakfast is considered the most important meal of the day, capable of boosting energy and productivity in a big way.

Getting a healthful breakfast on the table every morning requires a combination of the microwave, a high flame under the omelet pan, some savvy shopping, and, sometimes, a few simple preparations the night before.

The Basic Egg

The egg you eat is one of about 250 that a poultry-farm chicken lays in a year, one of about 390 billion produced annually in the world. It weighs about 2 ounces and provides 6.5 grams of protein, which is about 13% of the recommended daily intake. It has 80 calories and healthy amounts of iron, phosphorus, and thiamine. The problem with the egg is that it is very high in cholesterol, all of which is contained in the yolk. To reduce cholesterol, try making your omelets with a combination of whole eggs and egg whites. Or serve your eggs "over easy," but accompany them with a few slices of orange or melon instead of bacon or sausage, and spread the toast with "fruit-only" jam, not butter.

Boiled Eggs

You could serve soft-boiled eggs in the shell, as the English prefer, but then you would need egg cups. A more down-home approach is to break the egg into a bowl with some bite-sized pieces of toast. This is especially good to serve the kids if they're laid up with a sore throat and are having trouble swallowing.

Ingredients *(serves two)*
4 very fresh extra-large eggs

Equipment
Medium saucepan
Slotted spoon

1. Fill a medium saucepan ²/₃ full with water and bring to a boil on *high* heat.
2. Reduce the heat to *medium* and gently lower the eggs into the water with a slotted spoon.

How to Cook The Perfect Hard-Boiled Egg

Place cold eggs in a saucepan or pot and cover with cold water. Bring the water to a boil, then reduce the heat to a simmer. Simmer for 12 minutes. Plunge the eggs immediately into cold water to stop the cooking and to make them easy to peel right away.

3. Simmer for 3 minutes for regular soft-boiled eggs, or for 4 minutes if you like the yolks a bit harder.

4. Remove the eggs with a slotted spoon. Hold the hot eggs in a cloth or a doubled paper towel and gently crack the shell at the top with the back of a spoon. Peel away enough shell so you can ease the spoon into the egg. Scoop out the yolk and carefully scrape the white from the inside of the shell. Serve immediately with toast, as soft-boiled eggs cool quickly.

Scrambled Eggs

The secret is to get the pan nice and hot and to work quickly with the spatula.

Ingredients *(serves four)*

 8 large eggs
 1½ tablespoons butter or
 margarine

Equipment

 Large nonstick sauté pan
 Medium bowl
 Whisk
 Short spatula

1. Break the eggs into a medium bowl and beat with a whisk.

2. Put a large nonstick sauté pan on *high* heat and let it get hot, about 30 seconds.

3. Spread the butter or margarine around the pan. When it stops sizzling, pour in the eggs. Let the bottom set for about 10 seconds. Then, with the spatula, scrape the cooked eggs up from the bottom and stir them.

4. When the eggs are the consistency that you like, remove them from the pan (or they'll keep cooking) and serve immediately.

Variations

If you want to add some pizzazz to your eggs but don't want to make omelets, add any combination of the following to the beaten eggs and cook as above:

■ Small pieces of ham or cooked bacon

■ Grated cheese (cheddar, Swiss, Gruyère, feta, or any hard cheese)

■ Bits of smoked salmon

■ Any one of these fresh or dried herbs: oregano, basil, thyme, or chives

■ Thin slices of salami, pastrami, or corned beef

■ Sautéed chopped onion, mushrooms, bell pepper, or zucchini

Fried Eggs

To get eggs "over easy" without breaking the yolks, do what an experienced short-order cook does: Brush your spatula with a bit of oil, slip it under the frying eggs, and ease them over gently.

Ingredients *(serves two)*

 1 tablespoon butter
 or margarine
 4 large eggs

Equipment

 Large frying pan
 Spatula

1. Put a frying pan on *high* heat and let it get hot, about 30 seconds.

2. Spread the butter or margarine around the pan. When it stops sizzling, crack the eggs and open them just above the pan, easing the yolks onto the surface so they won't break when they land.

3. Fry the eggs until the whites are set, about 2 minutes. If you want "sunny-side up" eggs, lower the heat to *medium* and cook for 1 minute more. For "over easy," flip as described above and cook them for 30 seconds longer.

4. Use the spatula to carefully lift the eggs from the pan, as the yolks can still break. (If necessary, use the edge of the spatula to separate eggs that have run into each other while cooking.)

Tip

Put the bread in the toaster just after you begin to cook the eggs so the toast will be ready at the same time as the eggs.

Poached Eggs

Poaching is a cooking technique in which a food such as eggs, fruit, or poultry is cooked in liquid at or below the boiling point. Properly poached eggs on toast make an especially comforting breakfast. Serve these to Mom when she's spending the morning in bed.

Ingredients *(serves two)*

1 tablespoon white or cider vinegar
4 very fresh large eggs

Equipment

Large, deep-sided frying pan
4 small bowls
Slotted spoon

1. Fill a large, deep-sided frying pan ²/₃ full with cold water. Add the vinegar and bring to a boil on *high* heat.
2. While the water comes to a boil, break 1 egg into each of the 4 bowls, being careful not to break the yolks. If a yolk breaks, save the egg for something else and try another.
3. When the water boils, reduce the heat to *medium* so it is barely simmering. With a bowl tipped so that it's touching the water, let the egg slide gently into the water. Repeat with the remaining eggs, working quickly so that all of the eggs will be done at the same time.
4. Let the eggs simmer for 3 minutes, until the whites begin to get firm. Gently spoon some of the water over the yolks so they warm through. If the water begins to boil rapidly, reduce the heat a bit. When done, carefully remove the eggs with a slotted spoon and serve over toast or an English muffin.

Omelets

Great omelets depend as much on the proper proportion of eggs to the size of the pan as they do on the skill of the chef.

3 large eggs = 8-inch pan
(for 1 person)
5 large eggs = 10-inch pan
(for 2 people)
8 large eggs = 12-inch pan
(for 3 people)

The omelet will not set correctly with too many eggs in the pan, too few and it will cook too quickly. It is always better to make more omelets than to try to overload the pan with too many eggs. And since the cooking time for omelets is only about a minute, once you get in the groove, you can start cranking them out.

Ingredients *(makes one)*

About ½ cup filling (see below)
3 large eggs
1 teaspoon butter or margarine

Equipment

8-inch frying pan,
preferably nonstick
Medium bowl
Whisk
Spatula

1. Prepare the filling (if desired) and set aside.

2. Gently beat the eggs with a whisk in a medium bowl.

3. Put a small, preferably nonstick, frying pan on *high* heat and let it get hot, about 30 seconds. Spread the butter or margarine around the pan. When it stops sizzling, pour the eggs in all at once. Let the bottom set, about 15 seconds.

4. Slip a spatula about a third of the way under one side of the omelet. Lift up that edge and tilt the pan toward it so the loose, uncooked egg on top runs toward the area of open pan. Continue until there is no more loose egg on top.

5. Quickly spread your filling down the middle of the eggs. Fold the thicker side of the omelet over the filling.

6. Take the pan to the serving plate and use the spatula to nudge the omelet onto the plate.

7. Wipe the pan clean with a cloth or paper towel and start again, if desired.

Fillings

■ Grated cheddar, Monterey Jack, mozzarella, Swiss, Gruyère, Edam, or Parmesan or softer cheeses, such as Gorgonzola or feta, cut into small pieces

■ Ham, salami, or cooked bacon, cut into bite-sized pieces

■ Chopped onion, bell pepper, mushrooms, tomato, scallions (all can or should be sautéed briefly first)

■ Reheated leftover chili, or reheated refried beans, or tomato salsa (at room temperature)

■ A sprinkling of any combination of fresh or dried herbs, such as oregano, parsley, basil, rosemary, or, separately, tarragon (about 1 teaspoon per 4 eggs)

About Eggs

When considering eggs, freshness is key. The best eggs are bought from a local farmer—they have the most flavor. Organic and free range are also now widely available. There is no difference in taste or nutritional value between white and brown eggs. (The color of the shell is determined by the breed of hen that laid it.) For measurement purposes, especially in baking, it is important to have the right size eggs. Large or extra-large eggs are used in all of *Dad's* recipes. When buying eggs, check the date on the side of the carton and buy the freshest ones you can. Eggs are best used within 1 week of purchase, but will last up to 3 weeks in the refrigerator. Always store them in their carton. Here's a neat test to tell whether an egg is still fresh: Place an egg in a small bowl of water. If it is a fresh egg it will stay on its side; if it is an older egg it will stand straight up and float. Air always passes through the porous shell of an egg, but if so much air has permeated the shell as to make the egg buoyant, the egg has been sitting around too long and should be thrown away.

Pancakes

Pancakes can range from the ridiculous to the sublime depending on who mixed the batter and who flipped the cakes. These are light and nutritious.

Ingredients *(serves four)*

1 cup unbleached all-purpose flour

½ cup whole wheat flour

3 tablespoons sugar

2 tablespoons wheat germ (optional)

1½ teaspoons baking powder

½ teaspoon baking soda

½ teaspoon salt

1 large egg

1 cup milk

2 tablespoons butter or margarine, melted and cooled, or vegetable oil

1 teaspoon vanilla extract (optional)

Additional butter, margarine, or vegetable oil for cooking the pancakes

Pancake syrup, for serving

Equipment

Large frying pan or griddle

Medium bowl

Small bowl

Small pitcher (optional)

Whisk

Wooden spoon

Spatula

1. Using a whisk, mix together all the dry ingredients in a medium bowl.

2. Gently whisk together the egg, milk, melted butter or margarine (or vegetable oil), and vanilla in a small bowl.

3. Pour the wet stuff into the dry and stir with a wooden spoon until it is just combined. Do not overmix. At this point you may want to transfer the batter to a small pitcher so it will be easier to pour into the frying pan.

4. Put a large frying pan (or set your griddle) on *high* and let it get hot, about 30 seconds. Then reduce the heat to *medium*.

5. Spread about ½ tablespoon of butter or margarine around the pan. When it stops sizzling, pour the batter into the frying pan to the desired pancake size, as many as will fit without the edges touching.

6. Cook until craters *just begin* to form on top of the pancakes. Turn and cook for 1–2 minutes more for thin cakes, slightly longer for thicker ones. Serve immediately with butter or margarine and your favorite syrup.

Variations

Mix into the batter a cup of blueberries (fresh or frozen), thinly sliced strawberries, or diced peaches. Apples need to be thinly sliced and briefly sautéed before being added to the batter.

Slice a banana and, in a sauté pan set over *medium* heat, combine the slices with ⅓ cup real maple syrup. Cook just until warmed. Serve over the pancakes.

Tips

■ Commercial pancake mixes found in supermarkets aren't always great, but there are many mixes sold in country stores, at roadside stands, in health food stores (this is where you'll find whole grain mixes), or through food catalogs that are quite wonderful. If you discover one you like, save time by keeping it on hand for a quick and easy pancake breakfast.

■ If you have a crowd to feed and don't want to start serving until you've made enough to go around, keep the cooked pancakes warm for a few minutes on a baking sheet in a 200°F oven.

■ The first batch of pancakes may not turn out exactly right as the pan needs to reach the proper temperature. If your first pancakes took a lot longer to cook than the recipe indicated, raise the heat under the pan. Lower the heat if your first batch overcooked.

■ You may not need to add any butter to the pan after cooking the first batch.

French Toast

French toast was one of the few things my dad taught me to cook. With slight adjustments (he wasn't hip to the vanilla), this is his recipe.

Ingredients *(serves four)*

6 large eggs
½ teaspoon vanilla extract
Splash of milk
Dash of cinnamon (optional)
8 slices of bread
1 teaspoon butter or margarine

Equipment

Large frying pan or griddle
Pie pan or wide bowl
Whisk
Spatula

1. In a wide bowl or pie pan, whisk together the eggs, vanilla, milk, and cinnamon (if using).

Time-Saver

Uncooked French toast freezes very well. Soak the bread in the egg mixture, then lay the slices in a single layer on a baking sheet in the freezer for a few hours until the bread is frozen through, then transfer the frozen slices to a plastic freezer bag.

To serve: Put the frozen bread on a lightly greased baking sheet and bake in a preheated 400°F oven for 15 minutes. This technique works especially well with English muffins.

2. Dip each slice of bread into the egg mixture, turning a few times so the eggs soak into both sides of the bread.

3. Put a large frying pan (or set your griddle) on *high* heat for about 20 seconds, then reduce the heat to *medium*. (Unlike omelets, French toast needs to cook slowly.)

4. Add and swirl the butter or margarine around the pan. When it stops sizzling, add the bread. Cook for 3–4 minutes, until lightly browned. Turn and cook for 3–4 minutes more.

Tips

■ Whole wheat bread works just as well as white bread and is more nutritious.

■ For a variation, try French bread, cut diagonally into 1-inch-thick slices.

■ For a real Ukrainian effect, try thickly sliced challah bread.

■ If you're not using presliced bread, cut it into 1-inch-thick slices for French toast.

■ English muffins also make interesting French toast.

Breakfast in Bed

Some people think there is no better way to show their affection for a loved one than to appear at the bedroom door in the morning carrying a tray with freshly squeezed juice, hot coffee, and a sumptuous breakfast. Mother's Day, birthday, anniversary—any morning you want to make that special someone feel like a million bucks.

Slow Scrambled Eggs with Smoked Salmon, Sour Cream & Caviar

With its elegant presentation and delectable flavors, this breakfast begs for Champagne.

Ingredients *(serves two)*

4 slices homestyle white bread

4 eggs

¼ pound smoked salmon, finely chopped

2 tablespoons butter

2 tablespoons sour cream, at room temperature

2 ounces black caviar

Fresh fruit slices or whole berries

Equipment

Double boiler

Medium bowl

4-inch heart-shaped cookie cutter (optional)

Whisk

1. With a cookie cutter or a paring knife, cut and remove a heart shape from the center of each slice of bread. Discard the hearts or reserve for another purpose. Place the remaining bread in the center of two plates.

2. Whisk the eggs in a medium bowl. Stir in the smoked salmon.

3. Put 2 inches of water in the bottom of a double boiler. Put the butter in the top, and set the double boiler on *medium* heat. When the butter is melted, swirl it around to coat the pan, then add the eggs. Stir continuously with the whisk until the eggs are just about congealed, about 2½ minutes.

MENU

Slow scrambled eggs with smoked salmon, sour cream & caviar

Croissants

Mimosas

Café au lait

Fresh fruit

4. Remove the eggs from the heat and stir in the sour cream. Spoon a quarter of the eggs into each of the hearts. Top with the caviar and garnish the edge of the plates with alternating slices of fresh fruit or whole berries. Serve immediately.

Mimosa

For two mimosas, squeeze three fresh oranges. Fill half each Champagne flute with the orange juice, then add an equal amount of chilled Champagne.

Café au Lait

With this special breakfast, serve a cup of café au lait. Brew the coffee as usual, only slightly stronger, and add a pinch of cinnamon to the grounds. At the same time, warm some milk in a small saucepan. Pour equal amounts of coffee and milk into each cup just before serving.

Caviar Emptor

Fresh black caviar, such as osetra or sevruga, is usually available at specialty food shops. If you can't find fresh caviar, you may substitute the pasteurized or pressed caviar that is sold in supermarkets, although it is not comparable in taste. Beware that the distinctive fishy taste of caviar is not to everyone's liking. If desired, substitute a pinch of chopped fresh chives or parsley.

Hot Cereal

When I was a desultory lad of 22 and my grandfather was a vigorous codger of 91, I decided the best thing I could do was eat what he did. And one thing he ate every morning without fail was hot cereal.

Ingredients *(makes one bowl)*

⅓ cup old-fashioned rolled oats

¼ cup water

A bit of milk and brown sugar, maple syrup, or honey (optional)

Equipment

Microwave oven

Small microwave-safe bowl

1. Put the oatmeal and water in a microwave-safe bowl and cover loosely with plastic wrap.

2. Put the bowl in the microwave and cook on *medium* setting for 5–6 minutes. Mix well.

3. Add the milk and toppings of choice.

Variation

Mix in some fresh berries, banana slices, chopped apples, raisins, or flavored yogurt for the last 30 seconds of cooking.

Old-Fashioned Oatmeal

For stovetop oatmeal, bring the water to a brisk boil in a 1-quart saucepan. Use more water for thinner oatmeal; less water for thicker. Stir in the old-fashioned rolled oats and reduce the heat to *low*. Cook uncovered for 5 minutes, stirring frequently. Remove the oatmeal from the heat, cover, and let stand until it reaches the desired consistency. Mix well, then stir in the milk, sugar, maple syrup, or honey, if desired.

Puffed Pancake

This puffed pancake was one of the few foods my Dad made that we considered gourmet. It's a foolproof, impressive recipe.

Ingredients *(serves four)*

6 large eggs

1½ cups milk

1 cup unbleached all-purpose flour

3 tablespoons granulated sugar

1 teaspoon vanilla

¼ teaspoon cinnamon

6 tablespoons (¾ stick) butter or margarine

Jam, syrup, or honey, for serving

Equipment

12-inch cast-iron or ovenproof skillet

Blender

1. Preheat the oven to 425°F.

2. In a blender on medium speed, mix together the eggs, milk, flour, granulated sugar, vanilla, and cinnamon, until just combined, about 15 seconds. The batter should be a bit lumpy.

3. Melt the butter or margarine in a 12-inch cast-iron skillet by putting it in the hot oven for about 30 seconds.

4. Remove the skillet from the oven, spread the butter to coat the bottom and sides of the skillet, and pour in the batter. Return the skillet to the center oven rack and bake for about 20 minutes, or until the pancake is puffed and lightly browned. (Do not check before 17 minutes have passed, and close the oven door slowly and carefully after checking.)

5. Cut into wedges and serve immediately with jam, syrup, or honey.

Variations

The puffed pancake is nice accompanied by fresh slices of fruit, such as apples, bananas, berries, or peaches. If you serve apples, sauté them in a tablespoon of butter over *medium* heat for a few minutes while the pancake is cooking.

Tips

■ If the butter turns brown, it has burned and is unusable. Pour it out, wipe out your pan, and start again.

■ The pan must be exactly 12 inches across or the pancake will not puff.

■ If you don't have a blender, use a hand mixer or whisk, or pulse briefly in a food processor.

Frittata

Seen on antipasto tables in many trattorias, this classic Italian dish is like a quiche without the crust and cream—and it couldn't be easier to make.

Ingredients *(serves four)*

8 *large eggs*
4 *slices ham, prosciutto, Italian salami, or pepperoni*
1 *teaspoon dried oregano*
1 *medium zucchini*
1 *red bell pepper*
6 *button or wild mushrooms*
2 *shallots or 1 small onion*
3 *tablespoons olive oil*
½ *cup grated cheddar cheese*

Equipment

Large, nonstick frying pan with heatproof handle
Medium bowl
2 spatulas
12-inch serving plate (optional)

1. Preheat the broiler and arrange the rack in the lower third of the oven.

2. Lightly beat the eggs in a medium bowl. Cut up the meat into 1-inch pieces and add to the eggs with the oregano. Set aside.

3. Wash and dry the zucchini and bell pepper. Trim the ends of the zucchini, then cut it in half lengthwise, and cut the halves into ½-inch-thick slices. Core and seed the pepper and slice into ½-inch-wide strips. Cut these into 1-inch-long pieces. Slice the mushrooms thinly. Peel and cut the shallots or onion into thin slices.

4. Put a large nonstick frying pan with a heatproof handle on *medium* heat and let it get hot, about 30 seconds. Add 2 tablespoons of the oil and the zucchini, bell pepper, mushrooms, and shallots. Sauté for 6 minutes, stirring often, until the vegetables are soft.

5. Add the remaining tablespoon of oil to the pan and spread it to coat the bottom. Pour the egg mixture into the pan. Mix in the grated cheese and cook, stirring often, until the bottom half of the frittata is firm. (The top should be loose.)

6. Remove the pan from the stove and place it on the lower rack in your hot oven. Broil for 3–5 minutes or until the frittata puffs and browns.

7. Remove the pan from the oven and let it cool for a minute to set.

8. Transfer the frittata from the pan to the serving plate with 2 spatulas or serve directly from the pan. (Use a hot pad to hold the skillet handle; it will remain hot for a long time.)

9. Cut the frittata into wedges and serve.

Home Fries Supremo

I've often ordered eggs or even a sirloin steak, just to have something to eat with my home fries.

Ingredients *(serves four)*

   4 or 5 large potatoes
      (russet, red, or new potatoes)
   1 medium onion, peeled and cut into thin
      matchlike strips
   1 green bell pepper, seeded and cut into
      thin matchlike strips
   1 clove garlic, minced
   2 tablespoons corn oil
   1 teaspoon paprika
   Salt and pepper

Equipment

   Medium saucepan
   Large nonstick frying pan
   Colander

1. Cut the potatoes lengthwise into quarters. Cut the quarters into 1-inch-thick chunks, put them in a medium saucepan with just enough cold water to cover them. If using new potatoes, just cut them into quarters. Bring to a boil over *high* heat, then reduce the heat to *medium* and simmer for 10 minutes. The potatoes should be slightly undercooked. Drain in a colander and set aside.

2. When the potatoes are cooked and drained, put a large nonstick frying pan on *high* heat and let it get hot, about 30 seconds. Reduce the heat to *medium high,* add the oil, onion, and bell pepper, and cook until the onion is soft, about 6 minutes. Add the garlic and cook for 1 minute more.

3. Add the potatoes. Cook for about 15 minutes, turning the potatoes frequently so that all sides get browned. Add the paprika and salt and pepper to taste.

4. Cook for 5 minutes more, until the potatoes are crisply browned.

Time-Saver

The potatoes can be boiled the night before. Just cover them tightly and refrigerate.

Tip

For crispier potatoes, omit the paprika and stir in another tablespoon of oil 10 minutes before they are finished cooking and then place a heavy, heatproof dinner plate or another frying pan directly on the potatoes.

Muffins

Ingredients *(makes 12 muffins)*

2 cups unbleached all-purpose flour

3 teaspoons baking powder

¼ cup sugar

3 tablespoons wheat germ (optional)

½ teaspoon salt

1 large egg

1 cup milk

6 tablespoons melted butter or vegetable
  oil, plus extra for greasing muffin tin.

Equipment

12-cup muffin tin

Small bowl

Medium bowl

Wooden spoon

Whisk

1. Preheat the oven to 375°F.

2. Lightly grease a 12-cup muffin tin.

3. Mix the dry ingredients together in a medium bowl.

4. Gently whisk together the wet ingredients in a small bowl.

5. Pour the wet stuff into the dry. Stir with a wooden spoon until the ingredients are just combined. Do not overmix—the batter should be lumpy.

6. Spoon the batter into the muffin cups until each is ⅔ full.

7. Bake on the center oven rack for 20 minutes, or until the muffins are lightly browned and a cake tester inserted in the center of a muffin comes out clean.

8. Let the muffins cool in the tin for at least 10 minutes before removing them.

Variations

■ Add 1 cup fresh or frozen blueberries, fresh cranberries, or chopped apple to the wet ingredients before mixing with the dry. Use muffin tin liners instead of greasing the tin when making muffins with fruit.

■ Substitute 1 cup cornmeal for 1 cup of the unbleached flour. This is especially tasty with blueberries added to the batter as well, but be sure to use muffin tin liners.

■ Substitute 1 cup rolled oats for 1 cup of the flour. In a small bowl, pour the milk over the oats and let them soak for 1 minute. Then add the oats and ½ cup raisins to the rest of the wet ingredients. Proceed as directed in Step 5.

Time-Saver

The easiest, fastest way to have freshly baked muffins in the morning is to assemble the ingredients the night before. Just mix together the dry ingredients in one bowl, and the wet in another. Cover both bowls tightly with plastic wrap; refrigerate the liquids. Combine the wet and dry ingredients first thing in the morning and bake as directed.

Greasing a Pan

Fold a paper towel into quarters and use it to rub a very light coating of butter, margarine, shortening, or vegetable oil on the baking surface (both sides and bottom) of a pan, muffin tin, or baking dish. It is best *not* to use butter, as its burning point is too low. Vegetable oil sprays work well also and they save time as well as calories.

A Good Cup of Coffee & a Nice Cup of Tea

Coffee

Coffee beans are brown in warm climates and high altitudes, in places like Africa, Jamaica, Brazil, and, of course, Juan Valdez's home, Colombia. Different climates and soils produce beans with subtly different flavors and aromas. The beans are picked green, shipped to their destination, and then roasted, which turns them brown. The longer they are roasted, the darker and stronger the beans. French and Italian roasts, almost black in color, are two of the strongest-flavored beans and make rich, slightly harsh, but intensely flavored coffee. Viennese roast is light brown and produces milder, softer coffee with little aftertaste. There are many flavors in between. Often coffee emporiums sell what they call "house blends," mixtures of strong and mild beans that produce coffee with richer, more complex flavor than coffee made from one kind of bean. You can have your beans ground at the store, but your coffee will taste best if you grind the beans as you need them in your own home coffee grinder. For simpler, everyday coffee, a can of already ground, dark-roasted coffee, such as El Pico or Bustelo, will do just fine.

But whatever kind you buy, the amount of coffee is the same: 1 coffee measure (2 tablespoons) for each 6-ounce cup of water. Brew coffee, using any of the three methods on the following page and you're assured great results. Of course, the easiest way to make coffee is in an automatic drip machine. Simply follow instructions in the manual.

Manual Drip Method
(Beans should be ground medium fine.)

1. Bring a kettle of water just to the boiling point.
2. Fit a paper filter into the filter holder and measure the ground coffee into the filter.
3. Pour only a small amount of water into the filter to wet the sides of the paper and to just cover the grounds; let the water settle. Pour in the rest of the water very slowly, pausing to let it drip through.
4. Continue pouring water until the coffee has reached the desired level in the pot.

Plunger Method

(Beans should be ground medium.)

Freshness

The freshest beans obviously make the best coffee. Aficionados store their beans in the freezer and grind them immediately before brewing. Ground beans also stay fresher if refrigerated or frozen. Once the container is opened, ground beans lose their intensity after about a month and will produce only bland coffee after 2 months. Lots of supermarkets and delis offer "gourmet coffee beans." But if the beans have been sitting around for a while, they've probably lost their edge, and you're better off buying canned or vacuum-packed ground beans.

1. Bring a kettle of water to a boil.

2. While the water is heating, remove the plunger from the glass pot and measure the ground coffee into the bottom.

3. Fill the pot with as much water as you need. Insert the plunger so that it rests just at the water level, and the lid fits on the top, creating a vacuum.

4. Wait 5 minutes, then push the plunger down slowly. The coffee is now ready to pour.

Espresso-Stovetop Method

(Beans should be ground extra-fine.)

1. Fill the bottom section of the espresso maker with cold water up to the level of the little escape valve on the side.

2. Fit the filter section into the bottom section and fill the filter to the top with coffee. (Do not pack the coffee in.)

3. Screw the top on tightly and set the espresso maker on *medium* heat. When the top section is filled with coffee and it starts sputtering, the espresso is done.

Teas

Devout coffee drinkers may find this hard to believe, but tea is actually the world's most popular beverage. There are three main types of tea: black (the strongest flavored), green (an unfermented tea, with a mild, slightly bitter taste), and oolong (a subtle, delicate tasting tea). Herb teas are not made from tea leaves at all but are infusions of herbs, flowers, and spices.

To brew the perfect pot of tea, bring a kettle of cold water to a rolling boil. Warm a teapot by rinsing it out with hot water. Add 1 teaspoon of tea or 1 teabag per cup of water and "one for the pot." Pour the boiling water over the tea and leave it to brew for 3 to 6 minutes. If using loose tea, pour through a strainer (to catch the tea leaves) into cups.

BREAKFAST

The Yogurt & Fruit Breakfast

A simple bowl of yogurt and fruit or cereal is another quick and healthy way to start the day. And deciding what ingredients to mix in each morning's bowl can be fun for the kids.

Ingredients

Granola or wheat germ

Nuts, raisins, sunflower seeds

Assorted fruits, such as bananas, strawberries, blueberries, raspberries, pineapple, apples, or grapes

Plain or vanilla yogurt

1. Assemble the toppings in small bowls.

2. Spoon a cup of yogurt into a bowl for each person.

3. Let each person add the toppings of his or her choice.

About Yogurt

Yogurt comes in many styles—low-fat, lite, plain, flavored, creamy—you name it. You don't need to buy a national brand, but read the label carefully. Many of the fruit yogurts have a great deal of added sugar. As an easy alternative, buy plain yogurt and mix in "fruit-only" jam at home. The kids will like it just as much and won't be consuming unnecessary sugar. For Dad, any kind of lowfat or no-fat yogurt is the best bet, as it is lower in cholesterol than the nonreduced-fat yogurts.

Lunch

When I was a kid, lunch was definitely my Main Meal. Breakfast was hurried, dinner dragged on and required manners. But lunch was the meal to relish; you could get your hands dirty and lick your fingers. Even the language of lunch was fun; there were Dagwoods, Reubens, grinders, knockwursts, BLTs, malteds, and egg creams.

Lunch I liked.

For Dads, lunch can be a time for some culinary improvising with last night's leftovers, turning baked potatoes into stuffed skins, slicing London broil for steak sandwiches, using the remains of a roasted chicken for tacos or chilaquiles. Once you get the hang of it, you'll feel like the King of Lunch.

Six Sandwiches the Kids Will Eat

Peanut Butter & Jelly

Perhaps no other food more closely taps into the American zeitgeist. Transcending regional boundaries, ethnic backgrounds, and socioeconomic status, a peanut butter and jelly sandwich is part of every American childhood. I won't presume to tell you how to make one, but I do think you can tell a lot about someone by the proportion of jelly to peanut butter they prefer and whether they like smooth or chunky.

Variations

For a different taste sensation, omit the jelly and add one of the following to a peanut butter sandwich: sliced banana, sliced apples, or apple butter.

Tunafish Salad

Somewhere in America there is a luncheonette with a little sign behind the counter reading "Home of the First Tunafish Salad Sandwich" and we should

About Tuna

Solid white tuna packed in water is your best bet for sandwiches. It has the most distinct taste, the fewest calories, and holds up the best in tunafish salad. While solid white is a bit more expensive than chunk, flaked, or grated tuna, the meat is denser, so you wind up getting more for your money. Buy only tuna that has the "dolphin-safe" label, which means the fish from which it was made was caught without using nets that trap and kill many dolphins.

all be beholden to that spot. Whoever invented this sandwich made feeding kids a whole lot easier. Basic tunafish salad is essentially canned tuna and some mayonnaise. After that, it's anybody's ball game. Here's mine.

Ingredients *(makes four sandwiches)*
> *One 13-ounce can solid white tuna*
>   *in water*
> *2 ribs celery, finely chopped*
> *1 carrot, peeled and grated*
> *2 tablespoons mayonnaise*
> *2 tablespoons plain yogurt*
> *1 tablespoon Italian dressing or vinaigrette*
> *Salt and pepper*
> *8 slices bread*
> *Chips and pickles, for serving*

Equipment

Medium bowl
Fork
Spoon

1. Drain the liquid from the can of tuna. Empty the tuna into a medium bowl and flake it with a fork.
2. Add the celery and carrot.
3. Spoon in the mayonnaise, yogurt, and dressing. Add the salt and pepper to taste.
4. Mix well and spread on the bread for sandwiches. Serve with chips and a pickle.

Variations

The following can be mixed into the tuna salad to give it more zip:

- lemon juice
- curry powder
- grated red onion
- chopped dill
- chopped hard-boiled egg
- raisins
- chopped almonds or walnuts

BLT

Besides my own, the first initials I learned were BLT, for bacon, lettuce, and tomato sandwich. To a kid, it was an exotic concoction. Its double layers opened my eyes to a whole new dimension of sandwich-dom. The BLT was another entry on the short list of foods my dad liked to cook. He would cut it into triangles, arrange the triangles around the edge of the plate, points facing out, and fill the center with potato chips, just like they did at the local diner. There were even some frilly toothpicks set aside just for this enterprise.

Bread Box

No matter how you slice it, whole grain bread is better for you than white bread. When a grain of wheat is milled to make flour, the main ingredient in bread, its three parts—the bran (high in fiber), the germ (high in nutrients), and the endosperm (the nutritional weakling of the three)—are separated. All three are recombined to make whole grain flour, but only the endosperm is used to make white flour. Often white bread is enriched with vitamins but it is still no match for whole grain.

If your kids absolutely blanch at whole grain bread, look for "country white" or oatmeal bread. These have the smooth, mellow taste of white, but are often made without additives and are less airy, meaning there's more bread in the bread.

Some of the larger bakeries have tried to bake breads that combine the benefits of whole grain with the texture of white, but beware. Some airy "whole grain" breads are made with lots of additives and do not include enough whole wheat to make them nutritious. So look for "whole grain" on the package.

An official BLT is made up of two layers: lettuce and tomato along with a little mayo or butter on the upper deck, three or four slices of bacon on the lower deck, separated by the third slice of bread in the middle. BLTs can be made with only two slices of bread, but I wouldn't recommend it. Turkey, roast beef, or tuna salad can be substituted for the bacon, but then it becomes a club sandwich. And that's an easy next step.

Grilled Cheese

The grilled cheese sandwich is an important institution. For many people, men especially, it was the first food they cooked on their own. A grilled cheese sandwich is very easy to make, if you remember one simple rule: Cook it slowly. Once the pan is hot, grill the sandwich over *medium-low* heat. Placing a bowl or small plate on top to weight the sandwich down while it's cooking is also a good idea. Serve with chips, a bowl of tomato soup, and a glass of chocolate milk.

Ingredients *(makes one sandwich)*

    2 slices (about 2 ounces) cheddar,
        Monterey Jack, Swiss,
        or American cheese
    2 slices bread
    Pats of butter or margarine

Equipment

    12-inch frying pan
    Cereal bowl or heavy mug
    Spatula

1. Put the cheese between the slices of bread.

2. Spread a pat of butter or margarine on the outside of the top piece of bread.

3. Place a frying pan on *high* heat and let it get hot, about 30 seconds. Then reduce the heat to *medium low.*

4. Spread a teaspoon of butter or margarine in the pan. Arrange the sandwiches (you can make two at a time) in the pan, buttered side up, and set a weight on top of the sandwiches.

5. Cook on *medium-low* heat until the bottom of the bread is golden brown, about 5 minutes. You can't rush a grilled cheese sandwich—if you do, the bread will burn before the cheese melts.

6. Turn over each sandwich, replace the weight, and cook for 4 minutes more or until the bottom is golden brown.

7. Serve immediately.

Variations

For added flavor, place one or more of the following between the slices of cheese:

■ A slice or two of ham, prosciutto, or salami

■ Several pieces of cooked bacon

■ Thin slices of tomato, avocado, and/or red onion (that's for Dad, of course!)

Turkey Club

Now you can make this diner favorite right in your very own home. Serve with chips, pickles, and egg creams.

Ingredients *(makes four sandwiches)*

    ¹/₂ pound bacon
    12 slices bread
    1 pound sliced turkey
    Mayonnaise
    2 tomatoes, sliced
    Lettuce

Equipment

    Baking sheet
    Frilled toothpicks

1. Preheat the oven to 350°F.

2. Arrange the bacon in a single layer on a baking sheet. Bake in the center of the oven for 10–12 minutes, until the bacon is crisp. Transfer the bacon to paper towels to absorb the grease.

3. Lightly toast the bread.

4. Arrange ¼ of the turkey on a slice of bread. Spread the mayonnaise on a second slice and place it over the turkey, mayonnaise side down. Arrange 3 slices of bacon, sliced tomato, and some lettuce on the second slice of bread. Spread some mayonnaise on the third slice of bread and place it, mayonnaise side down, on top.

5. Cut each sandwich twice diagonally to make 4 triangles and place a frilled toothpick in each triangle.

Sloppy Joe

Another American classic, Sloppy Joe sandwiches make a great lunch on a chilly weekend afternoon—as long as your child's school didn't serve them more than three times that week. You can make Sloppy Joes by following the simple directions on a Sloppy Joes spice packet. Or brown 1 pound lean ground beef, drain off the fat, then add to the pan ½ cup ketchup, ½ cup tomato sauce, 1 tablespoon each red wine vinegar, Worcestershire sauce, and brown sugar, and a pinch of salt. Simmer for 15 minutes and pour the mixture over an open roll. This recipe serves four. For a leaner lunch, substitute ground turkey.

All-Star Sandwiches

Tuna Melt
Place tunafish salad and a slice of cheddar or American cheese on half an English muffin and melt under the broiler.

Salad in a Pita Sandwich
Stuff a pita with lots of greens, shredded carrot, cucumber slices, sprouts, sliced red onion, and chopped tomato. Add your favorite salad dressing and, if you like, some shredded Jarlsberg or crumbled feta cheese.

Deli Sandwich
A classic sandwich overstuffed with roast beef, turkey, salami, bologna, tongue, corned beef, or pastrami. Russian dressing is a must with the roast beef.

Egg Salad
Chopped hard-boiled eggs mixed with mayonnaise—the only sandwich I recommend eating on white bread.

Lox and Cream Cheese on a Bagel
A must for Sunday mornings. Hopefully your kid won't develop too much of a fondness for this expensive delicacy.

Chicken Salad Sandwich
Cut leftover chicken or turkey into chunks, add chopped celery, parsley, and just enough mayonnaise to hold them together.

Hero
Cut open a long loaf of Italian bread, lay it on a counter surrounded by cold cuts, cheeses, and condiments, and let the kids create their own.

Smoked Turkey with Cranberry Sauce
Tasty and refreshing; the cranberry flavor is a nice change. Serve with a bit of crisp lettuce on whole-grain bread.

Four All-American Lunches

They may not be haute cuisine, but you can't go wrong serving one of these for lunch. The only downside is that you may establish a reputation among your kid's friends, and they'll be showing up on a regular basis for Dad's homemade lunches.

Hamburgers

A hamburger is simply ground meat (sirloin, round, or chuck) that is shaped into a thick, slightly bulging patty, and grilled, broiled, or pan-fried. Thin patties don't count. Neither does meat mixed with egg, onion, bread crumbs, or herbs. Get fresh meat and cook it over *high* heat, and you'll turn out perfect burgers every time.

Ingredients *(serves four)*
>   1⅓ *pounds ground round, sirloin, or*
>   *chuck*
>   *4 hamburger buns*

Equipment
>   *Broiler pan or frying pan*

1. For broiling, shape the meat into 4 equal patties that are about 4 inches across and bulging slightly in the middle. For pan-frying, make the patties flatter. See Note.
2. Preheat the broiler or put the frying pan on *high* heat and let it get very hot, about 1 minute. If you have a well-seasoned pan, you won't need to add any oil when you're frying the burgers. The fat in the meat will be sufficient.
3. Broil the burgers 4 inches from the heat for 5–6 minutes, until they are brown and a crust has formed on the top. Turn them over and grill 5 minutes more for medium rare, 6 minutes for medium. Alternatively, panfry the burgers for 6 minutes, making sure they are not

touching in the pan. Turn them over and cook about 5 minutes more for medium rare, 6 minutes for medium. Reduce the heat slightly during the last few minutes if the pan begins to smoke.

Note

Do not cover the pan while the burgers are panfrying. This will steam them and make them mushy. If you're worried about grease splattering, get a splatter screen and rest it on top of the pan.

Toppings

■ Cheese—Add it during the last minute of cooking. It will melt very quickly under the broiler, so be attentive. If panfrying, add the cheese as soon as you flip the burgers so the cheese has time to melt.

Put in buns and serve with:
■ Sautéed mushrooms and onion
■ Bacon
■ Lettuce and tomato
■ Condiments of choice

Coney Islands

This is the "official" lunch in the greater Detroit area. Take a boiled hot dog and put it in a bun. Top it with yellow mustard, tons of chili (canned or homemade), and chopped white onion. Patrons of the legendary Lafayette Coney Island restaurant in downtown Detroit eat these with a knife and fork. But in the privacy of your own home, you can cheat a little.

Hot Dogs

Let's face it. Ball-park franks taste great only because you're at the game. Better franks—crispy on the outside and juicy inside—can actually be made in a frying pan at home.

Ingredients *(serves four)*

1 scant tablespoon vegetable oil
6–8 hot dogs (see Note)
6–8 hot dog rolls

Equipment

Frying pan

1. Place a frying pan on *medium-high* heat and let it get hot, about 45 seconds.

2. Spread a scant tablespoon of oil over the bottom of the pan and arrange the hot dogs in the pan so they aren't touching.

3. Cook for about 4 minutes, until the bottoms are brown. Turn the hot dogs and cook about 3 minutes more. Continue turning, so the hot dogs are lightly brown on all sides.

Note

Hebrew National Light or chicken and turkey hot dogs have less fat than regular franks.

Quick Macaroni & Cheese

This easy recipe puts to shame the boxes of macaroni and cheese sold in the supermarket.

Ingredients *(serves four)*

10 ounces small elbow macaroni

2 tablespoons butter

1½ tablespoons unbleached all-purpose flour

¾ cup whole or nonfat milk

1½ cups (about 6 ounces) grated cheddar cheese

Equipment

Large saucepan
Large frying pan
Colander
Whisk
Wooden spoon

1. Bring a large saucepan of water to a boil for the macaroni. Add the macaroni and cook until al dente, about 5–7 minutes. Drain in a colander.

2. While the water is coming to a boil and the macaroni is cooking, place the frying pan on *medium-low* heat and add the butter. When the butter is melted, sprinkle on the flour and stir continuously with the whisk until the butter and flour become a thick paste, about 2 minutes.

3. Increase the heat to *medium high* and add the milk. Stir continuously until the mixture thickens, about 5 minutes. Add the grated cheddar and stir with a wooden spoon until the cheese melts, about 2 minutes. Turn off the heat.

4. Drain the cooked macaroni, then add it to the pan with the cheese mixture. Stir the macaroni into the cheese mixture and serve.

Variations

■ Add 1 cup small ham cubes when you're mixing the cheese sauce and pasta.

■ Boil a few chunks of Polish kielbasa and serve with the macaroni and cheese for a hearty late-afternoon lunch or early supper.

Chef's Salad

Here's a salad that's a complete and healthy lunch. Follow this recipe or use your imagination to create another tasty and colorful combination.

Ingredients *(serves four)*

1 large head leaf lettuce

1 small head Romaine lettuce

1 cucumber, peeled and sliced

2 tomatoes, each cut into 6 wedges

1 red bell pepper, cut into strips

4 large hard-boiled eggs, cut in half

¼ pound ham, cut into thin strips

¼ pound Swiss cheese, cut into thick strips

¼ pound sliced turkey, cut into thick strips

½ cup black olives

One 4-ounce jar artichoke hearts, drained and quartered

1 cup Dad's Own Vinaigrette (page 165) or bottled dressing

Equipment

Large salad bowl

1. Wash and dry the lettuces. Tear the leaves into 1½-inch pieces and place in a large salad bowl.

2. Add half the cucumber slices, tomato wedges, bell-pepper strips, egg halves, ham, cheese, and turkey to the lettuce, and toss together.

3. Alternate the remaining cucumber slices, tomato wedges, bell-pepper strips, and egg halves around the edge of the bowl in a decorative pattern.

4. Arrange the remaining ham, cheese, and turkey in the center of the bowl.

Lunch Treats

Yogurt Smoothie

Here's a healthy alternative to a milkshake: In a blender, combine 1 cup lowfat plain yogurt with 1 banana, a few strawberries or blueberries, 2 ice cubes, and ½ cup orange or apple juice. Purée on high speed until everything is combined, about 1 minute.

Dad's Own Egg Cream

So named because the frothy white bubbles on top look like beaten eggs, or that's one of at least a dozen official theories. To make a real New York egg cream, pour about 2 tablespoons chocolate syrup into a tall glass, add about 2 inches milk, and stir well. Slowly fill the glass the rest of the way up with cold seltzer, stirring continuously. If necessary, let the foam subside and then add more seltzer. Insert a straw and think of Coney Island.

Trail Mix

Here's a fun-to-make, relatively healthy snack or dessert for kids. Mix together equal parts of any combination of the following: roasted almonds, shelled peanuts, sunflower seeds, raisins, chocolate or carob chips, coconut flakes, chopped dates, cashews, dried apples, dried peaches, and dried banana chips. Eat out of hand or swirl into yogurt.

Scatter the olives and artichoke hearts over the top.

5. Present the salad at the table. Pour on the dressing, toss, and serve.

Variations

Use any of the following instead of or in addition to the meats listed in the basic recipe: salami, cooked chicken breast, leftover London broil or steak, or bacon.

The Lunchbox

Kids mean school, and school means lunch, and lunch means a lunchbox. The lunchbox hasn't changed much over the years. Pictures of Red Ryder, The Lone Ranger, and Zorro have given way to Spongebob Squarepants and Superman. Zip-top bags have replaced wax paper. And juice packs show up more often than Thermoses. Otherwise, the basic components are the same:

Lunchbox Tips

■ Remember, your children have to eat in front of other kids, so don't turn their lunchboxes into exotic culinary adventures or the latest in macrobiotic cuisine.

■ Put lettuce between the tunafish and bread to keep the bread from getting soggy.

■ If your child's lunchbox will be sitting at room temperature for a while, prepare a sandwich that won't spoil in the heat, such as salami or peanut butter and jelly.

■ Use small, reusable plastic containers to save on plastic wrap and plastic bags.

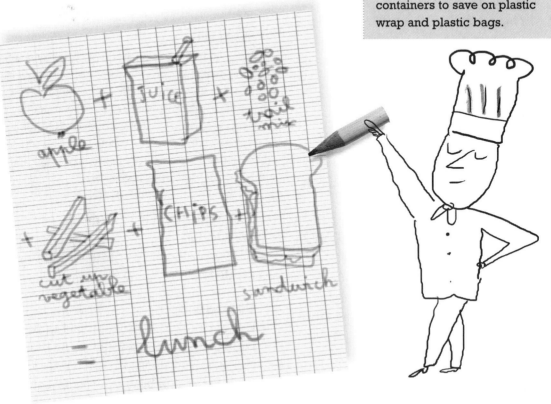

Instant No-Recipe Lunches

English Muffin Pizza

Have the kids top toasted English muffins with a spoonful of tomato sauce, cheese, veggies, salami, or anything they can find in the fridge. Put them on aluminum foil and place in the toaster oven until the cheese melts. Cool slightly, then dig in.

Yogurt Buffet

For healthful do-it-yourself sundaes, set a large bowl of vanilla yogurt on the counter along with granola, peanuts, and raisins, as well as fresh fruit, such as grapes, apple, or banana slices, pineapple chunks, or orange sections. Let the kids help themselves.

Tuna Patties

In a bowl, mash together 2 cans white meat tuna, 2 eggs, ½ cup grated cheddar, and ⅓ cup seasoned bread crumbs.

Let the mixture sit for 15 minutes in the refrigerator, then have the kids shape it into 8 patties. Fry the patties in a few tablespoons of oil in a large frying pan on *medium-high* heat until brown, about 3 minutes. Turn gently and fry for about 3 minutes more.

Macaroni & Cheese

Stock up on boxes of macaroni and cheese mixes from the health food store. You'll find several brands without added preservatives or hydrogenated oils. These handy meals always make kids happy.

Instant Burritos

Fill flour tortillas with a few tablespoons of canned chili with beans, grated cheddar, and shredded lettuce. Roll up and place, seam side down, in a lightly greased glass baking dish. Spoon on your favorite jarred taco sauce, cover the pan with aluminum foil, and bake in a preheated 350°F oven for 15–20 minutes.

Using Up Leftovers

Lunch is a great meal for using up leftovers. Two obvious ways to do this are to make sandwiches with leftover meat loaf or salads from the remainder of a cooked chicken or turkey. Here are three recipes that use leftovers in a slightly more adventurous fashion. None requires much preparation or cooking, but all are quite tasty. And if you have more or less of a particular leftover, feel free to improvise a bit.

Quick Leftover Lo Mein

This is a great dish to make with leftover shrimp (if you are ever lucky enough to have any), chicken, turkey, pork, beef, or just vegetables. Adding a handful of bean sprouts or snow peas makes it even more authentic.

Ingredients *(serves four)*

1–2 cups diced cooked chicken, meat, or shrimp
1 cup leftover cooked vegetables
¾ pound spaghetti
2 tablespoons corn oil, plus extra for tossing with the spaghetti
1 medium onion, cut in half and thinly sliced
¾ pound mung bean sprouts
¼ pound snow peas, strings removed
⅓ cup bottled Asian stir-fry sauce, such as ginger or teriyaki

Equipment

Pasta pot
Large, heavy frying pan or wok
Colander
Wok spatula, for stir-frying

1. Bring a large pot of water to a boil for the pasta. Add the spaghetti and cook until al dente, about 5 minutes. Drain in a colander, toss lightly in oil, and set aside.

2. Place a large frying pan or wok on *high* heat and let it get very hot, about 90 seconds. Add the oil and onion, and stir-fry until the onion is soft, about 1 minute.

3. Add the chicken, meat, or shrimp along with the sprouts and snow peas. Stir-fry for 2 minutes more.

4. Add the spaghetti and the Asian sauce to the pan. Cook, stirring continuously, until the sauce thickens and all the pasta is coated, about 3 minutes. Serve hot.

Asian Noodle Soup with Leftovers

Health food stores and most supermarkets sell ramen or other packages of Asian noodles with a variety of different-flavored powdered broths. They make a quick bowl of soup to which leftover meat, chicken, or vegetables can easily be added. Just cut the leftovers into small pieces and add them to the boiling water as you're stirring in the powdered broth.

Chilaquiles with Chicken, Tomatoes & Cheese

This "Mexican lasagna" is a tasty way to use leftover chicken, turkey, beef, or hamburger.

Ingredients *(serves four)*

1 23-ounce can crushed tomatoes

1 8-ounce jar red taco sauce, mild or hot

½ cup canned chicken broth or ½ bouillon cube dissolved in ½ cup hot water

1½ ounces taco seasoning mix

1 12-ounce bag unsalted tortilla chips

2 cups cooked chicken, cut into ½-inch strips (from about ½ roasted chicken) or cooked hamburger, steak, or turkey

1¾ cups (about 10 ounces) grated Monterey Jack or cheddar cheese

Equipment

Grater

Large frying pan

11 x 17-inch glass baking dish

1. Preheat the oven to 350°F.

2. Put the tomatoes, taco sauce, chicken broth (or water and bouillon), and seasoning mix in a large frying pan on *high* heat and cook until the mixture begins simmering, about 4 minutes. (If using the bouillon, make sure it dissolves completely.) Reduce the heat to *medium low* and cook the mixture for about 5 minutes more, stirring well to incorporate the spices. Turn off the heat and let the sauce sit until you are ready to use it.

3. Lightly oil an 11 x 17-inch glass baking dish. Break up the tortilla chips into large pieces and spread half of them over the bottom of the pan.

4. Spoon half the sauce over the tortillas. Arrange half the chicken pieces over the sauce. Sprinkle half the cheese over the chicken. Make another layer of chips, sauce, and chicken, and top it off with the remaining cheese.

5. Bake, uncovered, on the center rack of the oven for 25 minutes. Let sit for 5 minutes before serving.

Tips

If you're short on leftovers, poach 1½ pounds boneless chicken thighs (about 6) in an inch of water in a large covered frying pan for 8 minutes. Use *medium* heat so the water barely simmers.

Minestrone Deluxe

Make this when you have lots of leftover meat or poultry, vegetables, and pasta or rice.

Ingredients *(serves four)*

1 16-ounce can whole tomatoes,
    with liquid

1 23-ounce can minestrone soup

2 beef bouillon cubes

1–2 cups diced cooked meat, chicken,
    or turkey

1–2 cups cooked pasta or rice

1 cup leftover (or frozen) vegetables,
    cut into small pieces

¼ cup grated Parmesan cheese, for serving

Equipment

Medium saucepan

1. Chop the tomatoes coarsely.

2. Put all the ingredients except for the Parmesan in a medium saucepan and bring to a boil over *medium-high* heat.

3. Reduce the heat to *low* and simmer for 10 minutes.

4. Serve with a sprinkling of Parmesan over each bowl.

Dinner

The last thing most people want to do after a hard day's work is to come home and make dinner. But somebody has to do it and sometimes it has to be Dad. Whereas cooking for family or friends on the weekend is usually more a pleasure than a chore—you have the luxury of taking your time and stretching your culinary limbs by experimenting with a new dish—preparing dinner on a weeknight can be tricky. Let's say you don't even get started until 6:00 P.M. Factoring in your family's various schedules, the preparation time, cooking time, and cleanup, you could

DINNER

be drying the last dish at 9:30 and falling into bed five minutes later. But not if you plan, shop, and map out dinner in advance.

Plan your menus in advance. Dinner is probably the best meal to try to map out on a weekly basis. Then you can do your main course and staple shopping ahead of time, and you're free to do any preliminary preparations (marinating, defrosting, etc.) as required for each meal. All you'll need to pick up on your way home from work are some fresh items—like fish or vegetables.

To choose your main courses, think about your family's favorites and the ways you might alternate meat, chicken, fish, pasta, and soups in your menus. For instance, break up a series of heavy meals with a light pasta dish and a salad, or some fish. And though it seems impossible to determine whether red meat is the key to good health or the bane of our diets, it's probably best to serve it only a couple of nights a week at most. Once you've decided on a main course, the rest of the meal should fall neatly into place. Use the recipe serving suggestions featured in this chapter to help you fill out your menus with vegetables, a starch, and a salad.

Shop ahead. Nothing slows down a cook more than not having the necessary ingredients on hand. While you're planning your menus, create your shopping list. Also take a moment to check the cupboard to see what staples may need replenishing (see "The Cupboard" on page 23). A well-stocked pantry will not only make your cooking easier, but will also allow you to throw together a last-minute meal when necessary.

Prepare part of the meal beforehand. Starting from scratch when you walk in the door can make cooking dinner seem an insurmountable task, even for the most enthusiastic cook.

Taking just ten minutes the night before to ready the ingredients is time well spent. Another reliable time-saver is to wash and dry your salad greens in the morning, or even the night before, and pack them in well-sealed plastic bags, along with some paper towels to absorb moisture.

Prepare ahead and freeze. As you get used to shouldering the responsibility of making dinner, you may find it easier to give up a little time on a free night or the weekend to make a large batch of meatballs or a couple of pans of lasagna for freezing. It's nice to know that sometimes preparing dinner is merely a matter of remembering to defrost the entrée.

Mapping Out Dinner

Chicken, beef, fish, lamb, and pork are the traditional centerpieces of most American dinners. And while there are innumerable ways to prepare these foods as entrées, for the purposes of planning dinner, think about them in three groups: dishes that require little attention but long cooking times, dishes that require a lot of attention but take very little time to cook, and dishes that can be made in advance and reheated.

Plan dinner around what you have time to do. A roast chicken may take an hour and a half to cook, but once you've done your ten minutes of prep work, you have nothing to think about until it comes out of the oven. Serving this kind of entrée will give you a chance to get the rest of the meal together, open the mail, and talk with the kids. Sautéed fillet of sole takes only a few minutes to cook, but requires your full attention. This means making the side dishes and setting the table ahead of time.

If you make a stew or meat loaf in advance, all you need to do is reheat it and prepare your side dishes.

Coordinating the meal so that all of the different elements are done at the same time is probably the trickiest part of making dinner and will take some practice. Start with the food that takes longest to cook, jot down the cooking times of your other courses, and map it out from there.

Avoid planning a meal in which too many dishes require last-minute preparation. You can't fuss over a main course that needs sautéing, a sauce that needs stirring, and a broiled item that requires your watchful eye all at once. For example, if you are broiling swordfish steaks for the main course, make rice or microwave baked potatoes as a side dish. That way you'll be free to focus on the swordfish while the side dishes pretty much tend to themselves.

DINNER

Chicken Basics

Chicken is an ever-fashionable main course that lends itself to an infinite variety of dishes. You can buy it whole or in parts, with or without bones. No matter the form, chicken will give you lots of protein with less fat and cholesterol and fewer calories than red meat. You can reduce the calories and fat even further by removing the skin before cooking or eating.

Cuts & Parts

Broilers/fryers weigh $2^1/_2$ to $3^1/_2$ pounds and are suitable for roasting, broiling, or frying, or for stew and soup. Most chicken parts are cut from this size chicken.

Roasters are larger, more mature birds, weighing between 5 and 7 pounds. These should be used exclusively for roasting, as they are too large for frying or broiling. They can also be stuffed if you desire. You'll find that roaster parts are generally available at your market; the breasts make for especially delicious eating.

Stewing chickens (aka hens) are 1 year or older and weigh between 4 and 7 pounds. They are tougher than younger chickens but are full of flavor and make excellent soup or stew chickens.

Chicken parts can come in very handy if your kids have strong preferences for white or dark meat. Additionally, since white and dark meats have different cooking times, it's wise to cook one or the other. Boneless breasts make for quick and easy entrées, and are perfect for stir-fries. Your butcher can debone them.

Servings

The basic rule of thumb for chicken and turkey is $^3/_4$ pound of meat (with bone) per person. But it's just as easy to roast two chickens as one, or to add a couple of extra chicken breasts to the pan. You'll have great leftovers for the next day's lunch or dinner. Count on 4–6 ounces per person of boneless chicken.

Storage

When purchasing poultry, always check the expiration date on the packaging. The chicken should be cooked or properly frozen before that date. If you are not using the chicken right away, remove it from the packaging, rinse under cold water, and pat dry. Then wrap the chicken loosely in foil or plastic wrap and store in the refrigerator for up to 3 days.

To freeze chicken, wrap it in a freezer bag, seal well, label it, and store in the freezer for up to 3 months. Defrost all poultry in the refrigerator, not on the kitchen counter where risk of contamination from the salmonella bacteria is greater. Chicken parts will defrost overnight, a whole chicken in 24 hours. Chicken should be cooked soon after it is defrosted and should not be refrozen.

Roast Chicken

Roasting is the simplest way to cook a whole chicken. First remove the giblets (they're usually wrapped in paper inside the cavity) and rinse the chicken well, inside and out, with cold water. Pat it dry and pull off any globs of fat around the cavity. Next, squeeze half an orange or lemon over the skin and rub

it inside the cavity. Sprinkle the bird with salt, pepper, and a dash of paprika. Lay a few dots of butter on the back and legs and place the chicken in a roasting pan just large enough to hold it (use a rack if you've got one). Roast the chicken on the center rack of a preheated 350°F oven. Cook for 20 minutes per pound (about 1 hour 10 minutes for an average-size broiler/fryer), or until the juices run clear when a thigh joint is pricked with a knife.

Broiled Chicken

Broiling requires more attention than roasting. The chicken should be cut in half or in parts, rubbed with vegetable oil, seasoned with salt and pepper, and arranged in the broiler pan skin side down. Place the broiler pan 6 inches from the heat and broil for 20 minutes. Turn and broil for 20 minutes more. During the last 10 minutes brush the skin with a bit of butter or lime juice to keep it from drying out and turn if it starts to char. Marinating the chicken for several hours before broiling also keeps the meat from drying out.

Fried Chicken

Frying is the most difficult way to cook chicken. It requires careful monitoring of the temperature of the oil, otherwise the chicken turns into a soggy, greasy mess. There are as many authentic recipes for fried chicken as there are church suppers. The basic procedure calls for dredging (lightly coating) the chicken parts in flour, cornmeal, or seasoned bread crumbs, then frying a few pieces at a time in about $1/2$ inch of hot oil. Have a seasoned cook walk you through it the first time.

Sautéed Chicken

Sautéing boneless chicken breasts is quick and easy. Simply flatten the breasts a bit (see box, page 80) and dredge (lightly coat) them in flour or bread crumbs, if desired. Heat the sauté pan over *medium* heat, add a few tablespoons of oil, and sauté for 3–4 minutes until the underside is a nice medium brown. Turn and sauté for 3 minutes more.

DINNER

Perfect Roast Chicken

You *can* shove a chicken in the oven and forget about it for an hour or so and it will come out cooked. But with just a few simple touches, you can truly "roast" a chicken to golden-brown perfection.

Ingredients *(serves four)*

   1 4- to 5-pound chicken
   1 lemon
   1 small onion, peeled and cut in half
   4 tablespoons (½ stick) butter or margarine
   1 teaspoon salt
   Freshly ground black pepper
   1 sprig fresh rosemary or ½ teaspoon dried
   Additional salt and pepper

Equipment

   11 x 17-inch roasting pan
   Roasting rack
   4-inch metal skewer
   Carving fork
   Basting brush

1. Preheat the oven to 400°F.
2. Rinse the chicken inside and out under cold water, and pat dry.
3. Cut the lemon in half. Squeeze one half over the outside of the chicken. Rub the other half inside the cavity of the chicken, squeezing the juice against the bones. Leave that lemon half in the cavity along with the onion halves, 2 tablespoons of the butter, the salt, pepper, and rosemary. Close the cavity by folding the flaps of skin over the opening. Secure them further by threading a 4-inch metal skewer through the skin.

Cutting a Cooked Chicken

The key to easy cutting is a good pair of kitchen shears. After you've let the chicken cool for a few minutes, place it on a cutting board and, using the shears, cut through the breast to the back. Open the chicken up and you will see the ridge of the backbone. Use the shears to cut along each side of the backbone. Place the chicken halves, skin side up, on the cutting board and use the shears or a chef's knife to cut through the cartilage between the leg and the breast. If you meet with distinct resistance (bone), adjust the knife or shears slightly until you find the cartilage. If you want to separate the drumstick as well, bend it back away from the thigh and then cut the joint with shears.

4. Rub the breast side of the chicken with 1 tablespoon butter and place it on the roasting rack in the roasting pan, breast side up. Place the pan on the center rack of your oven.
5. After 30 minutes, turn the bird over to the other side with a carving fork. Rub on the remaining butter and continue roasting for 30 minutes more.
6. Turn the chicken breast side up and brush it with some of the pan juices. Roast it for 10–15 minutes more, until the leg and thigh move freely when jiggled or the juices run clear when the thigh joint is pricked with a knife.

Note

For a smaller (3–4 pound) chicken, roast for 25 minutes on each side and 10 minutes more breast side up.

Serving Suggestions

■ Serve with gravy and mashed potatoes, sweet potatoes, or rice.

■ Serve steamed or boiled broccoli, glazed carrots, or sautéed zucchini.

Oven-Baked Middle Eastern "Fried" Chicken

Here is an easy way to get crispy chicken without the mess and calories of frying.

Ingredients *(serves four)*

6 chicken legs
6 chicken thighs
1 cup plain bread crumbs
2 tablespoons coriander
1 tablespoon dried cumin
1 teaspoon onion powder
1 teaspoon garlic powder
1 teaspoon cinnamon
Dash of cayenne pepper
2 large eggs

Equipment

Large roasting pan
Roasting rack
Pie plate
Medium bowl
Aluminum foil

1. Preheat the oven to 375°F. Rinse the chicken pieces under cold water and pat dry with paper towels.

Simple Pan Gravy

Remove the roasted chicken, then, using a pot holder, tilt the roasting pan so the juice runs into one corner. Use a baster or serving spoon to skim off and discard the fat floating on the surface. Place the pan on top of the stove over *medium* heat. Add about $1/2$ cup water or white wine to the pan (large pans will require more liquid) and 1 tablespoon flour or cornstarch. Use a spatula to scrape up the bits of meat sticking to the bottom and stir regularly. When the liquid has reduced by half, transfer it to a bowl, along with any bits of meat stuck to the bottom of the pan. Add salt and pepper and serve with the chicken.

2. Combine the bread crumbs and all the spices in a pie plate and set aside. Beat the eggs in a medium bowl and set aside.

3. Dip each piece of chicken in the egg and let the excess drip off. One by one, lay the chicken pieces in the bread crumbs. Turn each one so the entire outside skin is coated with bread crumbs. Shake gently to remove excess.

4. Line a large roasting pan with aluminum foil and set the rack in the pan. Lay the breaded chicken on the rack and bake for 35–40 minutes, until the chicken is cooked through.

Variation

For chicken breasts, prepare in exactly the same way but bake for only 30–35 minutes.

Serving Suggestions

■ Serve with rice pilaf or home fries.

■ Serve with steamed spinach or steamed, boiled, or sautéed green beans.

DINNER

Chicken Breast Piccata

This is a simplified version of a classic Italian dish.

Ingredients *(serves four)*

2 whole skinless, boneless chicken breasts, split and flattened
2 large eggs
1 cup Italian-style bread crumbs
2 tablespoons olive oil
¼ cup white wine
¼ cup canned chicken broth
Juice of 1 lemon
2 teaspoons capers (optional)
Salt and pepper

Equipment

Large frying pan
Small bowl
Pie plate
Dinner plate
Serving platter
Spatula

1. Rinse the chicken breasts under cold water and pat them dry with paper towels. Beat the eggs lightly in a small bowl.
2. Put the bread crumbs in a pie plate.
3. Dip each chicken breast in the egg and let the excess drip off.
4. Dredge both sides of the breast in the bread crumbs and shake gently to remove the excess. Place the breasts on a plate.
5. Put a large frying pan on *high* heat and let it get hot, about 30 seconds. Add the oil and chicken breasts. Sauté the chicken for 3–4

Flattening Breasts

A whole chicken breast has two parts, one of which is usually considered a single portion. Most boneless breasts are sold already split. To flatten, lay 1 breast between 2 sheets of wax paper. Using the flat side of a meat mallet, pound the breast several times until it is about half its original thickness.

minutes, until the bottom is golden brown. Turn and cook for 3 minutes more. Reduce the heat to *medium* and sauté for 2–3 minutes more, until the chicken is cooked through. Transfer the chicken to a serving platter.
6. Add the wine to the pan and let it simmer and reduce, using a spatula to scrape up any bits of chicken stuck to the pan. Add the broth, lemon juice, and capers, if using. Cook and stir for another 45 seconds, until the liquid thickens slightly. Season with salt and pepper. Pour the sauce over the chicken breasts and serve immediately.

Variation

For Chicken Parmesan, preheat the oven to 350°F. Flatten the chicken breasts only slightly and follow Steps 1–5. When the breasts are brown on both sides, transfer them to a baking sheet. Spoon on a bit of tomato sauce, sprinkle on about a tablespoon of Parmesan, and top with a slice of mozzarella cheese. Bake until the cheese melts and the chicken is cooked, about 10 minutes. Serve over a bed of spaghetti.

Serving Suggestions

■ Serve with pasta or wild rice.
■ Serve boiled or steamed broccoli.

Chicken with Tomato & Sausage

This is a simple, hearty dish that the kids will love to eat with spaghetti.

Ingredients *(serves four)*

1 3- to 4-pound chicken, cut into 8 pieces

3 tablespoons olive oil, plus extra for tossing with the spaghetti

1 medium onion, thinly sliced

1 green or red bell pepper, thinly sliced

2 cloves garlic, minced

½ pound sweet Italian sausage, cut into ½-inch pieces

¼ cup dry white wine

1 28-ounce can whole tomatoes, drained and chopped

3 tablespoons tomato paste

1 teaspoon dried basil

1 chicken bouillon cube

1 teaspoon salt

Freshly ground black pepper

¾ pound spaghetti

Equipment

Large frying pan

Large pasta pot

Medium bowl

Large plate

Large platter

Slotted spoon

Spatula

Tongs

1. Rinse the chicken pieces under cold water and pat them dry with paper towels.

2. Place a large frying pan on *medium-high* heat and let it get hot, about 45 seconds. Add the oil, onion, and bell pepper, and sauté, stirring often, until soft, about 5 minutes. Add the garlic and sauté for 1 minute more. Transfer the vegetables to a medium bowl.

3. Raise the heat to *high* and add the sausage pieces to the pan. Sauté, stirring often, until the meat is cooked through, about 4 minutes. Use a slotted spoon to transfer the sausage to the bowl with the vegetables and discard the fat in the pan.

4. Return the pan to the burner and when it is very hot, after about 15 seconds, add the chicken pieces and cook until they are brown on all sides, using tongs to turn them. This should take about 5 minutes. Transfer the chicken to a large plate.

5. Add the wine to the pan and use a spatula to scrape up any bits of chicken stuck to the bottom.

6. Return the chicken, sausage, and vegetables to the pan. Add the tomatoes, tomato paste, basil, bouillon cube, salt and pepper. Bring the sauce to a boil, then reduce the heat to *low* and simmer, partially covered, for 30 minutes, until the chicken is thoroughly cooked. Stir occasionally.

7. While the chicken is simmering, boil the water for the spaghetti. Cook the spaghetti until al dente, then drain it and toss lightly with olive oil.

8. To serve, arrange the spaghetti on a large platter and use a slotted spoon to place the chicken and sausage over the pasta. Pour on enough sauce to flavor the spaghetti well.

Serving Suggestion

Serve with garlic bread and a tossed green salad or a Caesar salad.

Beef Basics

Thanks to its high fat and calorie contents, red meat has borne its share of criticism during the past few years. But that doesn't mean you should give up meat altogether. Instead, try to get in the habit of choosing the leanest cuts, such as eye of round, round tip, top round, tenderloin, and sirloin. Trim excess fat, and prepare small portions. And don't try to fight the fact that hamburgers are a major feature in most kids' childhoods.

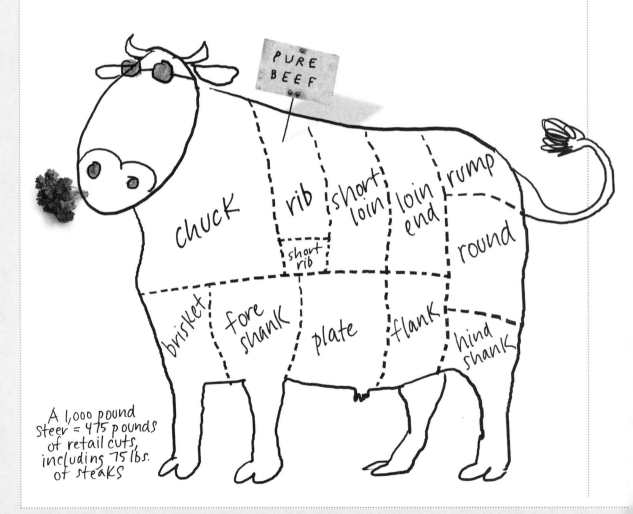

PURE BEEF

chuck   rib   short loin   loin end   rump

short rib

round

brisket   fore shank   plate   flank   hind shank

A 1,000 pound Steer = 475 pounds of retail cuts, including 75 lbs. of steaks

Cuts

Hitching up with a good butcher is the first step toward understanding (and obtaining) good cuts of meat. The second step is understanding that beef is cut from two types of muscle. Meat from muscles that are used infrequently, such as the loin and rib, will be tender. Cuts from more active muscles, such as the leg and shoulder, will be tougher. Tender cuts should be cooked quickly: broiled, roasted, or pan-fried; tougher cuts should be cooked slowly usually stewed or braised.

Whole fillet

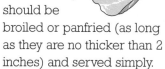

(or tenderloin) is the most tender and expensive cut of beef. It should be roasted whole in a very hot oven and can be sliced thin for an appetizer or slightly thicker for a main course.

Filet mignons

are 1- to 2-inch slices cut from the center part of the whole fillet and are best pan-fried in butter and oil. They can then be topped with herbs or different sauces.

Sirloin steaks are excellent and extremely flavorful cuts

taken from the rump end of the loin. They should be broiled or panfried (as long as they are no thicker than 2 inches) and served simply.

Porterhouse steaks

are taken from the shoulder end of the loin. They are usually cut thicker than sirloin steaks and are a little more tender as well. These should also be broiled and served simply.

Chuck steaks

come from the shoulder and are tougher and fattier than the loin cuts. They can be broiled, but are more commonly used for stews and roasts or ground for hamburgers.

Brisket is taken from under the shoulder. Look for the "first cut" of brisket, sometimes called the "plate," which is leaner and more flavorful than the second cut. Brisket is ideal for pot roast as it needs long, slow cooking.

Flank steaks

are thin, flavorful cuts taken from under the loin. These should be broiled and

can be served with any number of sauces, or can be rolled and stuffed with flavorful fillings. Leftover flank steak is also great in sandwiches and salads.

Chopped meat

is usually made from chuck, round, or sirloin. Chuck and round make for somewhat juicier—but fattier and more caloric—burgers. Leaner burgers are also very tasty. Hamburgers should be broiled, grilled, or panfried.

Roasts

are larger cuts of meat, usually weighing between 3 and 6 pounds. The most succulent are the rib roasts (with bone in), which will yield hefty portions. Other roasts come from the round or rump, which are both in the general vicinity of the tail. The top round and eye round are the most tender of these cuts. Chuck, bottom round, and rump roasts are flavorful but not as tender.

Ribs

are fatty and fun and will keep the kids busy at the table. They are easy to cook and can be prepared in a variety of ways.

DINNER

Servings

For boneless steaks, figure on $1/4$ pound per person. For bone-in cuts and roasts, figure closer to $1/2$ pound per person. For chopped meat, figure on $1/4$ pound per burger. For ribs, figure 1 pound per person. Leftover steak or roast beef will never go to waste, so don't hesitate to buy a little more than you need.

Storage

A roast will keep in the refrigerator for about 4 or 5 days. Whether storing in the refrigerator or the freezer, always rewrap beef in plastic and foil. Shape hamburger into patties before freezing and wrap individually so you can take out only what you need. Defrost meat in the refrigerator overnight, or in the microwave, removing the foil but leaving the meat in its plastic wrapping. Large roasts can take 2 to 3 days to defrost in the refrigerator. Meat should be cooked soon after it is defrosted and should not be refrozen.

The Meat Thermometer

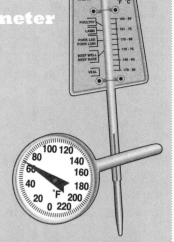

An all-purpose thermometer can take much of the anxiety out of cooking a roast. Avoid the old-fashioned meat thermometer that is placed in the meat before cooking, and get a good-quality instant-read thermometer to use at the end of cooking. Shortly before you think the meat will be done, open the oven and maneuver your meat or poultry so you have access to the thickest part of the roast or the thigh of a chicken or turkey. Insert the point to the center of the roast or thigh, making sure the tip is not touching a bone. Take a reading when the needle stops. Keep in mind that roasts continue cooking for about 10–15 minutes after they're removed from the oven.

Cooking Times

Different roasts have different cooking times depending on tenderness. The time guidelines below are minutes per pound for medium rare. Remember to preheat the oven and let the meat come to room temperature before cooking.

Cut	Weight	Temp.	Cooking Time per Pound
Whole fillet (tenderloin)	3–4 pounds	450°F	11 minutes
Rib roast (with bone)	4–6 pounds	300°F	28 minutes
Rib eye (boneless)	3–4 pounds	350°F	15 minutes
Roast beef (round, rump, chuck)	3–4 pounds	325°F	30 minutes
Whole brisket	5–6 pounds	375°F	35 minutes

Broiled Beef

Broiling is the most common way of cooking steaks, chops, and burgers. Thin cuts (1–1$\frac{1}{2}$ inches thick) should be cooked 3 inches from the heat. For thicker cuts (1$\frac{1}{2}$–2 inches thick), lower the meat to 4–5 inches from the heat, otherwise the outside will burn before the inside is done. Remember, this distance is not how far the rack is from the heat, but how far the actual surface of the meat is from the heat.

Stewed Beef

Stewing is the cooking of small pieces of meat in a covered pot in enough liquid to cover them. Vegetables and herbs are cooked with the meat to enhance the flavor. Stew meat on top of the stove over *low* heat or in a 325°F oven for several hours.

Braised Beef

Braising is the process of cooking meat slowly in a small amount of liquid, either on top of the stove or in the oven. Cook over *low* heat on the stove or in a 325°F oven.

Cuts such as chuck roast, brisket, and short ribs can all be braised. It's best to brown the meat first before adding the hot liquid. After adding the liquid and spices, cover the pot tightly. Onions, potatoes, carrots, and celery can also be added to the pot.

Roast Beef

Roasting is the proper method for cooking larger (over 2 pounds) pieces of meat. The meat should be arranged, fat side up, on a rack in a roasting pan just large enough to hold it. Using a rack keeps the bottom of the roast from steaming. If there is no fat on the roast, brush it lightly with oil or spread on a thin layer of mustard. Let the meat come to room temperature before putting it in the oven or it will take longer to cook.

Panfried Beef & Burgers

Panfrying is another method for cooking thinly cut steaks and burgers. They should be cooked in a small amount of margarine or oil in a preheated pan over *medium-high* heat. Fry until the bottom is brown, then turn the meat. Choose a pan that holds the meat comfortably. If the pan is too large, the drippings will start smoking before the meat is done. If the pan is too crowded, the meat will steam instead of fry.

DINNER

How to Cut an Onion

Onions are the most frequently listed ingredient in recipes. They are common to all cuisines and are used in both rustic and elegant dishes. For variation, instead of the common yellow onion, try the sweet Vidalia, or substitute another member of the onion family such as shallots, scallions, or leeks. Use red onion for salads or in sandwiches.

Peeling

1. Trim 1/2 inch from both the stem and root ends of the onion.

2. Cut through the skin lengthwise and peel it off, taking with it as little of the onion as possible.

Slicing

Using a chef's knife, cut crosswise in 1/4-inch-thick slices.

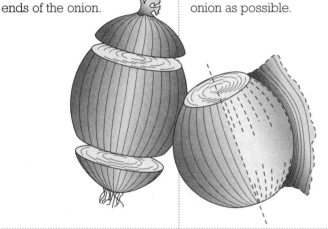

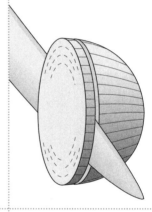

Chopping & Dicing

1. Using a chef's knife, cut the peeled onion in half lengthwise.

2. Place the flat side down and cut the onion crosswise in 1/4-inch-thick slices.

3. Hold the onion firmly together and give a quarter turn; cut in 1/4-inch pieces. (It will look like cross-hatching.) For even smaller pieces, continue to chop through.

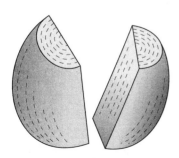

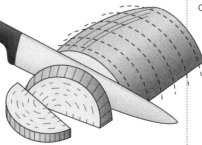

2 large carrots, cut into 1-inch rounds
1 large potato, cut into eighths

Equipment

Large frying pan or Dutch oven with cover

1. Rinse the roast under very cold water and pat it dry with paper towels.

2. Sprinkle the meat with the flour, then shake off any excess.

3. Place a large frying pan on *high* heat and let it get very hot, about 45 seconds. Add the vegetable oil and the meat and brown the meat on both sides.

4. Add the onions and garlic to the frying pan, arranging them around the meat. Add ½ cup water and the wine and ketchup to the pan and stir to incorporate. Sprinkle the onion soup mix on top of the meat.

5. When the liquid starts boiling, cover the pan and reduce the heat to *low*. Simmer the roast for 2½ hours, until the meat is very tender. Periodically spoon some of the sauce over the meat. If the sauce cooks away, add more water, ½ cup at a time.

6. Add the sliced carrots and potato pieces to the pan for the last hour of cooking.

7. To serve, let the roast cool for 10 minutes, then remove it from the pan juices. Slice the meat thinly and on an angle. Serve with the vegetables and pan juices.

Serving Suggestions

■ Serve over wide noodles.
■ Serve a mixed green salad or corn.

Variation

If you don't have a large enough frying pan or Dutch oven to cook the pot roast on the stove, you can also cook it in a preheated 325°F oven. After browning the meat in the frying pan (step 3), transfer it to a casserole. Add ½ cup water to the frying pan and, over *low* heat, scrape up any bits of meat that are stuck to the bottom. Then add the wine, ketchup, and onion soup mix and stir together. Transfer the liquid to the casserole and add the onions, garlic, carrots, and potato. Cover the casserole with foil and bake for 2½ hours, until the meat is tender.

Stuffed Flank Steak

This dish requires a lot of ingredients but not a lot of work. It not only tastes great, but looks very impressive on a platter, with the red tomato sauce complementing the green spinach stuffing. Hearty and rich, this dish will satisfy even the seemingly insatiable appetites of growing teenagers.

Ingredients *(serves four)*

Olive oil, for greasing the pan
1 10-ounce package frozen chopped spinach
¼ cup grated Parmesan
¼ cup bread crumbs
3 cloves garlic, minced
1 large egg
1 4-ounce jar roasted red bell peppers
1 medium flank steak (1½–2 pounds), butterflied by the butcher
2 ounces sliced prosciutto or Black Forest ham
2 cups Basic Tomato Sauce (page 182) or your favorite store-bought sauce

Equipment

9 x 16-inch roasting pan

Butcher's twine or heavy-duty uncoated all-cotton string

Small saucepan

Medium saucepan

Colander

Medium bowl

1. Preheat the oven to 350°F. Lightly grease a 9 x 16-inch roasting pan with olive oil. Cut five 8-inch pieces of butcher's twine. Set all aside.

2. In a small saucepan, boil the spinach in 2 inches of water until cooked through. Transfer to a colander and rinse with cold water. Take a small clump of spinach and squeeze out the water. Transfer to a bowl and repeat with the rest of the spinach.

3. Add the Parmesan, bread crumbs, garlic, and egg to the spinach, and mix together.

4. Drain the roasted peppers and cut them into ½-inch strips.

5. Lay the flank steak on the work surface and open it up. Arrange a row of prosciutto or ham slices lengthwise down the center. Spread the spinach mixture in an even layer over the prosciutto or ham. Arrange the red pepper strips down the center of the spinach.

6. Roll the meat lengthwise into a long log (like a jelly roll). Slip a piece of string under the center of the meat and tie it relatively tightly in a knot. Repeat down the length of the roll, tying the remaining 4 pieces of string at equal intervals.

7. Place the rolled meat in the roasting pan and roast on the center rack of the oven for 40 minutes, until the top is browned and the meat is cooked but still pink in the center.

8. Remove the pan from the oven and let the meat sit for 5 minutes before slicing.

9. While the meat is resting, heat the tomato sauce in a medium saucepan on *medium* heat until hot.

10. Cut the meat into 1½-inch slices, arrange them on a platter, and spoon a stream of tomato sauce down the center of the slices. Serve with the remaining sauce on the side.

Serving Suggestions

Serve with pasta or home fries, and snow peas or green beans.

London Broil

London broil is a good dish to make for a hearty last-minute dinner. It comes from a lean cut of beef, such as the top round, flank, or shoulder. It's best cooked to medium rare because it dries out if left in the oven much longer.

Ingredients *(serves four)*

2-pound London broil or flank steak, ¾- to 1-inch thick

1 clove garlic, peeled and cut in half

1 tablespoon vegetable oil

Equipment

Broiler pan

Basting brush

1. Preheat the broiler.

2. Rinse the meat under very cold water and pat it dry with paper towels.

3. Rub both sides of the meat with the cut side of the garlic clove, then lightly brush each side of the meat with the oil.

4. Lay the meat on the broiler pan and broil 2 inches from the flame for 6 minutes. Turn and broil for 5 minutes more.

5. Remove the meat from the oven and let it rest for 5 minutes before slicing.

Tip

London broil is best thinly sliced across the grain and on a slight angle.

Serving Suggestions

■ Serve with pasta dressed with a simple herb-and-butter sauce.

■ Serve a mixed green salad and steamed or boiled green beans.

Stir-Fried Beef & Broccoli

By taking advantage of the variety of Asian stir-fry sauces that are now widely available, you can whip up this meal in a flash. To make it even easier for Dad, many supermarkets sell beef that is already sliced.

Ingredients *(serves four)*

2 cups broccoli florets

2 tablespoons vegetable oil

1 pound sirloin or flank steak, thinly sliced into ½-inch wide strips

1 medium onion, thinly sliced

1 red bell pepper, seeded and cut into strips

¼ cup bottled Asian stir-fry sauce, such as teriyaki or ginger

Equipment

Medium saucepan with lid

Strainer

Paper towels

Large, heavy frying pan or wok

Medium bowl

1. Steam or boil the broccoli in the saucepan in ½ inch of water until it is cooked but still crunchy (about 3 minutes). Drain well and transfer to a double layer of paper towel so the florets will dry a little before stir-frying.

2. Place a large frying pan or wok on *high* heat and let it get very hot, about 90 seconds. Add the oil and swirl it around so it coats the bottom of the pan. Add the beef and cook, turning and stirring, until the meat loses its pinkness, about 3 minutes. Remove the beef and transfer to a medium bowl.

3. Add the sliced onion and pepper to the pan and cook, stirring continuously until the vegetables soften slightly, about 2 minutes.

4. Add the beef and broccoli to the pan, and stir to heat it through. Add the sauce and stir to lightly coat all the ingredients. Serve immediately.

Serving Suggestion

Serve with white or brown rice, Chinese noodles, or thin pasta.

Mexican Feast

Mexican food seems to appeal to kids and adults alike. You can get this fun meal ready and on the table in just 2 hours, using a combination of fresh and packaged or canned ingredients. Make all three entrées to serve twelve, or prepare a single entrée for four.

MENU

Tortilla chips

Salsa

Chicken burritos

Steak fajitas

Vegetarian tacos

Dirty rice

Lemonade ice-cream pie

Mexican beer

Assembling the Feast

In order to get everything on the table at the same time, enlist the help of a couple of youngsters to assist you during the last 20 minutes or so, when you are sautéing all the meat, assembling the burritos and tacos, and setting the accompaniments on the table.

The Day Before
- Make the ice-cream pie and freeze

Two Hours Before
- Broil the flank steak and cut into slices
- Cut the chicken into strips
- Make the chili for the tacos
- Shred the lettuce, put in a plastic bag, and refrigerate

One Hour Before
- Chop all the plum tomatoes, place in a bowl, and refrigerate
- Chop all the red onion, place in a bowl, and refrigerate
- Slice the yellow onion and refrigerate
- Grate all the cheese, place in a bowl, and refrigerate
- Make the rice
- Remove 16 tortillas from the refrigerator and wrap 8 of them in aluminum foil
- Preheat the oven to 275°F

Just Before Serving
- Sauté the steak, seasonings, and sauce
- Sauté the chicken, seasonings, and sauce
- Put the wrapped tortillas in the preheated oven
- Assemble the burritos and tacos
- Set the steak mixture, grated cheese, and flour tortillas on the table
- Set the rice on the table

The Shopping List
- 2 whole chicken breasts
- 3/4 pound boneless sirloin steak
- 1 1/2 pounds shredded Monterey Jack or cheddar cheese
- 1 1/2 pounds (about 10) plum tomatoes
- 1 head Romaine or iceberg lettuce
- 1 green bell pepper
- 1 red bell pepper
- 2 medium red onions
- 1 medium yellow onion
- 3 cloves garlic
- 2 28-ounce cans crushed tomatoes
- 1 12-ounce can red beans
- 1 8-ounce can corn, without sugar
- 2 chicken bouillon cubes
- 16 ounces mild or medium red taco sauce
- 1 4-ounce jar green taco sauce
- 1–3 cups converted rice
- 1 packet taco seasoning mix
- 1 packet chili seasoning mix
- 16 flour tortillas
- 8 taco shells
- vegetable oil
- 1–2 quarts high-quality vanilla ice cream
- 1–2 6-ounce cans frozen lemonade or limeade
- 1–2 store-bought graham cracker pie crusts

Steak Fajitas

To make fajitas, sauté sliced flank steak with sliced onion, bell pepper, and garlic, add sauce and spices, and serve at the table with flour tortillas and grated cheese.

Ingredients *(serves four)*

8 flour tortillas
¾ pound boneless sirloin steak
2 tablespoons vegetable oil
1 medium yellow onion, thinly sliced
1 red bell pepper, seeded and thinly sliced
3 cloves garlic, minced
¼ cup red taco sauce
¼ cup green taco sauce
½ packet taco seasoning mix
½ pound grated Monterey Jack
   or cheddar cheese

Equipment

Broiler pan
Large frying pan
Serving bowl

1. Preheat the broiler. Remove the tortillas from the refrigerator and let them come to room temperature while you are preparing the fajitas.

2. Place the steak on a broiler pan. Broil about 3 inches from the heat for 5 minutes. Turn the steak over and broil 4 minutes more until nicely browned. Transfer the steak to a platter and let it cool for about 10 minutes before slicing.

3. Cut the steak into thin slices and set aside on a plate.

4. Put a large frying pan on *high* heat and let it get very hot, about 1 minute. Add the oil and the sliced onion and bell pepper

and sauté, stirring constantly, until soft, about 5 minutes.

5. Add the steak slices and garlic and cook 1 minute more. Stir in the taco sauces and taco seasoning and cook until the mixture is heated through, about 2 minutes. Turn off the heat. Transfer the steak mixture to a serving bowl.

6. Place the tortillas on a dinner plate, and bring them to the table along with the steak mixture and grated cheese. Guests and family can assemble their own fajitas by placing a few tablespoons of steak across the middle of their tortilla, topping with grated cheese, then rolling the whole thing up.

Chicken Burritos

To make this burrito, you sauté sliced chicken, add sauce and spices, then place the filling in a flour tortilla with chopped tomato, onion, shredded lettuce, and grated cheese, and wrap it all up.

Ingredients *(serves four)*

8 flour tortillas
2 tablespoons vegetable oil
2 whole boneless chicken breasts, cut in half
   and sliced into ½-inch strips
½ cup canned crushed tomatoes
1 chicken bouillon cube
½ packet taco seasoning mix
¾ pound (about 5) fresh plum tomatoes
1 medium red onion
4 leaves Romaine lettuce or ¼ head iceberg
½ pound Monterey Jack or cheddar
   cheese, grated
1 6-ounce jar taco sauce

Equipment

Large frying pan
Medium bowl
4 small bowls

1. Preheat the oven to 275°F. Wrap the tortillas well in aluminum foil and place them in the oven.

2. Put a large frying pan on *high* heat and let it get very hot, about 1 minute. Add the oil and chicken strips and sauté until the chicken is opaque and just cooked through, about 5 minutes.

3. Add the crushed tomatoes, bouillon cube, and taco seasoning. Cook 2 minutes more, stirring often, until the sauce thickens. Be sure to break up the bouillon cube so it dissolves completely. Turn off the heat and cover the pan.

4. Cut the tomatoes lengthwise into quarters. Cut each quarter into ¼-inch slices and chop the slices roughly. Coarsely chop the onion.

5. Cut the lettuce into ¼-inch slices. Stack these and then cut them in half. Put the chopped tomato, shredded lettuce, chopped onion, and grated cheese in separate bowls.

6. Remove the tortillas from the oven. Open the package and place 2 tortillas on each dinner plate. Spoon 3 tablespoons of the chicken mixture down the center of each tortilla. Top the chicken with about 2 tablespoons each of grated cheese, chopped tomato and onion, and shredded lettuce.

7. Fold the bottom third of each tortilla over the filling. Fold the top third down so it overlaps slightly. Turn each burrito so the folded side faces down on the plate. Top each with taco sauce, if desired, just before serving.

Vegetarian Tacos

A Mexican feast is never complete without tacos.

Ingredients *(serves four)*

1 tablespoon corn oil
1 green bell pepper, seeded and coarsely chopped
1 28-ounce can crushed tomatoes
1 packet chili seasoning mix
1 12-ounce can red beans, drained
1 8-ounce can corn, without sugar, drained
¾ pound (about 5) plum tomatoes
4 leaves Romaine lettuce or ¼ head iceberg lettuce
½ pound grated Monterey Jack or cheddar cheese
1 medium red onion
8 store-bought taco shells, warmed, if desired

Equipment

Large frying pan with cover
4 small bowls

1. Put a large frying pan on *high* heat and let it get hot, about 45 seconds. Add the oil and the bell pepper and sauté, stirring often, until cooked through but still crunchy, about 5 minutes.

2. Add the tomatoes, chili seasoning, and red beans. When the mixture starts boiling, reduce the heat to *low*, partially cover, and simmer for 20 minutes. Stir the chili occasionally to keep it from sticking to the bottom of the pan.

3. Stir in the corn and cook until heated through. Turn off the heat.

4. Cut the tomatoes lengthwise into quarters, Cut each quarter into ¼-inch slices. Chop these roughly and set aside in a small bowl. Coarsely chop the onion. Put each topping in a bowl.

5. Cut the lettuce into ¼-inch slices. Stack these and then cut them in half. Put the lettuce in a bowl.

6. Place the taco shells on a platter. Fill each with about ¼ cup of the chili mixture. Top with the tomato, lettuce, cheese, and onion.

Dirty Rice

Dad's variation on the Cajun recipe, which is made with giblets, this "not so dirty rice" is a perfect accompaniment to a Mexican dinner.

Ingredients *(serves four)*

> 1½ cups water
> 1 cup canned crushed tomatoes
> 1 chicken bouillon cube
> 1 cup converted white rice

Equipment

> *Medium saucepan*

1. Bring the water, crushed tomatoes, and bouillon cube to a boil in a medium saucepan. Add the rice. When the liquid returns to a boil, stir once, immediately cover the pan, and reduce the heat to *low*.

2. Cook the rice for 18 minutes or until the liquid is completely absorbed.

Note

If you are making the entire meal for 12, triple this recipe and use a large saucepan.

Lemonade Ice-Cream Pie

A perfect way to cool the palate after a spicy Mexican feast. Make your life easier by preparing this pie in advance, up to 4 days before the dinner.

Ingredients *(serves six generously)*

> 1 quart high-quality vanilla ice cream
> 1 6-ounce can frozen lemonade or limeade (do not dilute)
> 1 store-bought graham cracker pie crust

Equipment

> *Food processor or blender*
> *Large bowl*
> *Rubber spatula*

1. Let the ice cream soften until it just begins to get runny. In 4 batches purée the ice cream in a food processor until light and creamy, about 15 seconds for each batch. If using a blender, purée the ice cream in 6 batches. Transfer the puréed ice cream to a large bowl.

2. Stir the frozen lemonade or limeade into the puréed ice cream until completely incorporated.

3. Transfer the mixture to the graham cracker crust, smoothing out the top with a rubber spatula. Place the pie in the freezer until ready to use.

4. Remove the pie from the freezer about 5 minutes before you want to serve it to let it soften.

Note

If you are serving the Mexican Feast for 12, make 2 pies.

DINNER

Lamb Basics

Lamb chops are my personal favorite food. Thick chops simply grilled to a luscious pink medium rare with a glass of Italian Barolo is the way I like to celebrate special occasions. Other cuts, such as roast leg of lamb and shoulder chops, are both flavorful and easy to prepare.

Cuts

Whole leg is one of the most popular cuts of lamb and is the basis  for many classic dishes. The whole leg comes either bone in and weighs 7–8 pounds, or boneless and weighs 5–6 pounds. Both should be roasted.

Butterflied leg of lamb is a boneless leg that has been trimmed and then opened up and slightly pounded out. Have your butcher do it.

Boneless loin roast, lean, flavorful, and succulent, is one of the  premier cuts of meat. The whole loin actually comes in 2 pieces and each should be rolled and tied before roasting.

Loin chops are cut from the loin and include the bone. Chops should be cut thick, about 1 1/2 inches.

Shoulder chops are also very flavorful but  are not nearly as lean as loin chops. They are cut thinner and can be either broiled or panfried.

Lamb chunks, which are great for stews or curries, are usually cut from the shoulder, although a friendly butcher might give you some from the leg, which are a bit leaner.

Rack of lamb is cut from the ribs, and while there is not a lot of meat, what there is is divine and expensive!

Servings

A whole leg of lamb (bone in or boneless) will serve 8 to 10 people. A rack of lamb serves 2 and a loin roast serves 6 people. Allow 2 lamb chops and 2 shoulder chops per person.

Panfried Lamb

Loin chops To fry, chops should be only 1-inch thick (thinner than those cut for broiling). Measure a scant 2 tablespoons olive oil (for 4 chops) into a large frying pan, place it on *high* heat, and let it get very hot, about 1 minute. Just when the oil starts smoking, place the chops in the pan so that they aren't touching. Panfry for 4–5 minutes. Then turn the chops and cook 3–4 minutes more. Don't let them go too long on the second side as loin chops overcook easily.

Shoulder chops Season with salt, pepper, and garlic powder and prepare as above. Because shoulder chops are streaked with fat, you need very little oil to cook them.

Roast Lamb

Leg of lamb, bone in

Preheat the oven to 400°F. Lightly oil a large roasting pan and rack. On the bottom of the pan, arrange 2 thinly sliced onions, 6 coarsely chopped cloves garlic, and 1 28-ounce can plum tomatoes, drained and coarsely chopped. Set a roasting rack over the vegetables and place the lamb on the rack. Rub the lamb with olive oil, salt, pepper, garlic powder, and rosemary. Roast for about 1 hour 15 minutes. Remove the lamb from the oven and let sit for 10 minutes before slicing. Skim the grease off the surface of the sauce in the roasting pan. Serve the lamb topped with the vegetables and sauce.

Boneless loin roast

Preheat the oven to 400°F. Lightly oil a roasting rack and place it in a roasting pan. Place the lamb on the rack and rub the roast with olive oil, salt, pepper, garlic powder, and rosemary. Roast for about 1 hour 10 minutes. Let the meat sit for 10 minutes before carving.

Broiling Lamb

Butterflied leg of lamb

Preheat the broiler. Open up the leg and arrange it on a broiler tray with the smooth side down. You can marinate up to 6 hours before cooking. If you haven't marinated the lamb, rub the top lightly with olive oil and sprinkle on some rosemary. Broil 4 inches from the heat for 6 minutes, then turn the meat and broil 6 minutes more. Lower the rack and broil 6 inches from the heat for 8–10 minutes, then turn and broil 6–8 minutes more. Cut into the meat at its thickest point. If it is pink, it is cooked to medium. The meat will continue cooking for about 10 minutes after it leaves the oven.

Shish kebab Preheat the broiler. Thread 1 1/2- to 2-inch cubes of lamb through metal skewers and arrange the skewers on a broiler tray. If you haven't marinated the lamb, brush the cubes lightly with olive oil and sprinkle on some rosemary. Broil 4 inches from the heat for 5–6 minutes. Turn them over and broil 5–6 minutes more. The cubes should be browned all over.

Loin chops Preheat the broiler. Arrange the chops on a broiler tray. Broil 1 1/4- to 1 1/2-inch chops 4 inches from the heat for 7 minutes. Then turn them over and broil 5–6 minutes more. For thicker 2-inch chops, broil 4 inches from the heat for 7 minutes, turn, and broil 4 minutes more. Then lower the chops to 6 inches from the heat and broil for 5 more minutes. The chops should be slightly springy to the touch.

Shoulder chops Broil 4 inches from the heat for 7 minutes. Turn and broil about 5 minutes more.

Loin Lamb Chops with Red Wine Sauce

Loin lamb chops fall into that elite category of foods, like lobster or Porterhouse steaks, that taste best when prepared as simply as possible. Thick chops, broiled medium rare, make for a perfect dinner. This classic red wine sauce, however, is a subtle enhancement and makes them absolutely sublime. The sauce is quite easy to assemble but does take about ½ hour to reduce.

Ingredients *(serves four)*

2 cups dry red wine

4 shallots, peeled and sliced

1 carrot, cut into 1-inch pieces

1 clove garlic, peeled and crushed

2 sprigs parsley

1 bay leaf

½ teaspoon dried thyme

1 cup homemade or canned chicken or
    beef stock (see Note)

3 tablespoons butter, cut into ¼-inch pieces

1 teaspoon cornstarch

Salt and pepper

8 loin lamb chops, cut 1¼–1½ inches thick

Sprigs of mint or parsley, for garnish

Equipment

Medium saucepan

Fine-mesh strainer

Small saucepan with cover

Small bowl

Broiler pan

1. Place the wine, shallots, carrot, garlic, parsley, bay leaf, and thyme in a medium saucepan and bring to a boil over *high* heat. Reduce the heat to *medium* and simmer, uncovered, until the liquid is reduced to about ⅔ cup, about 15 minutes. Add ¾ cup chicken or beef stock, increase the heat to *high,* and bring to a boil. Again reduce the heat to *medium* and simmer, uncovered, until the liquid is reduced to 1 cup, about 10 minutes.

2. Set a fine-mesh strainer in a small saucepan and pour the liquid through it. Set the small saucepan over *low* heat and stir in the butter, piece by piece. Mix the cornstarch with the remaining ¼ cup stock in a small bowl. Slowly drizzle this into the sauce, stirring continuously. Season with salt and pepper and simmer another 5 minutes, then turn off the heat.

3. Preheat the broiler.

4. Arrange the lamb chops on a broiler pan. Broil the chops 3 inches from the heat for 7 minutes on 1 side. Then turn the chops and broil for 5–6 minutes on the other side, depending on the thickness, for medium rare. For medium, broil 1 minute more on each side.

5. When the chops are done, remove them from the oven and let them sit for 3 minutes. Meanwhile, reheat the sauce over *low* heat for a few minutes, until it is hot. Spoon a thin layer of sauce over the bottom of each dinner plate and arrange 2 chops on each plate. Garnish with a sprig of mint or parsley.

Serving Suggestions

■ Serve with baked potatoes or spaghetti squash.

■ Serve asparagus and a mixed green salad.

Note

Do not replace the chicken or beef stock with bouillon cubes for this sauce. The seasonings in the bouillon will become too concentrated and will overpower the sauce.

Time-Saver

The sauce can be made a night ahead. Let it cool before transferring to a plastic container or a small bowl. Lay a piece of plastic wrap directly on the surface of the sauce to keep a crust from forming on the top. Tightly cover the container or bowl before storing in the refrigerator. Add another tablespoon or so of wine or stock when reheating.

Shoulder Lamb Chops with Garlic & Rosemary

Here is an easy and tasty way to prepare the "other" lamb chop. The aroma of the garlic sautéing will probably draw a crowd to the kitchen.

Ingredients *(serves four)*

1 tablespoon olive oil
8 shoulder lamb chops, trimmed of fat
10 cloves garlic, minced
8 shallots, peeled and finely chopped
1 cup chicken stock or 1 bouillon cube
  dissolved in 1 cup boiling water
½ cup canned crushed tomatoes
2 tablespoons tomato paste
1 teaspoon dried rosemary
Salt and pepper

Equipment

Large frying pan
Medium baking dish
Aluminum foil

1. Preheat the oven to 350°F.

2. Place a large frying pan on *medium-high* heat and let it get hot, about 45 seconds. Add the oil and 4 of the chops, and sauté them until they are brown, about 2 minutes. Turn the chops and cook them for 2 minutes more. Transfer the chops to a medium baking dish and brown the remaining 4 chops.

3. Pour out all but a bit of the oil from the frying pan. Return the pan to the stove and lower the heat to *medium*. Add the garlic and shallots, and sauté, stirring often, until soft, about 3 minutes.

4. Add the chicken stock or bouillon to the pan and simmer until it is reduced by half, about 2 minutes. Add the crushed tomatoes, tomato paste, rosemary, and salt and pepper, and cook until the sauce thickens, about 2 minutes.

5. Pour the sauce over the chops. Cover the baking dish with aluminum foil and place it on the center rack of your oven for 20–25 minutes, until the chops are cooked through.

Serving Suggestions

■ Serve with orzo or boiled new potatoes.
■ Serve beets, sautéed escarole, or zucchini.

DINNER

Pork Basics

In recent years, farmers have been working to raise pigs that yield leaner pork, and Americans have been rethinking their attitudes toward "the other white meat." Still, only the loin should be thought of as lean—although who can resist a slab of baby back ribs dripping with barbecue sauce or a succulent slice of glazed smoked ham? Just don't indulge too often. Instead, expand your repertoire of recipes that call for pork loin.

Cuts

Uncured pork cuts come from several different parts of the pig, including the shoulder, leg, and loin. But concern yourself primarily with meat from the loin, which is the most lean and comes whole or cut into chops.

Whole boneless loin of pork weighs 2 to 4 pounds and is a great dish to serve to a small crowd of 6 to 8 people.

Loin chops are simply bone-in cuts taken from the loin. These can be pan-fried, broiled, or baked. Because the meat is so lean, loin chops should be cooked quickly over *high* heat.

Crown roast is a circular arrangement of chops that have been scored, not separated. It is a majestic dish that can easily become the centerpiece at a dinner party for 6 to 8 people. Your butcher can prepare a crown roast for you.

Ribs come in 2 different sizes— country- style and baby back. Country-style have more meat on them. Baby backs are smaller but more succulent.

Cured pork comes in many shapes and sizes, from a small hock to an 8- to 18-pound ham. There are two processes for curing pork:

It can be soaked in brine or dry-cured with a mixture of salt, sugar, and spices. After curing, the pork is usually smoked.

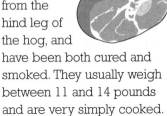

Smoked hams come from the hind leg of the hog, and have been both cured and smoked. They usually weigh between 11 and 14 pounds and are very simply cooked.

Servings

When buying boneless loin, figure on 6–8 ounces per person. Figure on 1 thickly cut (1 1/2-inch) loin chop per person. A 5-pound crown roast, stuffed, will feed 6 to 8 people. Because there is so much bone on them, buy at least 1 pound of ribs per person.

Storage

Store pork the same way you would chicken. Remember to cook refrigerated meat within 2 days of purchase.

Roast Pork

Roasting is the proper method for cooking a whole boneless loin or a crown roast. A loin roast can be marinated in many kinds of sauces, including Japanese and barbecue, and then simply roasted in the oven. The loin should be basted frequently with the sauce to help keep it from drying out. Cook either a crown or loin roast in a preheated 350°F oven for 20–22 minutes per pound or until the roast reaches an internal temperature of 150°–160°F on a meat thermometer. Thick chops can also be baked, but brown them first in a frying pan, to make them crispy.

Panfried Pork

Panfrying is a great way to cook chops, with or without the bone. The chops can be breaded or not, depending on your preference. Thinner chops should be fried over *medium-high* heat. Thicker chops should be browned quickly in the pan over *high* heat to get them crispy and seal in the juices. Then add $1/2$ cup apple juice, salt and pepper, reduce heat to *low*, cover, and simmer for 40 minutes. Thick chops can also be finished in a 350°F oven after browning. Cook for 20–25 minutes.

Baked Ham

Arrange the smoked ham, fat side up, in a roasting pan and place it on a low rack of a preheated 350°F oven. Add about an inch of apple juice or cider to the pan and cook for 15–18 minutes per pound. Then take the ham out of the oven and use a serrated knife to trim away the fat and rind. Cover the top of the ham with a sweet glaze, such as one made from 1 cup crushed pineapple mixed with 1 cup orange marmalade, and return it to the oven for 20 minutes or so, until the glaze is set.

Cooking Pork

Even though modern breeding practices have decreased the likelihood of contamination, it is still important to make sure your pork is cooked through and there is no pink in the center. At the same time, you need to watch that your pork doesn't get overdone as it tends to dry out quickly. It may be necessary to cut into a chop or the center of a loin to check whether it is done. Use a meat thermometer for roast pork.

Broiled Pork Chops

Broiling is an excellent method for cooking pork chops. For thin chops, broil 3–4 inches from the heat. For thicker chops ($1^{1}/4$ inches and up), lower the meat to 5 inches from the heat to keep it from drying out. Figure on 3–5 minutes per side, depending on the thickness. You must keep a close eye on the meat or it's likely to dry out.

Hunan Orange-Ginger Roast Loin of Pork

Using orange when roasting meats is traditional in the Hunan region of China. Here, the sweetness of the orange mixes with the pungent ginger and sesame to make for a lively sauce.

Ingredients *(serves six)*

¼ cup orange juice

½ cup white wine

¼ cup honey

¼ cup soy sauce

2 tablespoons sesame oil

1 tablespoon minced fresh ginger or
   1 teaspoon dried

½ cup apricot jam

2½- to 3-pound boneless pork loin

Equipment

Medium bowl

Small bowl

Large plastic container

Roasting pan

Meat thermometer

1. Mix together the orange juice, wine, honey, soy sauce, sesame oil, and ginger in a medium bowl. Place the apricot jam in a small bowl.

2. Place the pork loin in a plastic container just large enough to hold it. Pour the marinade over the pork, cover, and refrigerate for 6–12 hours.

3. Preheat the oven to 350°F.

4. Arrange the pork loin in a roasting pan and pour the sauce over it. Place the pan on the center rack of your oven and roast the loin for 1 hour 15 minutes.

5. After 1 hour 15 minutes, remove the roast from the oven. Take 3 tablespoons of pan drippings from the roasting pan and mix it with the jam in the bowl. Spoon the jam mixture over the loin and return it to the oven. Roast for 20–25 minutes more or until the meat reaches a temperature of 150°–160°F on a meat thermometer. Let the roast sit for 10 minutes before cutting into 1-inch slices.

Serving Suggestions

■ Serve with white, brown, or wild rice.

■ Serve sautéed green beans or broccoli.

Breaded Pork Chops

Start marinating the chops in the morning, and they'll be ready to be transformed into a quick and delicious entrée by dinnertime.

Ingredients *(serves four)*

Marinade

⅓ cup olive oil

Juice of 1 lemon

1 clove garlic, mashed

½ teaspoon dried thyme

½ teaspoon salt

Freshly ground black pepper

Chops

4 center-cut loin pork chops,
about 1½ inches thick

2 large eggs, lightly beaten

1 cup Italian-style bread crumbs

¼ cup grated Parmesan

2 tablespoons chopped fresh parsley
or 1 tablespoon dried

½ teaspoon dried thyme

Salt and pepper

1 tablespoon vegetable oil

Equipment

Large plastic container

Medium shallow bowl

Pie plate

Dinner plate

Large, ovenproof frying pan with cover

1. To marinate the chops, first trim away any excess fat and arrange them in a large plastic container in a single layer. Pour the olive oil and lemon juice over them, then add the garlic and sprinkle on the thyme, salt, and pepper. Turn the chops once so they are completely coated, cover the container, and refrigerate for 2–12 hours.

2. Preheat the oven to 325°F.

3. Remove the chops from the marinade and pat them dry with paper towels.

4. Beat the eggs in a medium bowl. Mix together the bread crumbs, Parmesan, parsley, thyme, and salt and pepper in a pie plate.

5. Dip the pork chops in the eggs and let the excess drip off. Dredge both sides of the chops in the bread crumbs and shake them gently to allow the excess crumbs to fall off. Lay the breaded chops on a dinner plate. (Wash the plate before reusing.)

6. Place a large ovenproof frying pan on *medium-high* heat and let it get hot, about 45 seconds. Add the vegetable oil and the chops and sauté them until golden brown, about 2 minutes. Turn the chops and cook for 2 minutes more.

7. Cover the pan and move it to the center rack of your oven for 20–25 minutes, until the chops are springy to the touch.

Serving Suggestions

■ Serve with bow-tie noodles tossed with olive oil and fresh parsley.

■ Serve tomato slices topped with chopped onion, lots of freshly ground black pepper, and a simple vinaigrette.

Pork Chop & Potato Casserole

This classic American casserole, held together with condensed mushroom soup, is guaranteed to warm your cockles on a cold winter night.

Ingredients *(serves four)*

1 tablespoon butter

1 can condensed mushroom soup

6 medium potatoes, peeled and thinly sliced

6 loin pork chops, about 1-inch thick

1 teaspoon garlic powder

Salt and pepper

½ teaspoon dried thyme

Equipment

8 x 12-inch baking dish
Small bowl

1. Preheat the oven to 350°F and use the butter to lightly grease a 8 x 12-inch baking dish.

2. In a small bowl, combine the mushroom soup with ½ can of warm water, stirring well. Set aside.

3. Arrange half the sliced potatoes in an even layer over the bottom of the prepared baking dish and season with salt and pepper.

4. Arrange the pork chops in a single layer over the potatoes. Season with the garlic powder and salt and pepper. Sprinkle on the thyme. Arrange the remaining potato slices over the chops.

5. Pour the mushroom soup over the top of the casserole so it almost reaches the level of the second layer of potatoes. If there isn't enough soup, add a little more water.

6. Bake the casserole, uncovered, on the center rack of the oven for 1 hour or until the potatoes are cooked and the liquid is almost completely absorbed.

Serving Suggestion

Serve with glazed carrots and a simple green salad.

Fish Basics

The sublime taste of fresh fish is best shown off in the simplest of preparations. In a hot pan with a little oil or butter, you can sauté a few fillets of sole in 5 minutes. Bay scallops take even less time to sauté. Salmon steaks can be baked in a lightly greased pan, and then need only a dash of salt and pepper and a spritz of lemon to finish them off. More complex sauces can be made for fish as well, but they are by no means a requirement.

How to Buy Fish

The easiest way to ensure that you are buying fresh, high-quality fish is to get it at a busy fish market with lots of turnover. When buying whole fish, look for plump, bright ones with good muscle tone. The eyes should be bright and slightly bulging. Saggy or sunken eyes are a sign of old fish.

Fillets are cut lengthwise from the backbone, so they are boneless. They are skinned and ready to cook.

A steak is a crosscut section of a cleaned, scaled fish cut at least $3/4$ inch thick from the

thickest part of the fish. Fillets and steaks should be moist and firm, and the flesh should be well toned. If it is soft or at all mushy, or if it has a film on the surface, look for something else.

DINNER

Cooking Times

The standard rule for cooking fish is 10 minutes per inch of thickness, as measured at the thickest point. However, if you are cooking the fish in foil, figure on 15 minutes per inch of thickness.

Servings

The rule of thumb for serving sizes is 6 ounces of fillet, steak, or whole fish per person. For brook trout, figure one trout per person. For shrimp, get $1/3$ pound of medium or large shrimp per person. For jumbo shrimp, judge by number (4 or 5 per person). For lobster, you'll need at least one $1^1/4$-pounder per person. When buying fillets, check to make sure that they are all of equal thickness. If they are not, oine piece will cook faster than the other and with fish, even 1 minute can mean the difference between succulent and dried out.

Storage

With fish, freshness is critical because its flavor and texture break down quickly. It's important to cook fish the day you buy it.

If you must keep your fish until the next day, follow this procedure: Remove the wrapping and dip the fish in a bowl of ice water with some freshly squeezed lemon juice which helps to slow down aging. Then pat the fish dry, wrap it in plastic, and place it on the bottom (the coldest part) of the refrigerator. If fish develops a mild fishy smell, use it in chowder. If the smell is pronounced and the fish feels filmy, discard it.

Broiled Fish

Broiling is a good method for cooking fattier fish, such as tuna, swordfish, and salmon, as they are sturdier and can withstand the intense heat. Broiling leaves the fish slightly crusty on the outside, which seals in the juices. Place the fish on a lightly oiled baking sheet. Sprinkle with a few teaspoons of water, lemon juice, or wine to keep it from drying out. Broil 4 inches from the heat. Thick steaks (1–$1^3/4$ inches) will need to be turned once after 6–7 minutes. Thinner steaks or fillets needn't be turned at all. Thin fillets ($3/4$ inch or less), such as flounder or sole, should not be broiled as they will dry out.

Panfried Fish

Like broiling, panfrying allows the fish to develop a crust on the outside while keeping the inside moist. Panfrying is also suitable for fillets too thin to broil. Before frying, lean fillets can be dipped in milk or a well-beaten egg, and dredged in flour, bread crumbs, or cornmeal to seal in moisture. Steaks cut from fatty fish, such as tuna, salmon, or swordfish, do not need to be coated before cooking. Small whole fish, such as brook trout, can also be panfried and do not need to be coated.

Heat the pan over *medium-high* heat until it is hot, about 30 seconds. Then add a few tablespoons of olive oil or a combination of olive oil and butter. Gently lay the pieces of fish in the pan, being sure not to crowd them together. Cook half the prescribed time and then turn the fish over. It's important to use a large spatula to turn a large fillet to keep it from falling apart.

Baked Fish

Baking is perhaps the easiest way to cook fish and it gives you the most room for error. Fillets, steaks, and whole fish can all be baked with very good results. Simply arrange the fish in a lightly oiled baking pan and bake in a preheated 400°F oven for 10 minutes per inch of thickness. Whole fish which have been scaled and gutted by the fishmonger can be stuffed with a combination of herbs, sautéed vegetables, nuts, and bread crumbs. Another way to enhance the flavor is to place the fish on a bed of thinly sliced, lightly sautéed vegetables, such as onions, celery, or carrots. Chopped garlic and/or fresh ginger are two of the best herbs for fish. A bit of wine or soy sauce added to the bottom of the pan makes a delicate sauce that can be served over the fish.

Fish Baked in Foil

Baking in foil is an almost foolproof way of cooking moist fish. Place a 9-inch square of foil on the work surface and lightly oil or butter it. Lay the fish in the center and sprinkle it with salt and pepper and a dot of butter. You can also add a marinade of 1 tablespoon soy sauce, white wine, or broth, and a pinch of chopped scallions, fresh ginger, or garlic. Pull the top and bottom sides of the foil together and fold them down to make a loose package. Then fold the ends securely. Place the foil in a baking pan and bake in the middle of a preheated 400°F oven for 15 minutes per inch of thickness.

Poached Fish

Poaching is simply cooking the fish in a small amount of water and lends itself to cooking thin fillets and smaller whole fish. Keep the water just barely simmering. If it boils too rapidly the fish will be tough. Fillets and small whole fish can be poached in a covered sauté pan on top of the stove. Bring $1/2$ inch water to a simmer, add the fillets (in 1 layer) or the whole fish and cover the pan. Increase the heat until the liquid is simmering again, then quickly lower the heat. Start timing now, following the 10-minute-per-inch rule.

A fish poacher enables you to cook large fish because it has an insert that allows you to raise and lower the fish into the hot liquid. Bring a few inches of water to a boil in the bottom of the poacher. Lower the fish into the pan and let the liquid return to a boil. Proceed as above.

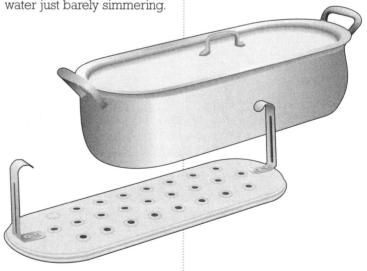

Fish Primer

These fatty fish are best for broiling, baking, and grilling. Meatier than flatfish, they can be cut into steaks or thick fillets. Use these fish in chowders and pasta sauces, as they won't flake and dissolve into the liquid.

	Description	Sold as	How Dad likes to cook it
Bluefish	Dark flesh; oily; distinctive, slightly fishy flavor	Whole fish; fillets	Broil fillets topped with thinly sliced onion, bell pepper, and chopped bacon. Or cut fillets into chunks and use in tomato-based pasta sauces.
Cod	Sweet; slightly fishy; firm flesh	Fillets; steaks	Cod can be bland on its own, so bake fillets or steaks smothered with Basic Tomato Sauce (page 182) or favorite store-bought sauce.
Mackerel	Oily, grayish flesh; slightly fishy flavor	Fillets	Simple preparation suits mackerel well. Marinate fillets in soy sauce marinade (page 248) for 1 hour before broiling.
Salmon	Firm; pink to red flesh; distinctive flavor	Steaks; fillets	Bake fillets or steaks on a bed of thinly sliced onion, celery, and chopped garlic that has been sautéed until soft. Leftover salmon makes for a great lunch.
Swordfish	Dense; fatty; slightly dark flesh	Steaks	Marinate in a soy sauce marinade (page 248) for 1 hour before grilling or broiling.

	Description	Sold as	How Dad likes to cook it
Tuna	Fatty; dark flesh; strong, distinctive flavor	Steaks	Because tuna is very fatty and has a pronounced flavor, it takes well to a marinade of garlic, olive oil, and lemon juice; apply $1/2$ hour before broiling.

These fish are lean and delicate and yield thin fillets that are best poached, cooked in foil, baked whole, or gently sautéed. They cook up quickly and their mild flavor makes them family favorites.

	Description	Portion	How Dad likes to cook it
Black Sea Bass	White flesh; mild flavor	Whole fish; fillets	Broil or bake whole in pan, filled to $1/8$ inch with white wine or water. Brush with soy sauce during last 2 minutes of broiling.
Flounder & Sole	White flesh; mild flavor	Whole fish; fillets	Flounder and sole are usually interchangeable in recipes. Dip fillets in milk, then dredge in bread crumbs. Gently sauté in butter and serve with a sprinkling of fresh lemon juice.
Halibut	White flesh; mild sweet flavor	Fillets	Bake, smothered with sautéed shallots and mushrooms (button or wild or a combination). Halibut cooks very quickly; watch carefully.
Red Snapper	White, firm, slightly sweet	Whole fish; fillets	Sprinkle fillets with fresh lemon juice, chopped parsley, and chives, and then bake in foil.

Red Snapper Baked in Foil

Baking in foil is one of the easiest ways to cook fish. This technique also helps to keep fish moist and flavorful.

Ingredients *(serves four)*

1 tablespoon butter
4 red snapper fillets, 4–6 ounces each
1 tablespoon lemon juice
1 teaspoon chopped parsley
Salt and pepper

Equipment

Four 9-inch squares of aluminum foil
11 x 17-inch baking sheet

1. Preheat the oven to 375°F.
2. Place four 9-inch squares of aluminum foil on the counter and butter them lightly.
3. Lay 1 fillet in the center of each piece of foil. Sprinkle each fillet with lemon juice, parsley, and salt and pepper.
4. Bring together the top and bottom ends of the foil and fold together, without pressing on the fillets, until you have a neat package. Now fold over the sides, being careful not to press too close to the fish.
5. Arrange the foil packets on the baking sheet and bake for 10 minutes.
6. Slit open the packets with a knife and ease the fish and its juices onto a plate.

Serving Suggestions

■ Serve with herbed baked new potatoes.
■ Serve steamed snow peas, sugar snap peas, or asparagus.

Fillet of Sole with Saffron & Tomato Cream Sauce

This is an elegant dish for when Dad wants to show off. The saffron has a sublime flavor and turns the sauce bright yellow, which always intrigues the kids.

Three Foil Sauces

These pungent sauces can be used to spice up seafood baked in foil.

■ Spoon 1 tablespoon crushed tomatoes in the center of each lightly buttered square of foil, and sprinkle with a pinch of parsley and oregano. Lay the fish fillets on top of the tomato and season them lightly with salt and pepper. Fold and bake as described in recipe for Red Snapper Baked in Foil.

■ Lay 6 large, peeled and deveined shrimp on the center of each lightly buttered piece of foil. In a small bowl, mix together 4 teaspoons vermouth or white wine, 4 tablespoons finely chopped prosciutto, and 4 teaspoons chopped scallions. Spoon $1/4$ of the mixture over each group of shrimp. Season the shrimp lightly with salt and pepper and a spritz of lemon. Fold and bake about 8–10 minutes in a preheated 350°F oven.

■ Lay a 6-ounce sea bass fillet on the buttered foil. In a small bowl, mix together 4 teaspoons soy sauce, 4 teaspoons lemon juice, 2 teaspoons chopped fresh ginger, and 2 teaspoons chopped scallions. Spoon $1/4$ of the mixture over each sea bass fillet. Fold and bake 10 minutes in a preheated 350°F oven.

Ingredients *(serves four)*

½ teaspoon dried saffron threads

1 16-ounce can whole tomatoes, well drained

1 tablespoon butter, plus extra for greasing the aluminum foil

3 shallots, minced

¾ cup white wine

¾ cup heavy cream

4 sole or flounder fillets (about 6 ounces each)

Salt and pepper

4 cups cooked rice, for serving

¼ cup chopped fresh parsley, for garnish

Equipment

9 x 12-inch baking dish

Aluminum foil

Small bowl

Large frying pan

1. Preheat the oven to 350°F. Lightly butter a 9 x 12-inch baking dish as well as a piece of aluminum foil large enough to cover it.

2. Put the saffron threads in a small bowl. Add a few tablespoons warm water and let the threads soften.

3. Chop the tomatoes lengthwise into quarters and then into 1-inch chunks. Set aside.

4. Place a large frying pan on *medium* heat and add 1 tablespoon butter. When the butter stops sizzling, add the shallots and sauté until soft, about 3 minutes, stirring often. Increase the heat to *high*. Add the wine and cook until the liquid is reduced by half.

5. Add the cream and the saffron with the water and cook, stirring constantly, until the liquid is reduced by half, about 2 minutes. Add the chopped tomatoes and turn off the heat. Let the sauce sit while you cook the sole.

6. Arrange the sole fillets on the prepared baking dish in a single layer and lightly salt and pepper them. Cover the fish with the prepared aluminum foil, buttered side down. Bake on the center rack of the oven for 7 minutes.

7. A few minutes before the fish is done cooking, reheat the sauce over low heat.

8. Spoon enough cream sauce onto each dinner plate to cover the bottom. Using a spatula, gently place the fish on top of the sauce. Arrange rice around the fish, and garnish with a bit more sauce and the chopped parsley.

Cajun Baked Salmon

This awe-inspiring dish couldn't be easier to prepare: It's simply a matter of sprinkling the spices on the salmon steaks and throwing them in the oven. The Cajun flavor enhances the natural taste of the salmon.

Ingredients *(serves four)*

1 tablespoon onion powder

1 tablespoon garlic powder

1 tablespoon paprika

1 tablespoon chili powder

1 teaspoon dried oregano

½ teaspoon dried rosemary

½ teaspoon salt

Pinch of cayenne pepper

Vegetable oil, for greasing the baking pan

4 salmon steaks, cut 1 inch thick

2 cups salsa, if serving fish at room
temperature

1 lime, cut into quarters

Equipment

Small bowl

9 x 12-inch baking pan

Aluminum foil

1. Preheat the oven to 325°F.

2. Combine all the spices through the cayenne pepper in a small bowl and set aside.

3. Line a 9 x 12-inch baking pan with aluminum foil, then lightly grease the foil with vegetable oil.

4. Sprinkle half the prepared spice mixture over the top of the salmon steaks. Place the steaks, spiced side down, on the aluminum foil-lined baking pan and sprinkle on the remaining spice mixture.

5. Bake the salmon, uncovered, on the center rack of the oven for 12–14 minutes, until the fish flakes when tested with a fork.

6. Serve the fish immediately with wedges of lime, or let it cool about 1 hour and serve at room temperature topped with salsa and garnished with lime wedges.

Baked Mackerel with Sun-Dried Tomatoes & Herbs

The sauce of tomatoes and herbs gives this fish a distinctive flavor. Fresh herbs are best with this dish, but if they're not available, soak the dried herbs overnight in the oil and sun-dried tomatoes.

Ingredients *(serves four)*

Vegetable oil, for greasing the casserole

4 ounces sun-dried tomatoes in oil

1 clove garlic, mashed

¼ cup parsley leaves

1 teaspoon fresh oregano or ½ teaspoon dried

½ teaspoon fresh or dried rosemary

½ teaspoon salt

2 fillets (1½ pounds) mackerel

Equipment

9 x 14-inch casserole

Blender or food processor

1. Preheat the oven to 375°F. Lightly grease a 9 x 14-inch casserole.

2. Remove the sun-dried tomatoes from the oil and finely chop them. Save the remaining oil.

3. Put the garlic, herbs, salt, and 3 tablespoons of the oil from the tomatoes in a blender or food processor. Blend until just puréed.

4. Lay the fish in the prepared pan. Spread the herb mixture over the fish. Sprinkle on the chopped sun-dried tomatoes.

5. Bake for 12–15 minutes on the middle rack of the oven, until the fish begins to flake.

Serving Suggestions

■ Serve with fusilli or radiatore in a light herb sauce.

■ Serve mixed greens sprinkled with diced red, yellow, and green bell peppers.

Panfried Flounder

This is a very quick way to cook any fillet of white-meat fish. The Parmesan and garlic add extra zip.

Ingredients *(serves four)*

> ½ cup bread crumbs
>
> 3 tablespoons Parmesan
>
> 1 clove garlic, minced
>
> 3 tablespoons finely chopped fresh parsley
>
> Salt and pepper
>
> 2 large eggs
>
> 4 flounder fillets (4–6 ounces each)
>
> 2 tablespoons vegetable oil
>
> 1 lemon, cut into wedges

Equipment

> Large frying pan
>
> Pie plate
>
> Medium shallow bowl
>
> Dinner plate
>
> Spatula

1. Mix the bread crumbs, Parmesan, garlic, parsley, and salt and pepper in a pie plate. Beat the eggs in a medium shallow bowl.

2. Dip each fillet in the egg and let the excess drain off. Lay both sides of the fillets in the bread crumb mixture and shake gently to release excess crumbs. Lay the breaded fillets on a dinner plate.

3. Place a large frying pan on *medium-high* heat and let it get hot, about 45 seconds. Add the oil and the fish fillets and cook until they are lightly browned, about 3 minutes. Turn the fillets with a spatula (being careful not to break the fish) and cook the other side for 2 minutes.

4. Lower the heat to *medium* and cook until the fish flakes, 1–2 minutes more. Lightly season with salt and pepper and a spritz of lemon and serve hot.

Variations

This dish also works with sole, trout, or snapper fillet. For thicker pieces of fish, like mackerel, cod, or scrod, preheat the oven to 350°F. Sauté the fish in an ovenproof frying pan for 2 minutes on each side until lightly browned, then put the pan in the oven and bake until the fish flakes, about 4–6 minutes.

Serving Suggestions

■ Serve with garlic bread.

■ Serve with endive salad or steamed broccoli.

Shellfish Primer

Shrimp, scallops, lobster, clams, and mussels are the most popular shellfish. Shrimp and scallops have usually been frozen and are defrosted by the fishmonger before selling. They will last a day in your refrigerator, after which they should definitely be cooked. Lobsters, clams, and mussels are sold live. It is best to cook and eat lobster the day it is purchased. Clams and mussels in their shells can be stored in the refrigerator covered with a damp towel for several days.

	Description	Portion	How Dad likes to cook it
Shrimp	Comes in 3 sizes: jumbo (9–15 per pound); extra large (16–20 per pound); large (26–30 per pound); and medium (31–44 per pound).	1/4 pound per person	Barbecue jumbo shrimp. Use large ones for shrimp cocktail. Sauté medium shrimp with shells on in oil and garlic and add to spaghetti sauce.
Bay & Sea Scallops	Bay scallops are small and more tender than the larger sea scallops; both are creamy white, sweet, and mildly fishy.	1/4–1/3 pound per person	Sauté with chopped shallots, sliced mushrooms, and lots of garlic, then deglaze the pan with white wine and pour over the scallops; garnish with fresh parsley.
Mussels	Deep purple oblong shells	1/2 pound per person, shells on	Look for cultivated mussels. Steam in a few inches of white wine seasoned with lemon juice, parsley, and chopped garlic.
Lobster	Deep purple shells; alive with claws intact	At least a 1 1/4 pound lobster per person, shell on	Boil and serve with melted butter, for dunking. Drain well in sink before serving.

Cajun BBQ Shrimp

Once the shrimp are prepared this dish is easy to make and it will give your kids a little taste of New Orleans.

Ingredients *(serves four)*

1½ pounds large shrimp
4 tablespoons (½ stick) butter or margarine
2 tablespoons Worcestershire sauce
3 tablespoons ketchup
1 tablespoon Cajun or Creole seasoning
¼ teaspoon cayenne pepper
Juice of 2 lemons
3 cloves garlic, minced
1 bay leaf

Equipment

9 x 11-inch casserole
Medium saucepan
Whisk

1. Preheat the oven to 450°F.

2. Peel and devein the shrimp. Keep refrigerated until ready to use.

3. Melt the butter or margarine in a medium saucepan. Remove from the heat. Whisk in the Worcestershire sauce, ketchup, Cajun seasoning, cayenne pepper, lemon juice, garlic, and bay leaf.

4. Arrange the shrimp in a single layer in a 9 x 11-inch casserole, then pour the butter mixture over the shrimp.

5. Bake on the center rack of your oven for 3 minutes. Turn the shrimp and bake for 2 minutes more.

6. Transfer the shrimp to a serving platter and pour on any remaining sauce.

Peeling and Deveining Shrimp

The good news about shrimp is that it's easy to cook. The bad news is that it's a pain in the neck to prepare. Allow yourself about 20 minutes per pound.

Removing the Shell

1. Hold the shrimp firmly just above the tail between your thumb and first two fingers.

2. With your other hand, pull away the body. The tail should now come loose easily.

3. Strip away the rest of the shell by peeling from the underside. It should come away in one or 2 sections. Remove the shells from all the shrimp before starting to devein.

Deveining

Lay the shrimp on its side and with a sharp paring knife make a shallow slit along the back from the head almost to the tail (about $1/8$ inch into the shrimp). This will expose the "vein," which can be lifted out with the point of the knife. Scrape away any residual dirt.

■ Lay ice cubes on top of the shrimp to keep them cold during cleaning.

■ Cover the shrimp well in the refrigerator, as they tend to share their shrimpy aroma with other foods.

Serving Suggestions

■ Serve with rice or crusty bread to soak up any leftover sauce.

■ Serve diced tomato and onion, and corn-on-the-cob.

DINNER

Stir-Fried Scallops with Red Pepper Peas & Baby Corn

I like to make this colorful and lively dish on hot summer evenings when I'm tired of barbecuing. It's light and festive and needs only some rice or thin noodles to accompany it.

Ingredients *(serves four)*

1 cup chicken broth, plus 1 tablespoon

2 tablespoons soy sauce

1 tablespoon white wine or dry sherry

1 teaspoon sugar

2 teaspoons cornstarch

1 tablespoon oil

1 small red bell pepper, cored, seeded, and cut into ¼-inch strips

1 small red onion, thinly sliced

8–10 ears canned baby corn, patted dry

1 pound scallops (if using sea scallops, cut them in half)

2 cloves garlic, minced

1 tablespoon fresh ginger, minced, or 1 teaspoon ground ginger

½ cup frozen peas, thawed

Equipment

Small bowl

Large, heavy frying pan or wok

1. To make the sauce, in a small bowl stir together the chicken broth, soy sauce, white wine or sherry, and sugar. If using the ground ginger, add it now and stir it into the sauce.

2. In a small bowl, dissolve the cornstarch in the 1 tablespoon broth and set aside.

3. Place a large, heavy frying pan or wok on *high* heat and let it get very hot, about 90 seconds. Add the oil, bell pepper, onion, and baby corn, and stir-fry until the pepper softens, about 3 minutes. Add the scallops and stir-fry until they begin to get opaque, 3–4 minutes depending on their size. Add the garlic and fresh ginger (if using) and stir-fry 1 minute more.

4. Add the sauce and the frozen peas. As soon as the sauce starts simmering, add the cornstarch mixture and stir to combine. Continue cooking another minute or so until the sauce begins to thicken and a nice glaze begins to form on the vegetables and scallops. Serve immediately.

Rice & Potatoes

Packed with complex carbohydrates, rice and potatoes are two of the best foods you can eat. Either can be served as a side dish or spruced up and turned into a main course. A baked potato with lots of nutritious toppings can be a meal in itself—one that both the kids and Dad sometimes prefer to fancier dishes—and rice served with beans provides as much protein as a meat-based entrée. Rice comes in several varieties, white and brown being the most common. Brown rice, with its outside bran layer intact, is more nutritious than white rice, although "converted" white rice is more nutritious than plain white rice.

Although rice and potatoes are two of the easiest dishes to cook, both can become disastrous blobs if you don't know the few basic rules in this chapter.

Boiled White Rice

Though any long-grain white rice will do, converted (aka parboiled) rice, which is soaked and steamed under pressure before it is milled, has greater nutritional value than regular white rice and tends to be less sticky.

Ingredients *(serves four)*

> *4 cups water*
> *2 cups long-grain white rice*
> *1 teaspoon salt (optional)*
> *1 tablespoon butter or margarine (optional)*

Equipment

> *Medium saucepan with lid*

1. Bring the water to a boil in a medium saucepan over *high* heat.
2. Add the rice, salt, and butter (if using).
3. When the liquid returns to a boil, immediately cover the pan and reduce the heat to *low*.
4. Cook for 17–20 minutes, depending on the nature of your stove's *low* setting. Turn off the heat and let the rice sit, covered, for 5 minutes.
5. Fluff with a fork before serving.

Variation

For more flavorful rice, cook it in chicken or beef broth instead of water, or add 1 bouillon cube per cup of boiling water.

Basic Rice Pilaf

With just a few simple touches, plain rice can become an exciting side dish. For pilaf, rice is sautéed in butter or oil before cooking in stock. Pilafs are variously seasoned and often contain other ingredients such as chopped vegetables, poultry, or nuts and raisins.

Ingredients *(serves four)*

> *2 tablespoons butter, margarine, or vegetable oil*
> *2 small onions, finely chopped*
> *1½ cups white rice*
> *3 cups canned chicken broth or 3 bouillon cubes dissolved in 3 cups boiling water*
> *½ teaspoon dried basil*
> *½ teaspoon salt*
> *Freshly ground black pepper*

Equipment

> *Large frying pan with cover*

1. Place a large frying pan on *medium-high* heat until hot, about 45 seconds. Add the butter, margarine, or oil and the onions and sauté them for 3 minutes.
2. Add the rice and sauté, stirring continuously, until it starts to become transparent, about 2 minutes.
3. Add the broth, basil, salt, and pepper, and bring to a boil.
4. When the liquid boils, immediately cover the pan and reduce the heat to *low*.
5. After 20 minutes, turn off the heat and let the rice sit, covered, for 5 minutes. Fluff with a fork before serving.

Variations

■ **For curried rice:** Omit the basil and add 1½ tablespoons curry powder to the onions after cooking them for 3 minutes, then cook for 1 minute more. After 15 minutes of cooking, add ¼ cup raisins or currants and ¼ cup chopped walnuts or slivered almonds to the rice, and cook for 5 more minutes.

■ **For Mexican rice:** Omit the basil. After the rice is cooked, stir in 3 tablespoons room-temperature sour cream, ¼ cup grated Fontina, Monterey Jack, or white cheddar cheese, and ¼ cup chopped green bell pepper or pimiento. Let the rice mixture sit covered for 5 minutes before fluffing and serving.

Basic Brown Rice

It is no myth that brown rice is more nutritious than white rice. It has considerably more protein, vitamins, potassium, and dietary fiber. Unlike white rice, brown rice is added to cold water that is then brought to a boil rather than being added to boiling water.

Ingredients *(serves four)*

3 cups water
1½ cups short- or long-grain brown rice
½ teaspoon salt

Equipment

Medium saucepan with cover

How to Cook Rice

1. Carefully measure your rice and water.
2. Turn the heat down to *low, immediately* after the water with the rice in it returns to a boil (for white rice) or begins boiling (for brown rice).
3. Set the timer and don't lift the lid until the timer goes off.

1. Measure the water into a medium saucepan. Add the rice and salt.
2. Bring to a boil, uncovered, over *medium-high* heat. This should take 5–7 minutes.
3. When the water begins boiling, immediately cover the saucepan and reduce the heat to *low*.
4. Cook for 50 minutes. (Do *not* lift the lid.) Remove the saucepan from the heat and let the rice sit, covered, for 5 minutes.
5. Fluff with a fork before serving.

Variation

You can enhance the flavor of brown rice by using chicken or beef broth instead of water, or by adding a bouillon cube or a tablespoon of miso soup powder to the water.

Tip

If the kids can't quite get used to the taste of brown rice, mix it in with some white rice. It's easy to cook in the same pot. Bring 1 cup brown rice and 3 cups water to a boil in a medium saucepan. Cover and reduce the heat to *low*. After 30 minutes, stir in ½ cup white rice. Raise the heat momentarily to *high* to return the water to a boil, then reduce the heat to *low*, cover, and simmer for another 20 minutes. Remove the saucepan from the heat and let sit, covered, for 5 minutes. Fluff with a fork before serving.

Baked Wild Rice

The sweetness of grapes complements the strong, nutty flavor of the rice (and is a big draw for the kids). This dish goes well with meat, chicken, or salad and is perfect for a small dinner party.

Ingredients *(serves six)*

1½ tablespoons oil

1 medium onion, finely chopped

1 carrot, grated

¼ pound shiitake or button mushrooms, sliced

1 scallion, chopped

1 clove garlic, minced

1½ cups wild rice

3 cups canned chicken broth or 3 bouillon cubes dissolved in 3 cups boiling water

½ pound seedless green grapes (optional)

Equipment

Large, ovenproof frying pan with cover

1. Preheat the oven to 375°F.

2. Place a large ovenproof frying pan on *medium-high* heat and let it get hot, about 45 seconds. Add the oil, onion, carrot, mushrooms, and scallion, and sauté, stirring frequently, until the onion is soft, about 6 minutes. Add the garlic and cook for 1 minute more.

Wild Rice

Wild rice is not technically a rice at all, but the seed of a wild grass native to the Great Lakes region. Originally it was harvested by Indians who would paddle their canoes next to the plants and shake the seeds onto the bottom of their boats. It is now cultivated commercially and is available in most markets.

Wild rice is very high in fiber, protein, and vitamin B. And while it is the most expensive kind of rice, it cooks to four times its original size, so a little goes a long way. Because wild rice and brown rice have the same cooking times, you can easily mix them together and cook them in the same pot. Cook wild rice exactly as you would plain brown rice and prepare the baked variation at left.

3. Add the rice to the pan and sauté, stirring continuously, until the rice is hot, about 2 minutes.

4. Increase the heat to *high,* pour in the broth, and let it come to a boil. When it does, immediately cover the pan and place it in the hot oven. Be careful not to tilt the pan or the hot liquid will spill. Bake for 45–55 minutes or until the rice if fluffy and the dark brown shell opens a bit to reveal the whitish inside.

5. While the rice is baking, slice the grapes in half and set aside. Scatter them over the rice for the last 10 minutes of cooking.

6. Remove the pan from the oven and let it sit, covered, for 5 minutes before serving.

Kasha

Kasha, or buckwheat groats, are the gently roasted kernels of the buckwheat plant. A staple food of the Russian steppes, kasha is packed with protein and vitamins. When combined with bow-tie noodles, it becomes the classic Jewish dish, "kasha varnishkas."

Ingredients *(serves four)*

　*2 cups canned chicken broth or 2 bouillon
　　cubes dissolved in 2 cups boiling water*
　1 large egg
　1 cup buckwheat groats
　1 tablespoon margarine or vegetable oil
　Salt and pepper

Equipment

　Small saucepan
　Medium bowl
　Large frying pan with cover

1. Heat the broth in a small saucepan until hot.

2. As the broth is heating, beat the egg in a medium bowl. Add the buckwheat groats and stir well to combine.

3. Place a large frying pan on *high* heat and let it get very hot, about 45 seconds. Add the margarine or vegetable oil and the egg-coated buckwheat groats. Cook, stirring constantly to break up the lumps, until the mixture dries and the buckwheat groats are mostly separate, about 2 minutes.

4. Add the hot broth to the frying pan, cover, and immediately reduce the heat to *low*. Simmer for 12 minutes. Remove the cover and check the kasha. If the kernels are still hard, replace the cover and continue

Canned Broth and Bouillon

Chicken or beef broth can be used in place of water to add extra flavor when making rice, casseroles, and sauces. Or instead of canned broth, bouillon cubes or powder can be mixed with boiling water. Bouillon is more highly seasoned than canned broth, and is usually a bit saltier. Part or all of a bouillon cube can be added directly to a soup, stew, or sauce to enhance the flavor. Just be sure to stir well to dissolve the cube completely.

cooking for 3–5 minutes longer, adding a bit of water if necessary. When the kernels are soft, turn off the heat. Let the kasha sit covered for 5 minutes. Season with salt and pepper and fluff with a fork before serving.

Variations

■ **Kasha varnishkas:** While the kasha is simmering (Step 4), add ¼ pound medium bow-tie noodles to a pot of boiling water and cook for about 8 minutes or according to the package instructions. Drain the noodles in a colander and transfer them to a large bowl. Add the kasha and mix together.

■ **Kasha pilaf:** In a large frying pan over *medium* heat, sauté 1 chopped onion, a few sliced mushrooms, and a chopped red bell pepper or carrot in a tablespoon of oil or butter. When the vegetables are soft (about 5 minutes), turn up the heat to *high* and add the uncooked kasha and egg mixture. Continue cooking as instructed in Step 3 of the basic kasha recipe.

The Basic Potato

Potatoes are the classic American side dish, expertly filling up that section of the plate between the meat loaf and the green beans. The potato is rich in protein and vitamin C and has only a modest number of calories, 100 for a five-ounce baked potato. There are several types of potato available; the most popular are:

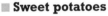 **Sweet potatoes**
Long and orange or slightly larger and rounder, these are suitable for baking, roasting alongside meats, frying, or for use in casseroles.

■ **Maine or all-purpose potatoes**
Roundish, about the size of a racquetball, these are best when boiled.

■ **Idaho or russet potatoes** Large and oblong, these are the sturdiest and best for baking.

■ **New potatoes** These small red or white taters are sweeter and more moist than other varieties. They stand on their own with just some butter or herbs or can be cast as the blushing star of potato salad.

Boiled Potatoes

For boiling, use new potatoes or all-purpose potatoes. Peel the potatoes or scrub them well. If they are very large, cut them into quarters. For good results, the trick is to start boiling potatoes in *cold* water and to keep the water barely simmering as they cook. This will keep the potatoes from becoming mealy or from turning into overcooked mush.

Bring the water and potatoes to a boil over *high* heat. As soon as the water boils, reduce the heat to *medium-low* and let the potatoes simmer. Rapidly boiling water will cause the potatoes to fall apart. Cook the potatoes until they begin to soften, 12–15 minutes. Test by pricking them with a skewer or the tip of a paring knife. If it goes in easily but with some resistance, the potatoes are done. They will continue cooking a bit longer after you remove them from the water. Drain the potatoes in a colander.

Serve boiled potatoes with a bit of butter or margarine, salt and pepper, and a sprinkling of fresh parsley.

Baked Potatoes

Look for potatoes of uniform hardness with no dark spots, cracks, or sprouting "eyes." Serve baked potatoes accompanied with a pat of butter or margarine, or a tablespoon of sour cream or yogurt with chives.

Oven Method

Preheat the oven to 350°F. Select potatoes that are about the same size and scrub them well. Prick the potatoes with a skewer or a fork in about 10 places. Place the potatoes directly on the center rack of the oven and bake for 1 hour or until soft when pricked with a fork. Let rest a few minutes before slicing them lengthwise.

Variation

It might take ten extra minutes, but it will turn plain old baked potatoes into a real taste treat. Slit the cooked baked potato in half and scoop the insides into a bowl. Add 2 tablespoons milk, 1 teaspoon butter, and salt and pepper, then mash the ingredients together. Put the mixture back into the skins, sprinkle grated cheddar or Parmesan cheese on top, and put under the broiler for about 5 minutes or until the top is brown.

Microwave Method

The skin will not be as crusty, but this way you can have a baked potato on the spur of the moment rather than waiting an hour. Scrub, then prick the potatoes as directed for the oven method. Arrange the potatoes at least 1 inch apart around the edge of a microwave turntable or on the bottom of the microwave. This positioning will allow the energy to hit them from all sides. Bake on the *high* setting for the specified amount of time:

1 potato 4–5 minutes
2 potatoes 7–9 minutes
3 potatoes 9–11 minutes
4 potatoes 11–14 minutes

Cook for half the allotted time, then turn the potatoes over. Finish cooking and remove the potatoes when they are still slightly firm. Wrap the potatoes individually in aluminum foil and let them rest for 5 minutes before serving.

Note

For microwave ovens with less than 650 watts of power, add 1–2 minutes to the cooking times.

Oven-Roasted Potatoes

For roasting, use new potatoes or any baking potato. Count on about $1/2$ pound per person. Cut the larger potatoes into $1^{1}/2$-inch pieces. Preheat the oven to 375°F. Using vegetable oil, grease a 9 x 14-inch casserole and arrange the potatoes in an even layer. Melt 3 tablespoons butter in a small saucepan and use a pastry brush to coat the potatoes with it. Sprinkle the potatoes with salt and pepper and place them on the center rack of your oven. Roast the potatoes for 30 minutes, then turn them over and roast for 20 minutes more. Use a skewer or the tip of a paring knife to see if the potatoes are done. They should be soft on the inside with a deep golden brown crust outside.

To Roast with Meat

Peel; then parboil the potatoes for about 12 minutes. Add them to the roasting pan about $1/2$ hour before the meat is done, turning them so that the meat juices cover all sides.

Mashed Potatoes

Every dad can be an expert at making mashed potatoes. My Dad would have Mom cook the potatoes for him. Then he'd enter the kitchen with the debonair manner of a master safe-cracker and coolly practice his art with the potato masher.

Ingredients *(serves four)*

> 2 pounds all-purpose
> potatoes, or new
> potatoes
> $1/4$ cup milk
> 2 tablespoons butter or
> margarine
> Salt and pepper

Equipment

> Vegetable peeler
> Medium saucepan
> Small saucepan
> Colander
> Medium bowl
> Potato masher or hand-
> held electric mixer

1. Peel the potatoes, then cut them into $1/2$-inch slices or in half if using new potatoes. Follow the instructions for boiled potatoes, cooking the slices in a medium saucepan until you can pierce them easily with the tip of a paring knife, about 15 minutes.

2. As the potatoes cook, heat the milk in a small saucepan over *medium-low* heat until hot. Do not boil.

3. Drain the cooked potatoes in a colander and immediately transfer them to a medium bowl. Add the hot milk and the butter or margarine, and mash with a potato masher or hand-held electric mixer set at medium speed until smooth. Season lightly with salt and pepper. Serve immediately (mashed potatoes cool quickly).

Tips

■ To keep mashed potatoes hot for up to 15 minutes, cover the bowl and set it in a large pan of hot water. Set the pan over *low* heat but don't let the water boil.

■ Don't use a food processor to mash potatoes as it turns them into wallpaper paste.

French Fries

French fries are a cinch; the hardest part is cutting them into thin sticks.

Ingredients *(serves four)*

4 medium baking potatoes
Approximately 3½ cups vegetable oil

Equipment

Vegetable peeler
Large saucepan
Slotted spoon
Paper towels
Baking pan

1. Preheat the oven to 200°F.

2. Peel the potatoes and slice about ½ inch off each end. Cut the potatoes into ½-inch slices. Stack 3 slices together and cut them lengthwise into ¼-inch sticks. Wrap the cut potatoes in a dish towel to keep them from browning.

3. Pour the oil into a large saucepan to a depth of about 1 inch. Heat the oil over *high* heat, 2–3 minutes. As a test, place 1 potato stick in the oil; if it sizzles immediately and starts cooking rapidly, the oil is ready.

4. Using a slotted spoon, gently lower half of the potato sticks into the oil and stir. Fry the potatoes until golden brown, about 8–10 minutes.

5. Using a slotted spoon, transfer the French fries from the hot oil to several layers of paper towels to drain. Transfer the drained potatoes to a baking pan and place in the oven to keep warm.

6. Let the oil get hot again (about 30 seconds) before making your next batch.

Oven-Roasted Fries

An easy substitute for French fries, these potatoes are just as tasty and have considerably less fat.

Ingredients *(serves four)*

1 tablespoon oil, for greasing the baking sheet
4 large baking potatoes or 2 pounds (about 16) new potatoes
1 teaspoon garlic powder
1 teaspoon salt
Freshly ground black pepper
1 tablespoon butter or margarine, melted

Equipment

11 x 17-inch baking sheet
Small saucepan
Basting brush or spoon
Spatula

1. Preheat the oven to 375°F. Grease an 11 x 17-inch baking sheet with the oil.

2. Scrub the potatoes well. Cut them into ½-inch rounds. Arrange the rounds in rows on the baking sheet, overlapping slightly. Sprinkle with the garlic powder, salt, and pepper.

3. Put the baking sheet in the center of the hot oven. After 30 minutes, brush or drizzle the tops of the potatoes with the melted butter using a basting brush or spoon. Continue baking for another 12 minutes or until the potatoes are golden brown. Serve immediately, removing the potatoes from the pan with a spatula.

A Baked Potato as a Meal

What's for dinner, Dad? Next time you hear that question and haven't had a second to think about food, try one of the easiest meals ever. Bake a potato (it will take only ten minutes in the microwave), split it open on a plate, and let your kids heap on any of the toppings suggested below. Heated-up leftovers are great for this. But just about anything goes!

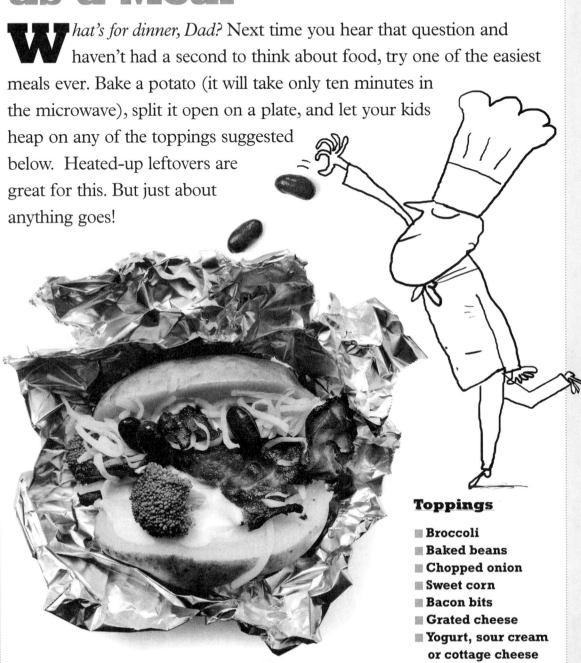

Toppings

- Broccoli
- Baked beans
- Chopped onion
- Sweet corn
- Bacon bits
- Grated cheese
- Yogurt, sour cream or cottage cheese

Stuffed Potatoes with Bacon & Cheese

Serve these with a bowl of soup or chili for dinner and you'll knock the kids' socks off. This is a great way to use up leftover baked potatoes.

Ingredients *(serves four)*

4 large russet or Idaho potatoes, baked (see page 125 for instructions)

½ cup milk

2 large eggs

1 cup (about 4 ounces) grated cheddar, Gruyère, or Swiss cheese

½ teaspoon salt

Freshly ground black pepper

Pinch of nutmeg

2 links sweet Italian sausage, cooked, or 4 slices bacon, cooked

¼ cup grated Parmesan (optional)

Equipment

Medium bowl

Small saucepan

11 x 17-inch baking sheet

Potato masher or hand-held mixer

1. Preheat the oven to 350°F.

2. Slice the baked potatoes in half lengthwise. Scoop out the center, leaving ¼ inch of shell. Mash the pulp in a medium bowl and set aside.

3. Heat the milk in a small saucepan until it's just hot. Do *not* let it boil.

4. Add the hot milk to the potato pulp and mix well with a potato masher until the potatoes are smooth. Beat in the eggs, one at a time, then stir in the grated cheese, salt, pepper, and nutmeg.

5. Crumble the cooked sausage or bacon into small pieces and stir into the potato mixture.

6. Spoon the mixture into the shells, heaping it in the center. Sprinkle with the Parmesan (if using).

7. Arrange the filled shells on an 11 x 17-inch baking sheet. Bake on the center rack of the oven until the filling puffs and bubbles, about 20 minutes. Serve immediately.

Tips

■ Chopped ham, salami, or prosciutto, or finely chopped scallion can be used if there's no leftover bacon or sausage or if you don't feel like cooking any.

■ Unbaked filled potatoes can be tightly wrapped in plastic and stored overnight in the refrigerator. Add 8 minutes to the baking time if you're putting cold potatoes in the oven.

Pan-Roasted New Potatoes

You may find yourself roasting a chicken just because you have a hankering for these potatoes and want something to go with them.

Ingredients *(serves four)*

2 pounds (about 12–14) small
*   new potatoes*

1½ cups canned chicken broth or
*   1½ bouillon cubes dissolved in*
*   1½ cups boiling water*

2 tablespoons butter or margarine

1 tablespoon fresh thyme
*   or 1 teaspoon dried*

1 teaspoon chopped fresh rosemary
*   or ½ teaspoon dried*

2 tablespoons chopped fresh parsley

Salt and freshly ground black pepper

Equipment

Large frying pan with cover

1. Scrub the potatoes well. Cut them in half and fit as many as possible in one layer in a large frying pan.

2. Pour the broth over the potatoes. Bring the liquid to a boil over *medium* heat, cover the pan, and cook until the broth is almost gone, about 20 minutes.

3. Just before the liquid is boiled away, reduce the heat to *medium low* and add the butter or margarine. Add the thyme and rosemary (if using dried herbs), and salt and pepper. Continue cooking, uncovered, shaking the pan often, for another 10 minutes. The potatoes should be soft but not mushy, with a deep golden brown crust. Add a bit of water to the pan if the potatoes start to burn.

4. Sprinkle on the thyme and rosemary (if using fresh herbs), and the parsley, and season with salt and pepper. Serve immediately, or cover and keep warm in a 250°F oven for up to 15 minutes.

Vegetables

The great thing about vegetables is that the less you do to them, the more nutritious and flavorful they are. Unfortunately, many people have gotten into the habit of using canned veggies or smothering fresh ones with cheese or sauce to entice their kids to eat them. But the best way to retain the distinct flavor and texture of vegetables is to steam or stir-fry them.

Fresh vegetables are always preferable, but frozen peas, spinach, corn kernels, and cauliflower taste okay if cooked for slightly less time than instructed on the package. Avoid canned vegetables with these few exceptions: artichokes, corn packed in water, and stewed tomatoes.

Getting your kids to eat vegetables (let alone the 3–5 servings a day recommended by the USDA) can be a battle. Be resourceful: put carrot sticks or cucumber slices on your child's lunch plate instead of potato chips. Add a cup of frozen peas or cut green beans to your tomato sauce. It also helps to give your children a choice: "Okay, kids, what do you want tonight? Broccoli or cauliflower?" Then hold them to their decision.

Cooking the Basic Vegetable

When cooking vegetables, less is more. To preserve color, flavor, and nutrition, we recommend the following methods. Cooking times are for crunchy (al dente) vegetables. For vegetables without any crunch, cook a bit longer but not so long that they become mushy and dull.

Boiling

Bring 1–2 inches of water to a boil in a saucepan on *high* heat. Add the vegetables. (Do not fill more than halfway with vegetables.) When the water returns to a boil, reduce the heat to *low,* cover the pan tightly, and simmer for the prescribed amount of time. To blanch vegetables, boil a full pot of water, plunge the vegetables in, and remove after 30 seconds to 1 minute. Rinse vegetables under cold water.

Steaming

Fill a medium-sized pot with 1–2 inches of cold water. Set the vegetable steamer in the pot. (The water level should not reach the bottom of the steamer.) Place the vegetables in the steamer and cover the pot tightly.

Bring the water to a boil on *high* heat. When the water boils, reduce the heat to *low* and steam for the prescribed amount of time.

Micro-waving

Unless a recipe states otherwise, put the vegetables in a microwave-safe bowl  just large enough to hold them comfortably. Add 2 tablespoons water and cover tightly with microwavable plastic wrap. Cook on *high* heat for the prescribed amount of time. (Times given in this chapter are for large, high-wattage microwave ovens. Small, low-wattage oven owners should add 30% more time.) Remove the vegetables from the microwave, let them sit, covered, for a few finished cooking, then lift the plastic carefully.

Steam for Health

Steaming is the most healthful way to cook vegetables. It also intensifies the color, so vegetables look vibrant on the plate. When you boil vegetables, many of the nutrients get lost in the water, but steaming prevents this because the water doesn't come in contact with the vegetables. Steaming takes a few minutes longer than boiling or cooking in the microwave, but it also leaves you more margin for error. Vegetables mistakenly left steaming for a few extra minutes will probably stay crunchy. When steaming, just remember to turn the heat down once the water boils; otherwise you'll wind up with a scorched pot.

Stir-Frying

Heat 2 tablespoons vegetable oil in a heavy frying pan or wok on *high* heat and let it get very hot, about 1 minute. Add the cut-up vegetables all at once and fry, stirring continuously, until they are cooked but still slightly crunchy, usually about 4 minutes. Add 1 minced clove of garlic and/or 2 tablespoons soy sauce, and stir-fry for 1 minute more before serving. There are a number of interesting Asian sauces available in supermarkets that you can add instead of plain soy sauce.

Photo Finish: Timing

To be sure your vegetables are done at the same time as the rest of the meal, follow these steps:

1. Clean and cut the vegetables and prepare them for cooking, whether conventionally or by microwave. This can be done early on in the dinner preparation or even in the morning (just keep the veggies covered and refrigerated).

2. If the main course is a roast meat or fowl, start the vegetables just before you take the roast from the oven. Remember, both roast meat and fowl need to sit for 10 minutes before they are sliced, which is enough time for vegetables to cook.

3. If your main course takes a short time to cook, such as sautéed fish fillets or boneless chicken breasts, start cooking the vegetables just before you begin sautéing.

Artichokes

Artichokes are surprisingly easy to prepare and the involved process of eating them makes them especially appealing.

Freshness

Fresh artichokes are distinguished by their bright-green color, tightly packed leaves, and absence of brown spots.

Preparation

Pull off tough outside leaves. Cut off the entire stem and trim about ½ inch from the top. Trim the tip of each leaf with scissors. Rinse well.

Portion Size

1 artichoke per person.

Cooking

To steam: Place the artichokes, stem side down, in a pot just large enough to accommodate them. Add 2 inches water, 2 teaspoons salt, and 2 lemon slices. Bring the water to a boil on *high* heat. When the water boils, immediately turn the heat to *low,* cover, and steam for 35–45 minutes, depending on the size of the artichokes. They are done when a middle leaf can be pulled out with ease. Remove the artichokes from the pot with tongs and turn them over in a colander to drain.

To microwave: Loosely wrap each artichoke individually in plastic wrap. Cook 1 artichoke for 7 minutes;

Curry Dip

With its subtle curry flavor, this quick dip is a great accompaniment for artichokes.

Ingredients

3 tablespoons sour cream
3 tablespoons mayonnaise
1 teaspoon curry powder
¹/₂ teaspoon garlic powder
¹/₂ teaspoon salt
Dash cayenne pepper

Equipment

Medium bowl
Wooden spoon

Mix all the ingredients together and refrigerate until ready to serve.

Note

2 tablespoons plain yogurt can be substituted for 2 tablespoons of the sour cream.

2 artichokes for 10 minutes; 4 artichokes for 12–15 minutes.

Eating

Place the artichoke in the center of a plate. To eat, gently tug on a leaf to remove it, then scrape off the meaty bottom portion of the leaf with your teeth. The rest of the leaf is inedible. After all the leaves have been eaten, you'll have worked your way down to the choke, which is covered with fuzz and very small leaves. Cut off the fuzz and discard. Underneath is the meaty bottom, called the heart, which is a delicacy. The leaves and heart can be sprinkled with lemon juice or dipped in different sauces, such as melted butter, a vinaigrette, or hollandaise sauce.

Asparagus

Asparagus is a curious vegetable in that it has no real leaves, only small nibs that run along the stalk. No longer the expensive delicacy it once was, asparagus is now generally available year-round.

Freshness

Look for firm, green stalks. The cluster at the top should be tightly closed and firm.

Preparation

Stalks can be thin, medium, or wide. All need about 1 inch trimmed off the end. If you bend the stalk, it will break at the right point. Thicker stalks, those that are 10–12 to a pound, need to be trimmed and peeled. Use a vegetable peeler to gently scrape off the tough outer skin, working from the middle of the stalk down to the end.

Portion Size

6 stalks per person.

Cooking

To steam: Place asparagus in an asparagus steamer with the water boiling—4 minutes for thin stalks, 6 minutes for medium stalks, and 8 minutes for thick stalks. Asparagus should be cooked through but still slightly crunchy.

To boil: Use a wide pot or deep frying pan to accommodate the asparagus. Fill halfway with water, add 2 teaspoons salt, and bring the water to a boil. Add the asparagus all at once. Cook 4 minutes for thin stalks, 6–7 minutes for medium stalks, and 8–9 minutes for thick stalks.

Orange Vinaigrette

In a small mixing bowl, whisk together $1/4$ cup orange juice, 2 tablespoons red wine vinegar, 2 tablespoons lemon juice, 2 teaspoons Dijon mustard, $1/2$ teaspoon salt, and freshly ground black pepper to taste. Drizzle in 1 cup olive oil and continue whisking until completely combined. Spoon lightly over chilled asparagus. *Makes about $1^1/2$ cups.*

To microwave: Because of their delicacy and quick cooking time, it is not advisable to cook asparagus in the microwave.

Serving

Asparagus is traditionally served with hollandaise or béarnaise sauce. Just as satisfying is a bit of butter, salt, and pepper. It can also be served chilled with a tangy vinaigrette (see box, above).

Beets

Like great actors in bad plays, beets have been cast poorly, canned in water or in jars of sweet syrup. But fresh medium-sized beets, simply cooked, can be a surprisingly wonderful addition to a meal.

Freshness

Beets should be hard with no wrinkles, bruises, or soft spots. Choose beets that are slightly larger than a golf ball.

Preparation

Trim the stems, leaving about an inch. Rinse gently. (Do not scrub or you could puncture the skin, which will cause the juice to run during cooking and cause a considerable loss of flavor.)

Beet & Cucumber Salad

Peel 4 cooked beets and 1 hothouse cucumber, slice thinly, and place in a medium bowl. In a small bowl, mix together $1/4$ cup plain yogurt, 2 tablespoons mayonnaise, 2 teaspoons chopped fresh dill or 1 teaspoon dried, and $1/4$ teaspoon salt. Pour the dressing on the vegetables and toss them gently. *Serves four.*

Portion Size

2 medium-sized beets per person.

Cooking

To boil: Put the beets in a pot and add water to cover them halfway. Cover the pot and bring the water to a boil. Reduce the heat to *low* and simmer for 35–45 minutes. When soft, transfer the beets to a large bowl of cold water. Slip off the skins with your fingers as soon as the beets are cool enough to handle.

To bake: Trim the stems and place the unwashed beets in an aluminum foil-lined casserole. Bake in a 325°F oven for about 1½ hours. Peel the skin with a paring knife when the beets are cool enough to handle.

To microwave: Trim the stems and wrap each beet loosely in plastic wrap. On *high* setting, cook ½ pound of medium beets for 12–13 minutes. Cook 1 pound for 16–17 minutes. Peel the skin with your fingers or a paring knife when the beets are cool enough to handle.

Serving

Slice the beets and serve dotted with butter and a sprinkling of dill, salt, and pepper; or sprinkle with white vinegar.

Broccoli

Broccoli is always available and is highly nutritious, boasting large amounts of vitamins A and C. It also scores high in iron, calcium, and potassium content. Like other members of the cabbage family, it has been shown to be helpful in the prevention of some kinds of cancer.

Freshness

Look for bunches that have abundant florets with tightly packed buds. Also look for the thinnest stalks. Avoid any bunches with yellowing areas or buds that have begun to flower.

Preparation

Rinse the broccoli. Trim 1 inch or more off the stem, depending on how thick and tough it is. Snap off the florets and then slice the stalks into ½-inch medallions.

Portion Size

1 bunch (3 stalks) serves 4–5.

Sautéed Broccoli & Mushrooms

Pat dry 1 bunch boiled or steamed broccoli florets and set aside. Trim the stems of $1/4$ pound mushrooms and cut them into thin slices. Mince 1 clove garlic. Place a frying pan on *high* heat and let it get hot, about 30 seconds. Add 1 tablespoon olive oil, then the mushrooms and the broccoli. Sauté for 3 minutes, stirring often. Add the garlic and a pinch of salt, and sauté for 1 minute more. Season with freshly ground black pepper. *Serves four.*

Cooking

To steam: Steam for 8–10 minutes. Stems will be slightly crunchy.

To boil: Boil for 6–8 minutes.

To microwave: Microwave 3 cups florets for 4–5 minutes, stirring once.

Serving

Broccoli is great plain, seasoned with salt and pepper or topped with a sprinkling of freshly grated Parmesan cheese. Or serve with a simple sauce, heated until warm, of equal proportions fresh lemon juice and butter with a dollop of Dijon mustard.

Carrots

Carrots are inexpensive and are always available. Lightly seasoned and not overcooked, they make a tasty and highly nutritious side dish.

Freshness

Carrots are usually packed in plastic bags that are deceptively tinted orange, making it difficult to tell the color of the carrots inside. Try to find firm, bright orange carrots that have no sprouts at their tops. Carrots sold with green tops taste fresher and do not need to be peeled.

Preparation

Cut carrots into ½-inch circles or slice lengthwise in quarters and cut into 3-inch sticks.

Carrots with Orange & Mint

Bring 1 cup orange juice, 1 tablespoon butter, 1 tablespoon sugar, and a coin-sized slice of peeled ginger to a boil on *high* heat in a heavy saucepan. Add ½ pound sliced carrots and reduce the heat to *medium low*. Cook, uncovered, for 10–12 minutes, until the carrots are soft and the juice begins to thicken. Remove the carrots with a slotted spoon, discard the ginger, and sprinkle with chopped fresh mint. *Serves four.*

Microwaved Glazed Carrots

Mix together ½ pound sliced carrots with 1 tablespoon each brown sugar and butter in a microwave-safe casserole. Cover and microwave for 8 minutes, stirring once. *Serves four.*

Portion Size

1 medium-sized carrot per person.

Cooking

To steam: For firm carrots, steam for 8–10 minutes.

To boil: Boil for 6–8 minutes.

To microwave: For 5 carrots, microwave for 5 minutes, stirring once.

Serving

Serve carrots seasoned with a pinch of salt and pepper, and if you like, a bit of chopped fresh dill or mint.

Cauliflower

Perhaps because of its nonthreatening color and somewhat mild flavor, cauliflower is often popular with kids.

Freshness

Look for heads that are firm and white with no brown spots. The florets should be tightly packed. If the head develops a few brown spots in the fridge, simply trim them away. The rest is perfectly fine.

Preparation

Cut the head in half lengthwise. Using a paring knife, cut the florets from the main stalk. Cut any extra-large florets in half lengthwise.

Portion Size

1 medium-sized head serves 6.

Cooking

To steam: Steam for 8–10 minutes.

Curried Cauliflower & Potato

In a large frying pan on *high* heat, sauté 2 peeled and diced medium-sized potatoes in 2 tablespoons vegetable oil for 3 minutes. Add 2 cups cauliflower florets, 1 minced garlic clove, 1 tablespoon curry powder, and 1 teaspoon salt, and sauté, stirring continuously, for 3 minutes more. Add ½ cup chicken stock (or ½ bouillon cube dissolved in ½ cup boiling water) to the pan and bring the liquid to a boil. Immediately reduce the heat to *medium low,* cover the pan, and simmer for 12 minutes, until the potatoes are soft. Garnish with chopped fresh coriander or parsley. *Serves four.*

To boil: Boil for 6–8 minutes.
To microwave: For 1 medium size head, cut into florets, microwave for 4 minutes.

Serving

Serve with salt and pepper and an optional dot of butter or a sprinkling of freshly grated Parmesan, if desired.

Corn

The taste of the first locally grown ears of corn is bittersweet, for as delicious as they are, they mean that summer is nearing its end.

Freshness

Try to find a market or stand that sells fresh local corn. Peel back the husk a bit and check inside to see if the kernels are small, packed tightly, full and shiny, and that there are no shriveled areas or worm holes. Florida farmers now grow excellent hybrids, giving us sweet-tasting corn starting in late spring.

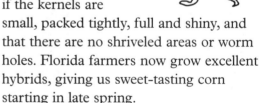

Preparation

Keep corn refrigerated and shuck as close to cooking time as possible.

Portion Size

1½ ears per person.

Corn Pudding

This is a great way to use up leftover cooked corn. With a sharp knife, scrape the kernels from 5 ears of cooked corn and transfer to a medium bowl. In a separate bowl, beat 3 large eggs with 1 cup cream, 1 cup milk, 2 tablespoons melted butter, 1 tablespoon sugar, and 1/2 teaspoon salt. Stir in the corn and transfer the mixture to a 9 x 9-inch buttered casserole. Bake in a preheated 350°F oven until the pudding is set, about 1 hour. *Serves four.*

Cooking

To boil: Place corn in a large pan with enough water to just cover the ears. Boil for 3–5 minutes.

To microwave: Wrap 4 ears of corn in microwavable plastic, microwave for 8 minutes (2 minutes each), turning once.

Serving

Serve with butter and salt and pepper. Extremely fresh corn, however, needs no enhancement. Give the kids corn holders or just run an ear under cold water for a few seconds until it is cool enough for them to hold.

Sautéed Green Beans with Garlic

Pat dry 3/4 pound of cooked al dente beans with paper towels. Heat 1 tablespoon olive oil in a heavy frying pan on *high* heat and let it get very hot, about 45 seconds. Add the beans and sauté, stirring often, for 2 minutes. Add 1 clove minced garlic and sauté for 1 minute more. Season with salt, pepper, and some dried basil or oregano. *Serves four.*

Green Beans

Fresh green beans are a far cry from the tasteless, waxy canned beans served in school cafeterias. They can be prepared in a variety of ways, none of which will remind you of the soggy green horrors of your youth.

Freshness

Look for firm beans of a rich green color without any shriveling at the ends. If you can get away with it, snap one and eat it. It should be crisp and slightly sweet.

Preparation

Rinse the beans and cut ¼ inch from each end. Cut in half or thirds if desired. This is about a 5–10 minute job that the kids can help you with.

Portion Size

¾ pound serves 4.

Cooking

To steam: For crunchy beans, steam for 6–8 minutes.

To boil: Boil for 5–7 minutes.

To microwave: For 1 pound of beans, microwave for 6–8 minutes.

Stir-fry: Green beans lend themselves very well to stir-frying. Just before they are finished cooking, add 1 clove minced garlic and 2 tablespoons soy sauce to the pan.

Serving

Serve plain beans with a dot of butter, and salt and pepper.

Mushrooms

America is finally waking up to the world of mushrooms. Wild mushrooms, such as shiitake, porcini, oyster, and even morel, are becoming popular in home kitchens. And with good reason, for their earthy taste can earn them a starring role in many intriguing recipes. Or they can be served as a side dish. Even the common button mushroom can enhance a recipe significantly.

Freshness

Mushrooms shouldn't have any slimy spots or other signs of decay. The membrane under the cap should be attached to the stem. Button mushrooms that are just slightly brown are fine for sauces, but only the freshest should be eaten raw in salads. *All* wild mushrooms should be cooked through before eating.

Preparation

Trim the stems of the mushrooms. Unless the tops have bits of dirt on them, they should not be cleaned. If there is dirt, brush it off or wipe the caps with a slightly damp cloth or paper towel. Never immerse the mushrooms in water. For most recipes, mushrooms are cut lengthwise into thin slices.

Portion Size

¼ pound per person.

About Dried Mushrooms

Italian porcini, French morel, and several different kinds of Chinese mushroom are available dried. To use these intensely flavorful fungi, simply let them soak in a small bowl of lukewarm water for an hour or so, until they are soft. Remove the mushrooms. Strain the liquid through a layer of cheesecloth or a fine-mesh strainer, then let the mushrooms sit for a minute on some paper towels before using. For extra flavor, add some of the strained soaking liquid to the recipe you are preparing.

Cooking

Do not boil or steam mushrooms.

To sauté: Heat 3 tablespoons butter, margarine, or oil in a large (non-iron) frying pan over *medium-high* heat until hot, about 45 seconds. Add 1 pound sliced mushrooms and cook, stirringoccasionally, until they are soft and lose their moisture, about 8 minutes. Mushrooms shrink considerably during cooking.

Peas

Besides being a real delicacy, fresh peas can also keep the kids busy. Have them shell the peas while you prepare the rest of the meal.

Freshness

The pods should be a deep green color. Before purchasing, snap one open and make sure the peas inside are glossy and full, and taste fresh and sweet.

In the Pod

Sugar snaps and snow peas are very popular with the kids. In both cases the whole pod is eaten. Before cooking, snap off the stem and peel away the string that runs along the length of the pod. Snow peas are available all year. Sugar snaps are one of the first vegetables harvested and show up for a short time in the beginning of the summer. Both need only a quick cooking, either blanched, steamed, or sautéed for 2–3 minutes.

Peas with Cream & Almonds

In a medium frying pan, melt 2 tablespoons butter on *medium* heat. Add $^3/_4$ pound fresh peas and $^3/_4$ cup heavy cream. Cook until the peas are soft and the cream thickens, about 10 minutes. Stir in $1^1/_2$ tablespoons sugar and $^1/_4$ cup slivered almonds. *Serves four.*

Preparation

Shell the peas. Do not rinse before cooking.

Portion Size

About ¾ pound per person (weighed before shelling).

Cooking

To boil: For peas with a bite to them, boil for 6 minutes. Boil 8 minutes for softer peas.

To microwave: For ½ pound of shelled peas, microwave for 3 minutes, stirring once.

Serving

Serve peas with a pinch of salt and pepper, or an optional dot of butter.

Spinach

Popeye notwithstanding, kids don't often take to spinach. Nevertheless, it's extremely nutritious, a cinch to prepare, and tastes good to most adults.

Freshness

Spinach is most often sold prewashed in 1-pound plastic bags or not very well washed in tied bundles. Avoid bags or bundles with leaves that are dark and moist or yellowed.

Preparation

Pinch off the stems and put the leaves in a large bowl filled with cold water. Swish the leaves around and lift them from the water into a colander set in the sink. Pour out the water from the bowl, rinse out any grit that has collected on the bottom, and fill the bowl again with cold water. Return the spinach to the bowl and swish it around again. Then lift out the leaves and shake off the excess water. It is now ready for cooking. Packaged "prewashed" spinach needs to be rinsed only once.

Spinach with Cheese

Cook 2 pounds spinach, drain it well, and chop finely. Put the spinach in a medium bowl and stir in $^1/_4$ cup heavy cream, $^1/_4$ cup milk, 1 beaten egg, 1 teaspoon salt, and a pinch of nutmeg. Transfer to a buttered pie plate. Top the mixture with $^1/_4$ pound grated cheddar or mozzarella. Bake in a preheated 350°F oven for 20 minutes, until the cheese melts and the spinach is warm. *Serves four.*

Portion size

A generous ¼ pound uncooked spinach per person.

Cooking

To boil: Put the spinach in a large, heavy-bottomed pot with a tight-fitting lid. Do *not* add water. The water remaining on the leaves from washing will be enough to cook the spinach. Cover the pot and turn the heat to *medium low*. Cook for about 6 minutes, until all the leaves are wilted. Turn the spinach a couple of times with tongs while it is cooking to keep the bottom leaves from burning.

To microwave: For 1 pound of spinach, microwave for 6–8 minutes, stirring twice.

Serving

Transfer the spinach to a colander to drain. Serve immediately with a light seasoning of salt and pepper.

Zucchini & Tomatoes

Preheat the broiler. Heat 2 tablespoons olive oil over *high* heat in a heavy ovenproof frying pan large enough to accommodate all of the zucchini (it all needs to touch the surface of the pan) for about 45 seconds. Add 1 finely chopped medium onion and sauté for 2 minutes, stirring often. Add ³/₄ pound zucchini cut into ¹/₂-inch rounds and sauté for 5 minutes. Add 1 minced garlic clove and cook for 1 minute. Add a 14-ounce can of drained whole tomatoes, roughly chopped. Cook for an additional 5 minutes. Turn on the broiler. Stir 1 teaspoon each of dried oregano, basil, and salt into the vegetable mixture. Sprinkle with ¹/₄ cup grated Parmesan cheese. Cook under the hot broiler for 2 minutes. *Serves four.*

Zucchini

The thinnest zucchini are best. Kids may not eat them plain, but mixed with tomato sauce and sprinkled with Parmesan, they become a popular side dish.

Freshness

Zucchini should be very firm with no scrapes or bruises.

Preparation

Zucchini need to be rinsed well. Rub them with your hand to get rid of stubborn fuzz and grit. Trim both ends and cut into ½-inch rounds. Or slice lengthwise into quarters and cut into 3-inch sticks.

Portion Size

1 small zucchini per person.

Cooking

Do not boil zucchini.

To steam: Steam for 6–8 minutes.

To microwave: For 3 small zucchini, in ¼-inch slices, microwave for 2½ minutes, stirring once.

To sauté: Heat 2 tablespoons olive oil in a heavy frying pan on *high* heat until it gets hot, about 30 seconds. Add the zucchini and sauté, stirring and turning often, until soft but still crunchy, about 5 minutes. Add 1 minced garlic clove and sauté for 1 minute more.

Serving

Sprinkle zucchini with a pinch of salt and pepper and some grated Parmesan cheese, if desired.

Two Fancy Dinners

fter just a bit of culinary cross-training, when your knives and sauté pan seem more like friends than strangers, you're ready to prepare a really special meal. Whether it's Mom's birthday, your wedding anniversary, or a promising first date, either of these elegant meals is sure to create a dramatic impression. First, some timely advice for smooth moves in the kitchen.

■ Do as much as you can the night before so you can have a few minutes to enjoy the pre-dinner wine and conversation. Lists of what can be prepared and stored ahead of time are noted for each menu.

■ Photocopy the recipes and tape them to the refrigerator or a cabinet where they're easy to see.

■ Go over the list of tasks that must be done just before serving so you don't forget any of them. Stay cool. The last thing you want to do during a romantic evening is to be jumping up and down like a jack-in-the-box.

A Light Summery Supper

These are foods you wouldn't want to share with just anyone. The tortellini is a light, festive starter. The fresh herbs add character to the salmon. Start your meal at sunset and you'll be savoring the airy strawberry mousse by the light of the midsummer moon. A glass of *eau de poire* would be a perfect ending to this meal.

The Timetable

The Night Before

■ Make the strawberry mousse.

■ Refrigerate the wine.

2 Hours Before

■ Chop the carrot, celery, and onion for the wild rice.

■ Make the prosciutto and tomato cream sauce.

■ Purée the herbs, shallot, garlic, olive oil, and mustard; mix together with the bread crumbs, salt, and pepper for the salmon, and set aside.

■ Arrange the salmon fillets on a baking sheet and coat thickly with the herb mixture. Cover the pan loosely with plastic wrap and refrigerate.

■ Make the salad dressing (see page 164).

■ Wash and dry the mixed greens for the salad and refrigerate in a plastic bag.

■ Halve grapes for the wild rice.

■ Set the table.

1 Hour Before

■ Cook the wild rice.

■ Bring a pot of water to a boil for the pasta.

■ Preheat the oven to 325°F.

■ Prepare the broccoli for steaming by cutting it into

florets and placing them in the steamer. If microwaving the broccoli, place the florets in a bowl with a few tablespoons of water and cover with plastic wrap.

■ Set up your coffeemaker so it is ready to go.

To Start the Dinner

■ Check the wild rice. When it's done, turn off the heat, add the grapes, and leave the pot covered until you're ready to serve.

■ Put the tortellini in the boiling water. Reheat the sauce over *low* heat. When the tortellini is done, top with the sauce, sprinkle with parsley and Parmesan, and serve.

■ Pour the wine.

■ Before you sit down for the first course, take a moment to place the salmon in the oven and set the timer for 12 minutes.

■ Start steaming or microwaving the broccoli.

■ Finish the first course.

To Serve the Main Course

■ When the timer rings, remove the salmon from the oven and place 1 fillet on each dinner plate.

■ Spoon on the wild rice, arrange some broccoli florets alongside, and serve.

MENU

Appetizer

Chicken tortellini with prosciutto & tomato cream sauce

Main Course

Baked salmon with herb crust

Wild rice with grapes

Steamed broccoli

Mixed green salad

Sourdough bread

Dessert

Strawberry mousse

Wine

California Chardonnay, French Muscadet, or Beaujolais

For the Salad

■ After you've finished the main course, it's fine to take a few minutes to throw the salad together.

■ Arrange the greens on salad plates and sprinkle on the dressing.

■ Turn on coffeemaker or put on water for tea.

For Dessert

■ Place a few whole strawberries on top of the mousse and serve.

■ Finish making coffee or tea and serve.

The Table Setting

This is a fancy table setting for a formal dinner, but why not do it up royally? If you are not serving soup or salad, simply leave out those pieces of tableware.

Butter knife

Water glass

Red-wine glass

White-wine glass

Dessert spoon

Bread plate

Dessert fork

Soupspoon

Soup bowl

Salad fork

Dinner fork

Dinner plate

Dinner knife

Teaspoon

Chicken Tortellini with Prosciutto & Tomato Cream Sauce

Ingredients *(serves two)*

2 tablespoons olive oil

2 cloves garlic, minced

2 ounces prosciutto, chopped

⅔ cup canned crushed tomatoes

¼ cup frozen peas

½ cup heavy cream

Salt and pepper

8 ounces fresh chicken tortellini (see Note)

Chopped parsley, for garnish

Grated Parmesan

Equipment

Medium sauté pan

Pasta pot

Colander

1. Place a medium sauté pan on *medium-high* heat and let it get hot, about 30 seconds. Add the oil and garlic and sauté for 1 minute. Add the prosciutto and sauté 1 minute more.

2. Add the crushed tomatoes and peas, reduce the heat to *medium,* and simmer for 10 minutes.

3. Increase the heat to *high* and add the cream. Cook until the cream reduces, about 1–2 minutes. Season with salt and pepper and remove from the heat.

4. Bring a pot of water to a boil for the pasta. Add the tortellini, and stir to make sure none are stuck together. Boil for 3–5 minutes, until cooked through, then drain in a colander.

5. If necessary, reheat the sauce over *medium* heat and pour it over the tortellini. Top with chopped parsley and grated Parmesan.

Note

If chicken tortellini isn't available, substitute another kind of tortellini.

Baked Salmon with Herb Crust

Because of the thick coating of herbs, this salmon doesn't need a sauce. Cooking it slowly at a low temperature keeps it moist.

Ingredients *(serves two)*

1 cup fresh parsley leaves

4 scallions, green part only

¼ cup fresh basil leaves or 1 teaspoon dried

6 stalks fresh chives or ½ teaspoon dried

2 shallots, peeled

1 clove garlic, peeled

¼ cup olive oil, plus extra for oiling the baking sheet

3 tablespoons plain bread crumbs

1 teaspoon Dijon mustard
Salt and pepper
2 salmon fillets (about 8 ounces each)

Equipment

Food processor or blender
Medium bowl
Baking sheet
Aluminum foil
Rubber spatula

1. Preheat the oven to 325°F.

2. Place the parsley, scallions, basil, chives, shallots, garlic, and ¼ cup olive oil in a food processor or blender and process until smooth.

3. Transfer the mixture to a medium bowl and stir in the bread crumbs, mustard, and season with salt and pepper.

4. Line a baking sheet with aluminum foil and oil the foil lightly. Arrange the salmon fillets on the foil. Using a rubber spatula, spread a thick coating of the herb mixture over the fish, making sure the fillets are covered right to the edge.

5. Bake the fish on the center rack of the oven until it flakes when pricked with a fork, 12–15 minutes. Serve immediately.

Wild Rice with Grapes

The simple addition of grapes turns wild rice into a special side dish.

Ingredients _(serves two)_

2 tablespoons vegetable oil
1 carrot, diced
1 rib celery, diced
1 small onion, diced
½ cup wild rice
1 bouillon cube
½ cup green seedless grapes, cut in half lengthwise

Equipment

Medium saucepan with cover
Slotted spoon

1. Place a medium saucepan on _medium-high_ heat and let it get hot, about 30 seconds. Add the oil and the diced carrot, celery, and onion, and sauté until soft, about 5 minutes.

2. Add the wild rice and cook, stirring constantly, until the rice is hot, about 1 minute.

3. Add 1½ cups water and the bouillon cube, and bring to a boil. Stir the rice, cover the pan, and reduce the heat to _low_. Simmer for 45–55 minutes, until the rice is cooked through.

4. Turn off the heat, add the grapes, stir, and cover until ready to serve. Serve with a slotted spoon in case there is any excess water.

Strawberry Mousse

Much easier than most mousse recipes, this one requires no cooking.

Ingredients *(serves four)*

2 quarts fresh strawberries
1 cup sugar
¼ cup fresh lemon juice
1 cup heavy cream
½ cup amaretto liqueur
Whites of 4 large eggs

Equipment

2 large bowls
Food processor or blender
2 medium bowls
Hand-held electric mixer

1. Set aside a few whole strawberries for garnish. Wash, hull, and cut up the remaining strawberries and put half of them into a food processor. Add the sugar and lemon juice and purée the mixture, transfer to a large bowl, then add the rest of the berries and purée the second half. Add that to the bowl of purée.

2. In a medium bowl, using a hand-held electric mixer set on medium-high speed, whip the cream until soft peaks form. Beat in the amaretto, then gently fold into the puréed strawberries.

3. In another medium bowl, beat the egg whites on medium-high speed until stiff. Gently fold the egg whites into the strawberry mixture.

4. Cover the mousse with plastic wrap and refrigerate for at least 2 hours or

overnight. Garnish with the reserved strawberries.

Variation

Replace 1 quart of the strawberries with 1 quart raspberries.

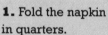

Special Touch

One finishing touch for an elegant table setting is a specially folded napkin. It's fairly simply and will let your guest know that she's not getting the Blue Plate Special. Use square cloth napkins made of heavy cotton or linen.

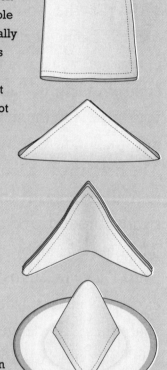

The "Quick Snap" is a simple triangular fold that every busperson learns early in his or her career.

1. Fold the napkin in quarters.

2. Fold it into a triangle.

3. Grasp the napkin in the center of the long side, placing your thumb on the bottom. Place your index finger and middle fingers, which are on the top side of the napkin, on either side of your thumb (like a modified fastball grip).

4. With a quick snap of the wrist, shape the napkin into a triangular tent and place it on the dinnerplate.

Wine Primer

Whether you're entertaining at home or dining at a four-star restaurant, you'll want to be able to choose an appropriate wine to drink with your meal. On the next pages you'll find information to help you make your choice. The best way to choose wine, however, is to find a local wine shop with a large stock, steady turnover, and a helpful salesperson. The days of snobby, effete wine merchants are over. They are, almost without exception, extremely enthusiastic about wine and anxious to share their knowledge. Tell the salesperson what you're serving, what you've liked and not liked about wines you've had before, and how much you want to spend. With a little help, you're sure to wind up with one or more special bottles of wine.

The simplest way to begin thinking about wine is to classify it into two groups: hearty, well-rounded, full-bodied wines and lighter, crisper wines. Wines in both groups differ subtly in taste and wildly in price. The labels chosen here are ones that are widely available and of consistent quality. Your local merchant may have access to certain smaller or more obscure labels or know of new labels that offer great taste and real value.

California

California vineyards name their wines not after the region or vineyard where they're grown (as is the custom in France), but after the predominant grape used in making the wine. These are the most popular varieties.

White Wines

Variety	Characteristics	Serve with	Price	Favorite Labels
Chardonnay	Fruity; full-bodied; smooth	Roast chicken; grilled fish; salmon; veal	$4–7 $18–20	Glen Ellen; Sonoma-Cutrer
Sauvignon Blanc	Light; crisp	Light fish or chicken dishes; cream sauces	$4–7 $10–12	Robert Mondavi; Silverado; Sterling

Red Wines

Variety	Characteristics	Serve with	Price	Favorite Labels
Cabernet Sauvignon	Fragrant; smooth	Roast meats or chicken; hearty pasta	$7–9 $18–22	B.V. Coastal; Napa Ridge; Hawk Crest; White Oak Vineyards
Merlot	Spicy; full-bodied; slightly tannic; slightly smoky	Lamb; grilled meats or fatty fish	$9–12 $13–16	Clos du Bois; Sebastiani
Pinot Noir	Spicy; slightly tannic; dry	Roast meats; steak; grilled tuna; lamb chops	$9–12	Napa Ridge; Robert Mondavi "Private Selection"
Zinfandel	Fruity; complex; slightly spicy	Grilled meats and fish; roast chicken; hearty pastas; lamb chops	$7–9 $10–15	Ravenswood; Segesio; Ridge

Rosé Wines

Variety	Characteristics	Serve with	Price	Favorite Labels
White Zinfandel	Fruity; slightly sweet; smooth	Chicken; fish; burgers; casual meals	$5–7	Beringer; Sutter Home

TWO FANCY DINNERS

France

Understanding the nuances of French wine is very complicated. There are many different vineyards in Bordeaux and Burgundy and each produces wines of varied tastes and finishes. However, you can count on certain wines to deliver distinctive tastes; full-bodied and light/crisp are the differentiating characteristics used here.

White Wines

Variety	Region Grown	Characteristics	Serve with	Price	Favorite Labels
Chablis	Burgundy	Dry; crisp; elegant	Chicken breasts; light fish dishes; cream sauces	$12–15 $40	Vocoret; Vocoret "Grand Cru"
Muscadet	Loire Valley	Full-bodied; fruity	Roast chicken; grilled fish; salmon	$8–12	Chereau "Carré"; Sauvion et Fils
Pouilly-Fuissé	Burgundy	Dry; subtle; crisp	Light fish dishes; cream sauces; light pasta sauces	$12–14	Georges Duboeuf
Vouvray	Loire Valley	Dry; soft; slightly sweet	Chicken; grilled fish; veal	$8–10 $18–20	B & G; Huet

Red Wines

Variety	Region Grown	Characteristics	Serve with	Price	Favorite Labels
Beaujolais	Burgundy	Fruity; soft; smooth	Chicken; fish; stews; burgers; pasta	$7–9	Georges Duboeuf; Louis Jadot
Bordeaux	Bordeaux	Rich; hearty; full-bodied	Roast beef; chicken; lamb	$7–9 $14–30	Mouton Cadet; Château Greysac; Château Meyney
Burgundy	Burgundy	Rich; hearty; full-bodied; strong	Roast meats; lamb	$8–10 $32–35	Louis Latour; Marquis d'Angerville

Wine Tip

Much is made of the rule, "Red wine with meat, white with fish or chicken." And you certainly would not serve a *grand cru* red Bordeaux with fillet of sole, nor a light Frascati with roast lamb. But some of the lighter and fruitier reds, such as Beaujolais, Barbera, or Valpolicella, are fine for roast chicken or grilled fish. And some of the heartier whites, such as a white Burgundy, will stand up to a veal chop.

Italy

Italy is known for its dry, crisp white wines and large, powerful reds. Of course there's also a lot of wine in between, like Barberas and Dolcettos, which are both light and fruity Italian reds. While the giant Italian wine labels that are distributed in grocery stores and less distinguished liquor stores may be unsatisfying, in a better wine shop you are bound to discover some wonderful Italian wines that rival the best of France and California.

White Wines

Variety	Region Grown	Characteristics	Serve with	Price	Favorite Labels
Frascati	Rome	Light; dry	Fish; hors d'oeuvres	$5–8	Fontana Candida
Orvieto	Tuscany	Light; crisp	Fish; chicken; veal	$7–9 $10–13	Antinori; Teruzzi & Puthod Vernaccia
Pinot Grigio	Friuli or Veneto	Fruity; crisp	Fish; seafood; chicken	$9–12	La Columbaia; Antica Corte; Bartenura

Red Wines

Variety	Region Grown	Characteristics	Serve with	Price	Favorite Labels
Barbera	Piedmont	Fruity; smooth	Pasta; veal; grilled fish	$9–12	Marchesi di Barolo; Bartenura
Barolo	Piedmont	Hearty; complex; full-bodied	Roast meats; hearty pasta	$20 $32–38	S. Orsola; Ceretto "Zonchera"
Dolcetto	Piedmont	Dry; elegant	Lamb; roast fowl; meat; pasta	$10–14	Marchesi di Barolo; Prunotto
Chianti	Tuscany	Full-bodied; fruity; slightly tannic	Meat; pasta	$7–10	Ruffino; Badia a Coltibuono

Wine Bargains

There are lots of very decent whites and reds in the $5 to $6 price range. Some are simply called "table wines" and can vary greatly in quality. Others are from some of the newer wine-producing countries such as Chile, Australia, and New Zealand. Ask your local wine merchant for his recommendations. Then take home four or five different wines and try them out. You really will taste the differences. The one you like most may even be the cheapest. Once you've found your favorite, pick up a case.

A Hearty Meal with a Mediterranean Flavor

To be alone together is cause for celebration and would make almost any menu a success. But this one with its earthy Mediterranean flavors and its balance of sweet and savory tastes makes it a meal to linger over and remember.

The Timetable

The Night Before

■ Prepare the poached pears. Remove them from the liquid after they are cool and refrigerate.

■ Make sure you have the wine you need.

2 Hours Before

■ Mince the shallots for the beef recipe and refrigerate in a bowl covered with plastic.

■ Stem and slice the mushrooms and seed and slice the red pepper for the beef recipe.

■ Make the salad dressing (page 164).

■ Wash and dry the mixed greens for the salad and refrigerate them in a plastic bag.

■ Assemble the prosciutto and melon or mozzarella and tomato on individual appetizer plates, wrap loosely in plastic, and refrigerate.

■ Peel, cut, and blanch the potatoes and drain them in a colander. Arrange the potatoes in the baking dish along with the garlic cloves, rosemary, and butter. Season with salt and pepper.

■ Set the table.

1 Hour Before

■ Open the red wine.

■ Preheat the oven to 450°F for the potatoes.

■ Cook the beef tenderloin through Step 4.

■ Remove the appetizer from the refrigerator and let it come to room temperature.

■ Put the potatoes in the oven.

■ Set up your coffeemaker so it's ready to go.

■ Remove the pears from the refrigerator and let them come to room temperature.

To Start the Dinner

■ Place the appetizer on the table.

■ When the potatoes are done, turn off the heat and leave the oven door closed until you're ready to serve the main course.

■ Finish the first course.

■ Pour the wine.

To Serve the Main Course

■ Return the vegetables and meat to the pan and reheat.

■ Transfer the meat and vegetables to dinner plates and spoon on the sauce.

■ Add the potatoes and serve.

For the Salad

■ When you've finished the main course, arrange the greens on salad plates and sprinkle on the dressing.

■ Turn on the coffeemaker or put on water for tea.

MENU

Appetizer

Melon & prosciutto or mozzarella with tomato & fresh basil

Main Course

Fillet of beef with wild mushrooms

Oven-roasted potatoes with rosemary & whole garlic cloves

Mixed green salad

Crusty French bread

Dessert

Poached pears with vanilla ice cream & orange liqueur

Wine

French Burgundy or Bordeaux, or California Merlot

For Dessert

■ Arrange the poached pears and ice cream on plates. Spoon on the berries and orange liqueur and serve.

■ Finish making coffee or tea and serve.

Melon & Prosciutto

Ingredients *(serves two)*

2 2-inch wedges cantaloupe, honeydew, or
   Crenshaw melon

⅓ pound prosciutto or Black Forest ham,
   thinly sliced by the butcher

2 lime wedges

1. Cut the flesh from the rind of the
melon and brush off any seeds.

2. Lay the 2 pieces of melon on a serving
plate and drape with the slices of
prosciutto.

3. Serve with a wedge of lime on each
side of the plate.

Mozzarella with Tomato & Fresh Basil

Ingredients *(serves two)*

½ pound fresh mozzarella

1 large vine-ripened tomato

6 fresh basil leaves

Extra-virgin olive oil

Salt and freshly ground black pepper

1. Cut the mozzarella into 6 slices.

2. Cut the tomato into 6 slices.

3. Rinse the basil and pat dry with a
paper towel.

4. Arrange 3 slices of tomato on each of
2 plates. Lean the slices of mozzarella on
the tomato. Lay a basil leaf on each slice
of mozzarella.

5. Drizzle on the olive oil and sprinkle
with salt and freshly ground black pepper.

The Triple Fold

This special napkin
has a pocket where
you can slip a little
note, a rose, two
tickets to the opera or
a professional
wrestling match, or
whatever seems
appropriate.

1. Fold the napkin in
quarters.

2. Arrange the napkin
so the free corners
are in the upper right.

3. Roll down the first
layer to just past the
center of the napkin.

4. Fold down the
second layer and tuck
the point under the
first fold.

5. Fold down the third
layer and tuck the
point under the second
fold. Make sure the 3
bands are of equal size.

6. Fold under the right
and left sides.

7. Place the napkin
just to the left of
the fork(s).

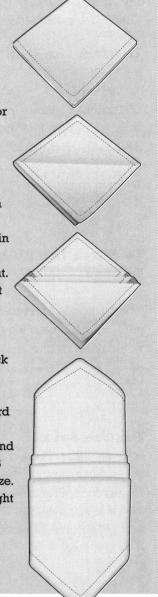

Fillet of Beef with Wild Mushrooms

The earthy flavor of the mushrooms complements the subtle flavor of the beef. Buy your fillet at a high-quality meat market.

Ingredients *(serves two)*

   3 tablespoons olive oil

   ⅓ pound shiitake mushrooms, stems discarded, caps cut into ¼-inch slices

   1 red bell pepper, seeded and cut into strips

   3 shallots, minced

   2 tablespoons butter

   ½ pound beef fillet, cut into ⅔-inch-thick slices

   ⅓ cup white wine

   ⅓ cup Marsala

   1 beef bouillon cube

   Salt and pepper

   Chopped parsley, for garnish

Equipment

   Large sauté pan

   Medium bowl

1. Place a large sauté pan on *medium-high* heat and let it get hot, about 45 seconds. Add the olive oil, mushrooms, and bell pepper, and sauté, stirring often, until they are almost tender, about 4 minutes. Add the shallots and sauté 3 minutes more, stirring frequently.

2. Transfer the vegetables to a medium bowl and return the pan to the stove. Increase the heat to *high* and add the butter.

As soon as the butter stops foaming, add the slices of tenderloin.

3. Brown the meat quickly, about 2 minutes on each side, then transfer to a plate.

4. Add the white wine, Marsala, and bouillon cube to the pan and reduce until the liquid is almost entirely evaporated, about 3 minutes.

5. Return the vegetables and meat to the pan. Cook just long enough to reheat the meat and vegetables, 1–2 minutes, turning the meat a few times. Season with salt and pepper, if desired. Serve immediately, pouring the pan juices over the meat. Garnish with parsley.

Oven-Roasted Potatoes with Rosemary & Whole Garlic Cloves

Ingredients *(serves two)*

   Olive oil, for greasing the pan

   2 medium-sized baking potatoes

   8 cloves garlic, unpeeled

   1 teaspoon chopped fresh rosemary or a pinch of dried

   2 tablespoons butter, cut into small pieces

   Salt and pepper

Equipment

   Medium saucepan

   9 x 9-inch baking pan

   Colander

1. Preheat the oven to 450°F.

2. Fill a medium saucepan halfway with water and bring to a boil over *high* heat.

3. Lightly grease a 9-inch square baking pan with the olive oil.

4. Cut the potatoes in half lengthwise. Cut each half into 4 wedges.

5. When the water boils, add the potatoes and blanch for 3 minutes.

6. Drain the potatoes well in a colander and transfer to the prepared baking pan.

7. Trim the nibs off the top of the garlic cloves (but do not peel them), and add the cloves to the potatoes. Sprinkle on the rosemary and dot with butter. Season with salt and pepper.

8. Bake in the center of the oven for 15 minutes. Turn the potatoes and bake for 15 minutes more or until browned all over and cooked through.

Poached Pears with Vanilla Ice Cream & Orange Liqueur

A simple yet elegant dessert that makes a fitting ending to a special meal. This recipe makes 4 pears, so that you can choose the 2 best ones for this dinner and save the others.

Ingredients *(serves four)*

4 Bosc pears

Approximately 1 bottle fruity red wine, such as Beaujolais or Zinfandel

1 cup sugar

Approximately 1 cup water

1 teaspoon vanilla extract

1 pint best-quality vanilla ice cream

½ pint whole raspberries, blueberries, or sliced strawberries

4 tablespoons orange liqueur

Equipment

Medium saucepan

Vegetable peeler

Ice cream scoop

1. Gently peel the pears, leaving the stems intact.

2. Combine the remaining ingredients through the vanilla extract in a medium saucepan and bring to a boil over *high* heat, stirring to dissolve the sugar. Reduce the heat to *medium* and place the pears in the pan.

3. Cover the pan and poach the pears until they are slightly soft, about 20 minutes. Remove the pan from the heat and let the pears cool in the poaching liquid, about 20 minutes.

4. Arrange the two best-looking pears and the berries on individual dessert plates and accompany with a scoop of ice cream. Pour 2 tablespoons of orange liqueur over the berries and serve.

Note

Leftover pears should be removed from the poaching liquid and refrigerated in a plastic container. They should last for about 2 days.

Salads

Salad can be as simple as a plate of leafy lettuce with balsamic vinegar and olive oil, or as complex as salad Niçoise with its eight-plus ingredients, or anything in between. There are really only two things that are essential to a successful salad: good fresh greens and a tasty dressing.

The versatile salad can be created out of almost any vegetable, raw or cooked, as well as poultry, fish, fruit, pasta, smoked meats, and a myriad of dressings. Served with a hunk of bread, some salads can be an entire meal.

Dad shouldn't overlook the benefits of getting the kids to eat even a small plate of leafy green lettuce with dinner. It's a great source of calcium and will get them started eating healthy foods.

SALADS

The Basic Salad

Greens can be prepared several hours ahead of time. Wash and pack them in plastic bags with a few sheets of paper towel to absorb the excess water.

For a salad with interesting colors and flavors, mix lighter leaves with darker ones and bitter salad greens with milder leafy ones. There is no exact formula to the basic salad, but figure on mixing in about half as many bitter greens as milder. There is also a wide assortment of packaged, pre-washed salad greens. Arugula and watercress stand nicely alone as the sole green in a salad. A combination of complementary greens with a good vinaigrette dressing makes a sophisticated salad, or greens can form a base for any of the vegetables on pages 162–163.

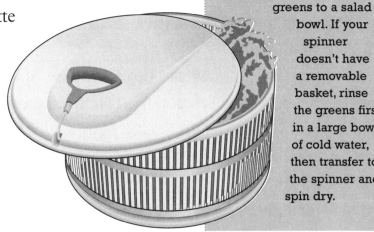

The Salad Spinner

The salad spinner is one of the greatest kitchen innovations of all time. It lets you rinse and dry greens with minimal work, which means a nutritious salad is never more than a few minutes away.

1. Discard any outside leaves that are tough or have brown spots.

2. To separate the leaves, cut across the base about 2 inches from the bottom.

3. Run each leaf briefly under cold water to wash off grit.

4. Tear the leaves into 1$\frac{1}{2}$- to 2-inch pieces and put the pieces in the spinner.

5. Fill the spinner with cold water and swish the leaves around. Remove the basket and let the water drain out. Pour out the water in the base of the spinner, reinsert the basket of lettuce and spin until dry. Transfer the greens to a salad bowl. If your spinner doesn't have a removable basket, rinse the greens first in a large bowl of cold water, then transfer to the spinner and spin dry.

Leafy Lettuces

Name	Appearance	Freshness	Taste	Salad Uses	Notes
Bibb	Small, vivid green leaves	No browning at edges; no large cracked leaves	Sweet, delicate, mild	Alone or with Romaine or bitter greens	Wash well; grit hides in folds
Boston	Somewhat round, spring-green leaves	No wilting or browning at tips or on stem	Sweet, mild	Alone or with leaf lettuces	Wash well; very gritty
Green or Red Leaf	Long, green or red-tipped leaves	No browning at tips or on stem; no mushiness at tips of red leaf	Light, mildly sweet	Alone or with bitter greens	Colors dress up a salad
Iceberg	Thick, sturdy leaves; tightly packed head	Firm and tightly packed; no brown spots	Crisp, mild	Alone or with Bibb or Romaine	Less dirt, but wash thoroughly
Romaine	Deep-green, long leaves	No dry, overgrown outside leaves, no brown spots	Crunchy, has some bite	Alone or with Bibb or iceberg	Wash well; very gritty

Bitter Salad Greens

Name	Appearance	Freshness	Taste	Salad Uses	Notes
Arugula	Dark, narrow leaves on stems	No yellow leaves or dark bruises; no large, dry, cracked outer leaves	Tangy, pungent	Alone or toss with leafy greens	Wash well to remove sand and grit; remove the stems
Belgian	White, conical leaves, looks like a cigar	Endive heads should be tightly wrapped	Subtly spicy	Slice thinly or add whole leaves; good contrast to milder flavored lettuce; with radicchio	Cut just before serving to prevent browning
Chicory	Long, frizzy light-green leaves	No brown or mushy spots	Slightly bitter	Add small amount to leafy greens	
Escarole	Broad, coarse leaves with wavy edges	No tough outer leaves	Slightly bitter	Add small amount to salads	Whitish inner leaves are best for salad
Watercress	Small, delicate leaves on long stems	Look for deep green leaves without any dark spots	Delicate, bitter	Alone; adds color and a sweetly bitter flavor to leafy greens; as a garnish	Wash gently as leaves bruise easily; trim away stems
Radicchio	Small, deep purple, tightly wrapped leaves	No yellowing edges; firm, not soft, leaves	Slightly bitter	Use a bit at a time to add color; with endive	Needs minimal washing; expensive, but keeps well

Once you've chosen your greens (see chart), you can build a salad with any number of vegetables, from the "garden variety" carrots and tomatoes to the more exotic fennel. Most vegetables can be prepared well in advance, but mushrooms, avocados, fennel, and endive should be sliced just before serving the salad, as they turn brown quickly. Dress the salad just before you serve it, tossing so that all the ingredients are coated.

Avocados

This vegetable-like fruit has smooth, mild flesh that complements the crunchy components of a salad and soaks up the flavors of the dressing. Choose avocados that yield to gentle pressure. Peel, then cut in half, twisting the halves around the pit to release them. Slice crosswise or cube.

Bell Peppers

Thin strips of bell pepper add crunch to a salad. The red, orange, and yellow varieties add vivid color.

Broccoli

Florets of broccoli complement any salad containing meat or poultry.

Cut the florets into pieces small enough to eat in 1 bite. To tenderize broccoli slightly, blanch (boil for 1 minute), then drain and cool under cold water.

Carrots

Peel first, then either grate, slice into thin rounds, or continue peeling and let the slivers fall into the salad bowl. Carrots with green tops are apt to be less woody than the packaged variety.

Celery

Kids relish the familiar flavor of celery in salads. Use the mild inner stalks, if possible, and slice very thin. Cut through a stalk lengthwise, then cut into $1/8$-inch pieces.

Cucumbers

Look for the thinnest, firmest ones, preferably unwaxed. Peel (if waxed) and slice thinly for salad. If they are very large, cut lengthwise and scrape out the seeds with a spoon before slicing.

Fennel

This is a bulb similar to celery, but it is rounder and has a slight licorice flavor that makes a piquant addition to a salad. Trim the bottom, then trim the stalks to within about $3/4$ inch of the bulb and cut the bulb in half lengthwise. Cut crosswise into thin slices for salad.

Mushrooms

For salad, use button mushrooms. They should be very white, and the membrane

connecting the cap and stem should be intact. Trim the stem, and slice the cap thinly just before serving, as mushrooms brown quickly. Do not use wild mushrooms in a raw salad as they must be cooked before eating.

Radishes

With their deep red skin and refreshingly peppery flavor, radishes can perk up a common salad. Slice them as thin as possible they are almost transparent.

Red Onion

Essential for a Greek salad. Peel, cut in half, and slice thinly. Wrap the remainder tightly in plastic and refrigerate. Look for firm onions with dry skin and no sprouting green shoots.

Scallions

(aka green onions) Many people feel scallions are essential to a good salad because they cut the vinegar and add a sharpness to the very mild taste of lettuce.

Wash and remove the small roots from the end. Chop the white bulb and green stalks for salad.

Snap & Snow Peas

Either can be included raw in a salad. Peel away the strings and rinse well. Do not buy peas if they are limp or pale.

Tomatoes

Use only vine-ripened tomatoes in salads. Off-season, your best bets are ripe plum tomatoes, cherry tomatoes, or the Israeli or Latin American tomatoes. Avoid packaged tomatoes and the generic, pale red tomatoes, sold as "slicing tomatoes," as they are mealy and tasteless. Nothing matches the taste of local farm stand tomatoes allowed to ripen on the vine, so grab them whenever you can (they're usually around between July and September).

What to Buy

Supermarkets like to pretend that vegetables have no seasons. They feel it is better to have tasteless waxed cucumbers at exorbitant prices in the middle of winter than not to have them at all. Increasingly though, you can get some tasty fresh produce—tomatoes from Israel and avocados from California or Florida—year round. You still need to shop with discretion, however. As a general rule all greens should have crisp, deeply colored leaves with no brown or soft spots or other signs of decay. Cucumbers must be firm; tomatoes should be firm (but not hard) and richly colored; carrots should be sprout-free. The maxim that great ingredients make great cooks is most true when it comes to making salad.

Zucchini

Use only small, thin zucchini for salad. Wash well, rubbing off any stubborn dirt or fuzz. Trim the ends and cut into paper-thin slices.

The Basic Dressing

There are some decent bottled vinaigrettes that you should keep on hand for use in a pinch, such as Newman's Own and Blanchard & Blanchard. But once you learn how easy it is to make your own dressing, the bottled ones may not seem as appealing. Remember dressing is meant to enhance the flavor of the salad, not smother it. Create salads with interesting and diverse flavors and dress them sparingly.

Olive Oil

The recent surge of interest in olive oil in the United States elevated this rustic food to a lofty status, with connoisseurs touting the virtues of oil costing upwards of $20 a bottle. While there are subtle distinctions among oils, you need not spend exorbitant sums to get a flavorful one.

You should, however, buy only "extra-virgin" olive oil to use on your salads. "Extra-virgin" comes from the first pressing of the olives and is, therefore, the purest and most flavorful oil. Subsequent pressings, designated superfine, fine, virgin, pure, or simply olive oil, are perfectly suitable for use in cooking. In fact, the subtle flavor of finer olive oils is lost at high temperatures. Olive oil does eventually become rancid, so store it in a cool, dry place and buy only as much as you can use in 6 months. In hot weather olive oil should be stored in the refrigerator. It will get cloudy and thick, but returns to normal when brought to room temperature.

Vinegar

The two kinds of vinegar most commonly used to make vinaigrette are red wine vinegar and white wine vinegar. Though most brands of vinegar look alike, they do have distinct differences in taste due to subtle differences in acidity. Try a few brands until you find one you like. Other kinds of vinegar include:

■ Balsamic vinegar, imported from Modena, Italy, is aged in barrels made of different kinds of wood. Its rich, pungent, slightly sweet flavor lends a distinctive taste to any salad.

■ Champagne vinegar is made from Champagne and has a slightly milder and sweeter flavor than white wine vinegar.

■ Herb-infused vinegars are made by steeping herbs, such as tarragon, chives, basil, or dill, in vinegar.

■ Fruit vinegars, such as raspberry or strawberry, are slightly sweet. These are especially well suited for dressing fruit salads.

■ Rice vinegar is made from fermented rice and is a frequent ingredient in a number of Eastern cuisines.

Dad's Own Vinaigrette

Because it is light, this basic vinaigrette enhances the salad. Heavier, gloppier dressings tend to swamp the delicate taste of interesting greens.

As a general rule, use one part vinegar to three parts oil.

Ingredients
(dresses a salad for eight)

¼ cup red or white wine vinegar (or balsamic vinegar)

1–2 cloves garlic, minced

1 teaspoon Dijon mustard

Salt and pepper to taste

¾ cup olive oil

Equipment

Medium bowl

Whisk

1. Combine all the ingredients except the oil in a medium bowl, and whisk for 15 seconds.

2. Add the oil in a slow, steady stream, whisking continuously until it is incorporated into the dressing.

3. Whisk again before using to recombine the oil and vinegar.

Variations

■ **Basil dressing** Gently whisk ¼ cup chopped fresh basil leaves into the dressing after the oil is incorporated. This dressing is excellent on a fresh tomato salad.

■ **Poppy seed dressing** Add 2 tablespoons sugar, 1 large egg, and 3 tablespoons poppy seeds to the vinegar mixture and whisk until smooth; then add the oil. This dressing is particularly good on spinach salad.

■ **Lemon and tarragon dressing** Substitute ¼ cup freshly squeezed lemon juice for the vinegar in the basic vinaigrette. Gently whisk in 1 teaspoon chopped fresh or dried tarragon after the oil has been incorporated.

■ **Anchovy dressing** Substitute ¼ cup freshly squeezed lemon juice for the vinegar, then add 2 anchovy fillets to the basic vinaigrette and purée. Use this dressing to make a great salad Niçoise.

■ **Parmesan dressing** Gently whisk ⅓ cup freshly grated Parmesan into the basic vinaigrette after the oil has been incorporated.

■ **Bacon and scallion dressing** Add 2 finely chopped scallions, 4 slices cooked and crumbled bacon, and 1 teaspoon bottled white horseradish to the basic vinaigrette and whisk until smooth. This dressing adds sparkle to a simple green salad.

Tip

Equal parts lemon juice can be used in combination with the vinegar in any of the vinaigrette recipes.

Chicken Salad

This old standby always seems to put the kids in a good mood and it doesn't take long to throw together, especially if you have a lot of leftover chicken. If you don't have any cooked chicken, allow a few hours for cooking and cooling a raw one.

Ingredients *(serves four)*

3 cups cooked chicken or 1 4–5 pound
    whole chicken or 2–3 whole breasts
2 stalks celery, cut into ½-inch slices
1 medium red onion, chopped
¼ cup chopped fresh parsley

Dressing

¾ cup mayonnaise
2 tablespoons sour cream
1 teaspoon mustard
1 teaspoon dried basil
1 teaspoon dried thyme
1 teaspoon salt

Equipment

Large pot with cover
Medium bowl
Large bowl
Small bowl

1. If using cooked chicken, skip the first 4 steps and proceed with Step 5. If not, bring a large pot of water to a boil. Add the chicken. When the water returns to a boil, lower the heat to *medium* and let the chicken simmer, partially covered, until the dark meat is just cooked through, about 1¼–1½ hours.

2. Transfer the cooked chicken to a medium bowl and let it cool, about 1½ hours.

3. When the chicken is cool enough to handle, peel the skin from the meat and discard it. Pull the meat from the bones, chop it into bite-sized pieces, and transfer it to a large bowl. (Be careful that no bones make their way into the bowl.)

4. Combine the dressing ingredients in a small bowl.

5. Add the celery, onion, and parsley to the chicken. Pour the dressing over the chicken and vegetables and toss.

Tips

■This salad can be stored for several hours in a tightly-covered plastic container in the refrigerator. Let the salad sit at room temperature for ½ hour before serving.

■ Once it is dressed, chicken salad cannot be frozen. Cooked chicken, however, freezes very well. Cut it into bite-size pieces and freeze in an airtight bag for up to a month. Let the chicken defrost overnight in the refrigerator before using it in the salad.

Variation

Curried Chicken Salad: Add ½ cup coarsely chopped walnuts and ½ cup raisins to the chicken. Eliminate the mustard, basil, and thyme from the dressing and substitute 1 tablespoon curry powder.

White Bean & Basil Salad

This salad plays the part of coleslaw in Northern Italy where it is sold in most *salumerie,* or corner delis. A really fine extra-virgin olive oil will enhance its flavor.

Ingredients *(serves four)*

2 10-ounce cans cannellini beans, drained
1 red bell pepper, cut into short, thin strips
½ cup fresh basil leaves or 3 teaspoons dried
4 tablespoons extra-virgin olive oil, or more if needed
1 teaspoon salt
Freshly ground black pepper

Equipment

Food processor or blender
Medium bowl
Colander

1. Put the beans in a colander and rinse them with cold water. Drain well and transfer to a medium bowl. Add the red bell pepper.

2. In a food processor or blender, combine the fresh basil with the olive oil and purée, adding more oil, 1 teaspoon at a time, if needed.

3. Pour the basil purée over the beans and peppers. If you're using dried basil, sprinkle it over the beans and then drizzle on the oil. Season with salt and pepper, then toss lightly.

Greek Salad

The feta cheese and olives are of Greek origin, but the salad itself is an American innovation. Feel free to add or subtract ingredients according to your family's tastes.

Ingredients *(serves four)*

1 head Romaine, iceberg, or leaf lettuce, or a combination
¼ pound feta cheese
2 tomatoes, quartered
1 cucumber, peeled and sliced
½ cup black olives
1 4-ounce jar marinated artichokes, drained and quartered
5 peperoncini (hot peppers; optional)
½ small red onion, thinly sliced
Dad's Own Vinaigrette (page 165), made with red wine vinegar

1. Wash and dry the lettuce well and tear into 1½-inch pieces. Place in a salad bowl.

2. Crumble the feta over the center of the lettuce. Arrange the tomatoes and cucumber around the edge of the bowl. Scatter the olives, artichokes, and peperoncini, if using, on top. Lay the onions over the cheese.

3. Present the salad at the table before adding the dressing sparingly, tossing, and serving.

SALADS

Caesar Salad

The pungent dressing livens up this simple salad of Romaine lettuce.

Ingredients *(serves four)*

1 large head Romaine lettuce

1 large clove garlic, minced

3 anchovy fillets, plus additional fillets for garnish, if desired

¼ cup white wine vinegar

2 tablespoons fresh lemon juice (from about 1 small lemon)

½ teaspoon Dijon mustard

½ teaspoon bottled white horseradish

½ cup olive oil

¼ cup grated Parmesan

4 tablespoons croutons, for garnish

Equipment

Medium bowl

Food processor or whisk

1. Wash and dry the lettuce well, tear into 1½-inch pieces, and place in a salad bowl.
2. Combine all the remaining ingredients except the oil, Parmesan, and croutons in a medium bowl or in a food processor. (If using a bowl and whisk, the anchovies must be finely chopped.) Whisk or process the mixture until it is smooth, about 30 seconds. Add the oil in a slow, steady stream until it's completely incorporated. Add the Parmesan and mix briefly.

Croutons

Boxed croutons are fine, but making your own is a snap and they taste much better. Any stale bread will do, though day-old French bread is preferable. Preheat the oven to 375°F. Cut the bread into ½-inch cubes. In a medium bowl, whisk together ¼ cup olive oil, 1 clove minced garlic, ½ teaspoon dried oregano, ½ teaspoon salt, and some freshly ground black pepper. Add the cubes of bread and toss them until they are lightly coated with the oil mixture. Spread the cubes of bread on a baking sheet and bake, shaking the pan occasionally, until crisp and golden brown, about 5–8 minutes.

3. Just before serving, pour ⅔ of the dressing on the lettuce and toss until it is lightly coated. Add more dressing if needed.
4. Garnish with croutons and additional anchovy fillets (if using).

Spinach Salad

The key to this simple salad is using the freshest spinach you can find. Look for spinach that isn't prepackaged. If that's unavailable, examine the packaged spinach well for mushy leaves.

Ingredients *(serves six)*

1 pound fresh spinach

10 strips bacon, cooked and broken into small pieces

2 scallions, chopped into thin rings

¼ pound button mushrooms, thinly sliced

Dressing

2 tablespoons lemon juice

2 tablespoons olive oil

¾ teaspoon salt

¾ teaspoon pepper

¼ teaspoon garlic salt

⅛ teaspoon dry mustard

¼ teaspoon sugar

1 tablespoon buttermilk

Equipment

Salad spinner

Small glass jar with cover

1. Pinch off the stems of the spinach and rinse the leaves well under cold water before drying in a salad spinner.

2. Transfer the spinach to a salad bowl. Arrange the bacon, scallions, and mushroom slices on top.

3. Combine the dressing ingredients in a glass jar, cover, and shake well.

4. Drizzle the dressing over the salad, toss, and serve.

Variation

Add walnuts or sliced avocado, or if you have an adventurous palate, try adding Roquefort or other blue cheese.

Waldorf Salad

Legend has it that Oscar Tschirky, the noted maître d' of the Waldorf-Astoria Hotel in New York City, created this famous salad in the 1890s. It's best to compose Waldorf salad on individual plates.

Ingredients *(serves four)*

2 heads Boston lettuce or 1 bunch leaf lettuce

2 ribs celery

2 apples, such as Granny Smith, McIntosh, or Golden Delicious

1 tablespoon mayonnaise

1 tablespoon plain yogurt

½ cup walnuts, coarsely chopped

Equipment

Salad spinner

Medium bowl

1. Wash and dry the lettuce leaves in a salad spinner, tear them into pieces approximately 4 inches square, and divide them among 4 salad plates.

2. Cut the celery ribs in half lengthwise, then cut them into approximately ½-inch pieces. Peel, then cut the apples lengthwise into quarters. Trim off the core and cut each quarter lengthwise into thirds. Cut each wedge into approximately ½-inch pieces.

3. Put the celery and apples in a medium bowl and add the mayonnaise and plain yogurt. Toss. Add the chopped walnuts.

4. Spoon helpings of the salad mixture over the lettuce leaves on the salad plates.

Carrot & Black Bean Salad

This refreshing, colorful main course salad takes time (about two hours). The effort might be lost on the kids, but this salad makes a distinguished luncheon for friends. You can make the dressing and cook the beans and rice a day ahead of time and refrigerate.

Ingredients *(serves four)*

¾ cup dried black beans, soaked overnight or for one hour in boiling water before cooking (or 16 ounces of canned black beans, drained and rinsed well)

1 cup brown rice

6 carrots

1 tablespoon plus 1 teaspoon olive oil

1 small red bell pepper

1 small green bell pepper

½ medium red onion

1 jalapeño pepper (optional)

½ cup pineapple juice

¼ cup freshly squeezed lime juice

1 tablespoon sugar

2 teaspoons finely grated ginger

½ teaspoon salt

½ small honeydew melon

¼ cup raw cashews

¼ cup shredded unsweetened coconut (available at health food stores; see Tips)

¼ cup raisins

Equipment

2 medium saucepans

Colander

Food processor with small shredder blade

Large frying pan

Large bowl

Small bowl

1. If you are using canned beans, proceed to Step 2. Otherwise, rinse the beans, then place them in a medium saucepan with 3 cups of water. Bring the water to a boil, reduce to a simmer, and cook the beans for about 1 hour, until tender. Drain in a colander, then cool to room temperature.

2. In another medium saucepan over *medium-high* heat, combine the 1 cup rice with 2 cups water. Bring the mixture to a boil, then reduce to a simmer, cover, and cook for about 50 minutes, until all of the water is absorbed. Cool to room temperature.

3. While the beans and rice are cooking, cut the carrots into sticks, then grate in the food processor using the small shredder blade specifically designed for this purpose. (If a food processor is unavailable, you can use a knife to cut the carrots into thin matchsticks but it's a tedious chore.)

4. Measure the oil into a large skillet over *medium-high* heat and let it get hot, about 45 seconds. Add the grated carrots and cook, stirring continuously, until the carrots are crisp-tender, about 5 minutes. Cool to room temperature.

5. Cut the bell peppers into ¼-inch dice. Coarsely chop the onion. Cut the jalapeño pepper in half, then remove the seeds and ribs and chop finely.

6. In a large bowl, combine the beans, rice, carrots, bell peppers, and onion. Cover and refrigerate until chilled, at least 1 hour.

7. In a small bowl, combine the jalapeño,

pineapple juice, lime juice, sugar, ginger, and salt.

8. Scoop the seeds out of the honeydew, then cut the honeydew half into 2 pieces, cut the flesh from the rind, and cut the flesh into ¼-inch dice. Coarsely chop the cashews.

9. Toss together the rice-and-bean mixture and the dressing. Stir in the honeydew, nuts, coconut, and raisins. Serve.

Tips

■You'll probably have to go to the health food store to get the unsweetened coconut. If it's too far out of the way, skip the coconut altogether. But, if you are going to make the trip, pick up the cashews, black beans, brown rice, and raisins there as well.

■If you are in a rush to cool the carrots, beans, or rice to room temperature, transfer them from the pans in which they were cooked to bowls and place them in the refrigerator for a little while.

Tuna, Chickpea & Smoked Cheddar Salad

This quick and easy salad is especially tasty with fresh basil and is great for picnics.

Ingredients *(serves four)*

2 6-ounce cans solid white tuna in water
2 ribs celery

1 15-ounce can chickpeas
1 6-ounce jar artichoke hearts in oil
1 4-ounce jar roasted red peppers
¼ pound smoked cheddar or any smoked cheese
¼ cup fresh basil leaves, or 1 tablespoon dried
¼ cup fresh parsley, chopped
¼ cup Dad's Own Vinaigrette (page 165)

Equipment

Medium bowl
Colander

1. Drain the tuna, empty it into a medium bowl, and flake it with a fork.

2. Rinse and dry the celery, then cut it on an angle into ⅛-inch slices. Add to the tuna.

3. Drain the chickpeas in a colander. Rinse them and shake the colander vigorously to remove the excess water.

4. Drain the artichoke hearts and cut them into quarters. Add to the tuna.

5. Drain the red peppers and chop them coarsely. Add to the tuna.

6. Cut the cheese into ½-inch cubes. Add to the tuna.

7. Wash, dry, and tear the basil leaves into ½-inch pieces. Add the basil and parsley to the tuna.

8. Drizzle on the dressing, toss, and serve.

Tip

This salad can be stored, without dressing, for several hours in a tightly covered plastic container in the refrigerator. Let the salad sit at room temperature for ½ hour before adding the dressing and serving.

Coleslaw

This is not the sodden version found in diners and school cafeterias across the country. Instead, it is a crisp, fresh-tasting side dish just begging for freshly grilled burgers or chicken.

Ingredients *(serves four)*

   1 medium head cabbage
   2 carrots
   1 small red onion

Dressing

   3 tablespoons mayonnaise
   2 tablespoons sour cream
   2 tablespoons corn oil
   2 tablespoons white wine vinegar
   1 tablespoon sugar
   2 teaspoons celery seed
   2 teaspoons salt

Equipment

   Large bowl
   Small bowl
   Food processor
   Whisk

1. Cut the cabbage lengthwise into quarters. Trim the core section from the bottom of each quarter. Put each quarter through the food processor, using the shredder blade. Transfer to a large bowl.

2. Grate the carrots in the food processor, using the small shredder blade. Chop the onion. Add the vegetables to the cabbage.

3. In a small bowl, whisk together all of the dressing ingredients.

4. Pour the dressing over the vegetables and, using your hands (it's the only way), mix everything together. Refrigerate until ready to serve.

Red Potato Salad

This recipe doesn't swamp the potatoes with dressing, but instead coats them lightly. There's no need to peel the potatoes. Besides contributing nutritionally, the red skins make the salad more colorful.

Ingredients *(serves four to six)*

   2 ½ pounds small red potatoes
   2 ribs celery
   1 medium red onion
   2 scallions
   1 red or green bell pepper
   ½ cup chopped fresh parsley

Dressing

   ½ cup mayonnaise
   2 tablespoons sour cream or additional mayonnaise
   1 tablespoon Dijon mustard
   1 tablespoon salt
   Freshly ground black pepper

Equipment

   Large pot
   Large bowl
   Small bowl
   Colander
   Rubber spatula (optional)

1. Rinse the potatoes, scrubbing off any spots of dirt with a potato brush or dish towel.

2. Put the potatoes in a large pot. Cover with cold water to about 1 inch above the potatoes and bring to a boil, uncovered, on *high* heat.

3. When the water reaches a boil, reduce the heat to *medium-low* and simmer the potatoes until just tender (when a paring knife can pierce the potatoes easily), about 15 minutes. Drain and cool in a colander.

4. While the potatoes are cooking, rinse and dry the celery ribs and cut them on an angle into ⅛-inch slices. Cut the onion in half and then into thin slices. Chop the green parts of the scallions into ½-inch pieces. (Discard the white parts.) Seed the bell pepper and cut it into short thin strips.

5. To make the dressing, combine all of the ingredients in a small bowl.

6. When the potatoes are cool enough to handle, cut them into quarters and transfer them to a large bowl. Add the vegetables and chopped parsley.

7. Pour the dressing on the potato mixture and gently combine with your hands or a rubber spatula. Refrigerate, covered, for at least 2 hours. Remove from the refrigerator ½ hour before serving.

Variation

Substitute 2 tablespoons plain low-fat yogurt for the sour cream to help reduce calories.

Watercress, Snow Pea & Melon Salad

This is a wonderful way to start a summer meal. The kids will love the touch of sweetness the melon adds.

Ingredients *(serves four or five)*

 2 bunches of watercress
 ½ pound snow peas or sugar snap peas
 ½ honeydew or cantaloupe
 ¼ cup Dad's Own Vinaigrette (page 165), made with lemon juice instead of vinegar

1. Wash and dry the watercress and divide it among salad plates.

2. Remove the strings from the snow peas or snap peas, rinse, and dry on paper towels. Arrange the peas over the watercress.

3. Cut the melon in half and remove the seeds, then cut each half into quarters. Cut the flesh from the rind and slice it into 1-inch pieces. Arrange 6–8 melon slices on top of the watercress.

4. Drizzle on the dressing just before serving.

Variations

■Three sectioned clementines can be used in place of the melon. Or try two 6-ounce cans mandarin orange slices, well-drained.

■Boston or green leaf lettuce can be used in place of the watercress.

■ Green beans or jicama can replace the snow peas.

Complete Meal Salads

Many salads, like the three that follow, are meals in themselves. Oftentimes, especially in summer, a salad with a good loaf of bread sounds and tastes better than any hot entrée you can imagine. The salads that follow, classic salad Niçoise, exotic-tasting Japanese beef, and Chinese-style chicken salad, all provide a full complement of meat or fish, vegetables, and carbohydrates. Other salads in *Dad's Own Cookbook* that can be served as complete meals are the Chef's Salad (page 67) and the Cold Tortellini Salad (page 192).

Salad Niçoise

This classic salad originated in the city of Nice on the French Rivera.

Ingredients *(serves four)*

- 6–8 *small red potatoes, cut in half*
- ½ *pound green beans or haricots verts (very thin French green beans)*
- 1 *head Romaine or leaf lettuce, torn into bite-sized pieces*
- 1 *red bell pepper, seeded and cut into ½-inch strips*
- 2 *6-ounce cans solid white tuna in water, drained*
- 3 *large hard-boiled eggs, shelled and cut lengthwise into quarters*
- 1 *medium red or yellow onion, sliced into thin rings*
- ½ *cup (about ¼ pound) pitted black olives (Niçoise or kalamata)*
- *Freshly ground black pepper*

Dressing

- 2 *garlic cloves*
- 5 *tablespoons freshly squeezed lemon juice (from 1 large lemon)*
- ½ *cup plus 1 tablespoon extra-virgin olive oil*
- 1¼ *teaspoons dried basil*
- ½ *teaspoon salt*

Equipment

- 2 *medium saucepans*
- *Colander*
- *Salad spinner*
- *Glass jar with cover*

1. Fill a medium saucepan with water and bring to a boil. Add the potatoes and boil for 10–15 minutes or until tender. Drain in a colander. Set aside to cool.

2. Bring another medium saucepan of water to a boil and blanch the green beans for 1 minute or the haricots verts for 30 seconds. Drain immediately in a colander and run under cold water to cool.

3. Wash and dry the lettuce in a salad spinner. Transfer to a salad bowl. Add the bell pepper, tuna, eggs, onion, olives, potatoes, and green beans, and stir gently to combine.

4. Combine the dressing ingredients in a glass jar. Cover and shake well.

5. Drizzle the dressing over the salad and toss well. Grind the pepper over the top and serve.

Variations

Artichoke hearts or sliced cucumbers can be substituted for the hard-boiled eggs.

Japanese Beef Salad

If your kids like meat, they'll love this salad. It can be made ahead of time for a no-fuss dinner.

Ingredients *(serves four)*

1¾ pounds flank steak, about ½-inch thick
½ pound green beans or snow peas
2 cups broccoli florets
1 red bell pepper, cut into strips
1 medium onion, thinly sliced
2 scallions, cut into ½-inch pieces

Dressing

¼ cup soy sauce
¼ cup white wine (or clear apple juice)
1 tablespoon sesame oil
1 tablespoon sugar
1 teaspoon garlic powder
1 teaspoon ground ginger

Equipment

Broiler pan
Medium saucepan
Medium bowl
Colander
Large bowl
Whisk

1. Preheat the broiler.

2. Place the flank steak on the broiler pan and broil 4 inches from the flame for 5–7 minutes on each side. Let the steak cool while you assemble the rest of the salad.

3. Fill a medium saucepan halfway with water and bring it to a boil. Fill a medium bowl with cold water. Trim the ends of the green beans or peel the strings from the snow peas. Blanch the beans or snow peas for 1 minute in the boiling water. Drain them in a colander and transfer them to a bowl of cold water. Repeat with the broccoli. Allow the vegetables to cool.

4. Slice the steak across the grain into very thin slices and transfer to a large bowl. Pat the broccoli and beans or snow peas dry with paper towels and add them to the beef along with the rest of the vegetables.

5. Whisk together the dressing ingredients in a small bowl. Pour the dressing over the salad and toss together.

Tips

■ This salad can be stored for several hours, without dressing, in a tightly covered plastic container in the refrigerator. Let the salad sit at room temperature for ½ hour before adding the dressing and serving.

■ To save time, the flank steak can be broiled that morning or the night before.

Chinese Chicken Salad

The slicing of the chicken, cucumber, and carrots takes a while; otherwise this salad is a cinch to make. If desired, prepare the dressing in advance.

Ingredients *(serves four)*

1 pound plain cooked chicken, cut into 3-inch strips

½ pound bean sprouts

1 medium cucumber, peeled, seeded, and cut into 3-inch matchsticks

2 large carrots, cut into thin 3-inch matchsticks

Dressing

3 tablespoons peanut butter or sesame paste (tahini)

2 scallions, chopped

⅔ cup chicken broth

3 tablespoons soy sauce

2 tablespoons rice vinegar (see Tip)

1 tablespoon dry sherry or rice wine (see Tip)

2 teaspoons sesame oil

2–4 cloves garlic, minced

1 teaspoon sugar

1 teaspoon salt

Chopped fresh cilantro, for garnish (optional)

Equipment

Large bowl

Glass jar with cover

1. Combine the chicken, bean sprouts, cucumber, and carrots in a large bowl.

2. Put the dressing ingredients in a glass jar, cover, and shake vigorously.

3. Drizzle the dressing over the salad and toss gently. Sprinkle the cilantro over the salad, if desired.

Tip

Cider vinegar can be substituted for the rice vinegar and dry white wine can be substituted for the dry sherry or rice wine.

Note

If you don't have any pre-cooked chicken in the refrigerator, place 1 pound boneless chicken breasts on a rimmed baking sheet, cover the pan securely with foil, and bake in a preheated 350°F oven for 20–25 minutes, until cooked through but still juicy.

Pasta

opular legend would have us believe that Marco Polo was responsible for carrying the idea of noodles back with him from China to Italy, but in actuality some form of pasta was being eaten in both places before Polo even set out on his voyage in 1271.

Whatever its history, pasta is loved today by children and adults alike and, fortunately, is very healthy, economical, and easy to prepare: You make the sauce or broth, cook the pasta, put the two together, and dinner (or lunch) falls neatly into place.

Some people still think of pasta as a plate of spaghetti with tomato sauce, a couple of meatballs, and a sprinkling of Parmesan cheese. But pasta possibilities are much more varied. This chapter covers the basics, like tomato sauce, lasagna, and macaroni casserole, and also explores more adventuresome dishes like penne with tuna, tomatoes, and roasted peppers; Asian noodles with chicken and ham; cold peanut noodles; and tortellini salad.

Pasta Primer

Pasta comes in many sizes, shapes, even colors; there are cords, tubes, ribbons, and special shapes like shells, wheels, and even butterflies. Two pastas, ravioli and tortellini, have fillings. When marrying sauce to pasta keep in mind a simple rule: the longer the pasta, the thinner the sauce. That means, use light sauces for delicate pastas like angel hair and chunky, heavier sauces for sturdy pastas like fusilli. One exception is fettuccine, which works best with thick cream sauces. Cooking times depend not on the size or length of the pasta, but on its thickness.

Fresh vs. Dried

Both fresh and dried pastas have their own virtues. Fresh pasta, which is usually made with all-purpose flour and eggs, is lighter and richer than dried pasta and shines when matched with light sauces. Fresh pasta is best when eaten the day it is made but can be stored in the refrigerator for about 4 days.

Dried pasta is made with a harder flour than fresh pasta and is, in most cases, suited to more robust sauces, for example, tomato and sausage, carbonara, or puttanesca sauces. Whenever possible, use imported Italian dried pasta, which is higher in quality than most domestic dried pastas. It doesn't absorb too much water and is pleasantly firm.

Name	Translation	Serve with	Cooking Time
Capelli d'angeli	Angel hair	Light marinara or oil-based sauces	Fresh: *2 minutes* Dry: *5 minutes*
Conchigliette	Little shells	Seafood sauces; marinara	Fresh: *3 minutes* Dry: *7–9 minutes*
Farfalle	Butterflies or bow-ties	Pesto or other oil-based sauces	Fresh: *3 minutes* Dry: *7–9 minutes*
Fettuccine	Small ribbons	Cream or oil-based sauces	Fresh: *3 minutes* Dry: *9 minutes*

Name	Translation	Serve with	Cooking Time
Fusilli	Twists	Marinara or pesto sauce	Fresh: *3 minutes* Dry: *10 minutes*
Lasagna	Broad-leafed	Layered with cheese and tomato sauce and baked	Fresh: *4 minutes* Dry: *10 minutes*
Linguine	Little tongues	Marinara or oil-based sauces	Fresh: *2–3 minutes* Dry: *5–7 minutes*
Macaroni	Elbows	Butter, cheese, and milk	Dry: *9 minutes*
Manicotti	Muffs	For stuffing and baking; marinara or cream sauces	Fresh: *3 minutes* Dry: *7 minutes*
Orecchiette	Little ears	Marinara or oil-based sauces	Fresh: *3 minutes* Dry: *7 minutes*
Penne	Pens	Hearty marinara with sausage; baked with cheese	Fresh: *3–4 minutes* Dry: *7–9 minutes*
Radiatore	Radiators	Pesto or cream sauces	Fresh: *3 minutes* Dry: *7–9 minutes*
Ravioli	Ravioli	Depending on filling, light cream sauce or butter or Parmesan	Fresh: *4 minutes*
Ruote	Wheels	Hearty marinara; cream sauces	Fresh: *3 minutes* Dry: *7 minutes*
Spaghetti	Strings	Any sauce; meatballs	Fresh: *2–3 minutes* Dry: *7–9 minutes*
Tortellini	Little twists	Depending on filling, light cream or oil-based sauces	Fresh: *4 minutes* Dry: *7–9 minutes*
Vermicelli	Worms	Fresh tomato sauce	Fresh: *2 minutes* Dry: *5 minutes*
Ziti	Bridegrooms	Hearty marinara or cream sauces	Dry: *10 minutes*

Pasta Sauce Primer

Don't be put off by the complexity of some pasta sauces. Quite simply all Italian sauces use either cream, tomatoes, or oil as their base. Cream sauces are cooked in a frying pan for a short amount of time. The cream is added last and reduced to the desired thickness. Tomato sauces are usually cooked in a large pot and allowed to simmer for at least an hour to thicken and enhance the flavor. Sauces using fresh tomatoes, however, are more often made quickly in a frying pan. The tomatoes are sautéed along with other fresh ingredients like basil and onions. Oil-based sauces are the fastest sauces, usually requiring only a quick sauté of the main ingredients in a frying pan with enough olive oil to coat the pasta.

Below is a quick reference guide for sauces. Those included in *Dad's Own Cookbook* are noted with stars. Others can be found in any number of Italian or pasta cookbooks. Most recipes use sautéed onions and garlic as prime ingredients.

Garlic

Dealing with garlic quickly and efficiently will propel you through many recipes. Garlic burns easily (making it bitter) and should be sautéed for no more than a minute or so.

Minced garlic
1. Separate the clove from the head of garlic.
2. Using a paring knife, trim off the stem end. Peel off the shell from the garlic clove.
3. Place the flat side of a chef's knife over the clove and smack it hard enough to mash the clove.
4. Chop the mashed clove until it is finely minced.

To prepare garlic for cooking, chop it with a knife. But for salad dressing, peel the clove, then use a garlic press to crush it fine enough to dissolve into the liquid.

Cream Sauces

Name	Ingredients	Cooking Time	Serve with
Alfredo	Cream, Parmesan, butter	*5 minutes*	Fettuccine
Carbonara*	Bacon, eggs, Parmesan, cream	*10 minutes*	Spaghetti, penne

Cream Sauces *(cont.)*

Name	Ingredients	Cooking Time	Serve with
Gorgonzola	Gorgonzola, cream, butter, Parmesan	*5 minutes*	Fettuccine, spaghetti, penne
Primavera	Zucchini, yellow squash, red bell pepper, cream, butter, Parmesan	*10 minutes*	Fettuccine, penne, small shells
alla Saffi	Asparagus, smoked ham, butter, cream	*20 minutes*	Spaghetti, fettuccine

Tomato-Based Sauces

Name	Ingredients	Cooking Time	Serve with
Amatriciana	Bacon, tomatoes, hot red pepper, Parmesan	*40 minutes*	Spaghetti, vermicelli
Bolognese*	Tomatoes, meat, peppers, carrots, wine	*2–4 hours*	Spaghetti, ziti, most shapes
Clam (red)	Clams, tomatoes, anchovies, parsley	*20 minutes*	Spaghetti, linguine
Marinara*	Tomatoes, wine, basil, oregano, stock	*1–2 hours*	Most shapes
Pescatore*	Shrimp, fish, scallops, tomatoes, fish stock	*20 minutes*	Spaghetti, linguine
Puttanesca*	Anchovies, garlic, tuna, olives, capers, tomatoes	*40 minutes*	Spaghetti, penne
Sausage and Basil*	Sausage, basil, tomatoes	*20 minutes*	Spaghetti, ziti
Siciliana	Eggplant, tomatoes, Parmesan, ricotta, basil	*40 minutes*	Spaghetti, ziti
al Tonno*	Tuna, roasted red pepper, tomatoes	*20 minutes*	Spaghetti, linguine

Oil-Based Sauces

Name	Ingredients	Cooking Time	Serve with
Broccoli and Garlic*	Broccoli, olive oil, Parmesan, garlic	*20 minutes*	Spaghetti, penne
Clam (white)	Clams, garlic, fish stock, olive oil	*20 minutes*	Spaghetti, linguine
Garlic and Oil	Garlic, olive oil, Parmesan	*10 minutes*	Spaghetti, linguine
Pesto	Basil, olive oil, Parmesan	*10 minutes*	Spaghetti, shells, orzo, penne
al Sarde	Sardines, fennel, olive oil, raisins, pine nuts, anchovies, saffron, tomato paste	*20 minutes*	Spaghetti, thick linguine

Basic Tomato Sauce

This tomato sauce can be used on its own or as the foundation for many different sauces.

Ingredients *(makes 2½ quarts, enough for 5–6 pounds spaghetti)*

1 tablespoon olive oil
1 large onion, finely chopped
2 ribs celery, finely chopped
2 large carrots, finely chopped
1 green bell pepper, seeded and diced
2 cloves garlic, minced
½ cup red or white wine
2 28-ounce cans crushed Italian plum
   tomatoes
1 6-ounce can tomato paste
3 tablespoons chopped fresh basil or
   2 teaspoons dried
3 tablespoons chopped fresh parsley
2 teaspoons dried oregano
1 tablespoon salt
Freshly ground black pepper

Equipment

Large, heavy pot with cover

1. Place a large pot on *medium-high* heat and let it get hot, about 45 seconds. Add the olive oil and the onion, celery, carrots, and bell pepper. Sauté, stirring often, until the vegetables are soft, about 10 minutes.
2. Add the garlic. Stir and cook for 1 minute more.
3. Increase the heat to *high*, add the wine, and cook until the liquid is reduced by half. Stir in the tomatoes, tomato paste, 2 cups water, and the basil, parsley,

oregano, salt, and pepper to taste.
4. When the sauce begins to bubble, turn the heat down to *low*, cover the pot halfway, and let the sauce simmer, stirring occasionally for at least 45 minutes, until it begins to thicken. Longer cooking time makes for a thicker, more intensely flavored sauce.

Tip

The flavor of tomato sauce will intensify if you let it sit for a day. If you have the time, make it a day ahead and refrigerate. Tomato sauce also freezes well. With this amount of sauce, you can freeze half of it. Let the sauce cool before either refrigerating or storing in well-sealed plastic containers in the freezer. Freeze the sauce in 2- or 3-cup containers so you can defrost only what you need for each meal.

Variations

■**With meat:** Brown 1 pound chopped beef, veal, or a combination of the two in a frying pan over *high* heat for 5–6 minutes. Transfer the meat to a colander to let the fat drain off. Add the meat to the sauce when you add the crushed tomatoes.
■**With sausage:** Brown ½ pound sweet Italian sausage meat in a frying pan over *high* heat for 5–6 minutes breaking it up into small chunks as it cooks. Transfer the meat to a colander to let the fat drain off. Add the sausage to the sauce when you add the crushed tomatoes. Sausage can also be used in combination with ground beef.
■**With mushrooms:** Thinly slice ¾ pound white or wild mushrooms or a combination of the two. Sauté these with the other vegetables.

■ **Puttanesca:** Coarsely chop any 3 or more of the following: 4 anchovy fillets, 2 tablespoons capers, 1 can tuna in oil (drained), a dozen pitted black olives, 1 4-ounce jar roasted Italian red peppers (drained), and 1 4-ounce jar artichoke hearts (drained). Add to the sauce when you add the crushed tomatoes.

Meatballs

These are the Titleists of meatballs. You can freeze half the batch and still feed a foursome with what's left.

Ingredients *(makes 24 meatballs)*

3 slices bread, crusts trimmed, broken into pieces

½ cup whole milk

2 pounds ground beef, or 1 pound ground beef and 1 pound ground veal

½ pound sweet Italian sausage meat, removed from casing

3 ½ cups Basic Tomato Sauce (opposite page) or your favorite store-bought sauce

2 large eggs

¼ cup grated Parmesan

1 teaspoon dried oregano

1 teaspoon dried basil

3 tablespoons olive oil

Equipment

12 x 16-inch casserole

Medium bowl

Large bowl

Large frying pan

Aluminum foil

1. Preheat the oven to 375°F. Lightly grease a 12 x 16-inch casserole with vegetable oil.

2. Put the bread in a medium bowl, pour in the milk, and let sit for 1 minute.

3. In a large bowl, combine the meats, the bread mixture, ½ cup of the tomato sauce, the eggs, cheese, oregano, and basil, using your hands if necessary.

4. Shape the meat mixture into 1½-inch balls by rolling them between your palms. Arrange the balls on a large platter or baking sheet.

5. Measure 1½ tablespoons of the oil into a large frying pan and place over *medium-high* heat for about 1 minute. Add half the meatballs and cook until brown on all sides, turning as needed, about 5 minutes.

6. Transfer the cooked meatballs to the prepared casserole and repeat with the remaining oil and meatballs. When all the meatballs are browned, pour the remaining 3 cups tomato sauce into the casserole and stir briefly so that all the meatballs are coated.

7. Cover the casserole dish with aluminum foil and bake for 30 minutes until the meatballs are firm and cooked through. Remove the foil and bake for 15 minutes more.

Tips

■ Meatballs can be made a day in advance and refrigerated.

■ To reheat, place the meatballs in a large saucepan with ½ cup tomato sauce and heat slowly on *medium low* for 12–15 minutes.

■ Cool the meatballs completely before freezing in a tightly sealed plastic container. Place a layer of plastic wrap directly on the meatballs to protect them against freezer burn. Defrost the meatballs in the refrigerator for 24 hours.

Dad's Own No-Boil Lasagna

Every time I make lasagna this way (without cooking the lasagna noodles first) I'm convinced it's not going to work. But it always comes out perfectly. Since it's both easy to make and a meal that nearly every kid loves, there's no reason not to double the ingredients and make two pans at once. Serve one for dinner and store the other in the freezer.

Ingredients *(serves six)*

1 pound ground beef

½ pound sweet Italian sausage, removed from its casing and broken into small chunks

5 cups Basic Tomato Sauce (page 182) or your favorite store-bought sauce

2 6-ounce packages frozen chopped spinach

24 ounces ricotta cheese

2 extra-large eggs

½ cup grated Parmesan

1 tablespoon salt

Olive oil or butter, for greasing the pan

1 pound lasagna noodles

1 pound mozzarella, thinly sliced or grated

Equipment

9 x 13-inch baking pan (see Tips)

Large frying pan

Colander

Medium saucepan

2 large bowls

Aluminum foil

1. Preheat the oven to 350°F.

2. Place a large frying pan on *high* heat and let it get very hot, about 45 seconds. Add the ground beef and sausage and brown, stirring frequently, until all the meat is cooked through. Transfer the meat to a colander and let the fat drain. Then transfer the meat to a large bowl, add the tomato sauce, and stir to combine.

3. In a medium saucepan over *medium-high* heat, cook the spinach in enough boiling water to cover, until cooked through, about 5 minutes. (The spinach can also be cooked in the microwave; see page 142). Transfer the spinach to a colander and rinse with cold water. Squeeze small clumps of spinach between your hands until the water is thoroughly extracted.

4. Transfer the spinach to a large bowl. Add the ricotta, eggs, ¼ cup of the Parmesan, and the salt, and mix well.

5. Lightly oil or butter a 9 x 13-inch baking pan. Spoon in just enough meat sauce to thickly cover the bottom. Cover the sauce with a layer of pasta, laying the strips lengthwise, side-by-side, and up to the edges of the pan.

6. Cover the pasta with ¼ of the remaining sauce and top with half the mozzarella. Cover the mozzarella with a second layer of pasta and spread the pasta with ⅓ of the remaining sauce.

7. Spread on *all* of the spinach-ricotta mixture in an even layer and cover it with a third layer of pasta.

8. Spread on ½ of the remaining sauce and top with the remaining mozzarella. Arrange a fourth layer of pasta and cover with a final layer of sauce. Sprinkle on the remaining ¼ cup Parmesan.

9. Cover the pan securely with aluminum foil and bake about 50 minutes, until the cheese melts and the noodles are cooked through.

10. Remove the lasagna from the oven and let rest for 5 minutes before serving.

Time-Saver

The meat sauce and the spinach-ricotta mixture can be prepared a day in advance, sealed in plastic wrap, and refrigerated.

Tips

■To freeze lasagna, let it cool, then wrap tightly in plastic wrap and cover with aluminum foil. If you plan to freeze lasagna, bake it in a disposable aluminum pan so you won't tie up one of your best baking pans in the freezer.

■To reheat a whole pan of frozen lasagna, unwrap it and place in a preheated 325°F oven for 30 minutes. Raise the temperature to 350°F and cook until heated through, about 20 minutes more. Cover the top of the lasagna with aluminum foil for the last 10 minutes of cooking so it won't dry out.

■Refrigerated leftover lasagna is best reheated in the microwave, which keeps it moist. Place a portion of lasagna on a plate and cover with plastic wrap. Reheat on *medium high*—4 minutes for 1 portion, 6 minutes for 2, 8 minutes for 4. Otherwise, spread a couple of tablespoons of tomato sauce on the bottom of a small casserole and lay the cold lasagna over the sauce. Cover the pan and heat in a 300°F oven until heated through, about 12–15 minutes.

Never-Fail Macaroni Casserole

While not the most elegant of meals, this easy casserole is high on the list of children's favorites.

Ingredients *(serves four)*

> *1 package #7 macaroni*
> *8- to 10-ounces extra-sharp cheddar cheese*
> *1 28-ounce can crushed tomatoes*
> *¼ cup seasoned bread crumbs*
> *1 tablespoon butter, cut into small pieces*
> *Freshly ground black pepper*

Equipment

> *Pasta pot*
> *2-quart casserole*
> *Colander*

1. Preheat the oven to 350°F. Lightly grease the casserole with margarine or vegetable oil.

2. Bring a large pot of water to a boil for the pasta. Cook the macaroni until al dente, about 7–9 minutes, then drain it well in a colander.

3. While the pasta is cooking, cut the cheese into thin slices.

4. Layer ⅓ of the cooked macaroni in the bottom of the casserole dish. Add ⅓ of the cheese slices followed by ⅓ of the tomato sauce. Repeat the layering 2 more times. Add pepper to each layer. Sprinkle with the bread crumbs and dot with the butter.

5. Bake for 45 minutes, until lightly browned.

Eight Steps To Pasta Heaven

1. The Big Pot

Use at least a 6-quart pot when cooking pasta.

2. The Water

One pound of pasta needs to cook in at least 4 quarts of rapidly boiling water. Less water will not allow the individual pieces of pasta to float freely, causing them to stick together. Bring the water to a fast rolling boil before adding the pasta.

3. The Oil

Add 1 tablespoon oil to the water. This helps prevent the pasta from sticking together.

4. The Salt

Add 1 teaspoon salt to the boiling water. This helps bring out the flavor of the pasta.

5. The Pasta

Add the pasta to the pot in a slow, steady stream. This will help keep the pieces separate and the water boiling. Push down strands of spaghetti as they soften. Once all the pasta is in the pot, stir quickly to keep it from sticking. Stirring occasionally during cooking helps keep thicker pasta, like ziti or lasagna, from sticking to the bottom.

6. The Timing

■ **Dried Pasta:** Begin timing the pasta when the water returns to a boil. Check the pasta about 1 minute before the time specified by the manufacturer by lifting a few strands or pieces from the pot, letting them cool a few seconds, then taking a bite. If the pasta is not yet done, continue cooking it and test every 30 seconds or so.

Pasta should not be overcooked, it should be al dente ("to the tooth")— tender but firm.

■ **Fresh:** Fresh pastas cook in a fraction of the time necessary for dried pastas. Begin timing as soon as the pasta is in the water. Check the pasta at the prescribed time. If it's not ready, check it again every 15 seconds or so.

7. The Draining

Drain the pasta in a large, stable colander set in the sink. Using pot holders, shake the colander vigorously to release any remaining water. Transfer to a bowl and toss with 1 tablespoon olive oil to keep the pasta separate. Some recipes recommend draining pasta in cold water, which stops the cooking process. I recommend doing this only when the pasta is going to be served cold.

8. The Serving

Pasta needs to get to the table fast as it cools quickly (even when it's not rinsed in cold water). Immediately after the pasta is drained, transfer it to the serving bowl or individual plates. Quickly

How Much to Cook

Type of Pasta	First Course	Main Course
1 pound dried pasta	8 servings	6 servings
1 pound fresh pasta	6 servings	4 servings

Timing

Check individual recipes or instructions on packages for recommended timing. Cooking time varies according to manufacturer and whether fresh or dried (homemade pasta cooks more quickly). But here are some general guidelines.

	Average Cooking Times	
Type of Pasta	1 Pound of Dried Pasta	1 Pound of Fresh Pasta
Angel hair, spaghettini, or other thin spaghetti-like pasta	5 minutes	2 minutes
Regular spaghetti	7 minutes	3 minutes
Fettuccine	8–9 minutes	3 minutes
Ziti, shells, fusilli	10 minutes	—
Lasagna	10 minutes	—
Ravioli, tortellini, and other filled pastas	—	4 minutes

pour on enough hot sauce to coat lightly, but not smother the pasta, then toss to combine. If serving on individual plates, you might want to put some sauce on the plate first, add pasta, then put more sauce on top.

Reheating

Place pasta in a heatproof bowl, add enough boiling water to cover pasta, let stand for 1 minute, and drain well.

PASTA

Fettuccine with Tomato, Sausage & Basil

This dish is best when made with fresh pasta and fresh basil.

Ingredients *(serves four)*

1 pound fresh fettuccine or ¾ pound dried

2 28-ounce cans Italian plum tomatoes, drained and coarsely chopped

½ cup fresh basil leaves, torn into pieces, or 2 tablespoons dried

1 tablespoon olive oil plus additional olive oil for tossing the pasta

½ pound sweet Italian sausage, cut into ½-inch pieces

2 cloves garlic, minced

Salt and pepper

Grated Parmesan, for serving

Equipment

Pasta pot

Large frying pan

Colander

1. Bring a large pot of water to a boil for the pasta. Add the pasta and cook until al dente. Drain in a colander and toss with some olive oil.

2. While the pasta water is coming to a boil and the pasta is cooking, heat the 1 tablespoon olive oil in a large frying pan on *medium-high* heat, about 1 minute.

Fresh Basil

When purchasing basil (or any other herb), look for leaves that are green all over. Yellowing leaves indicate that the herb is past its prime. Moist black spots indicate bruising.

Cleaning: Basil has a tendency to be gritty and needs to be rinsed thoroughly before using. To do so, pinch the leaves from the stalks and swish them in a bowl of cold water. Then remove the leaves from the water, lay them between sheets of paper towel, and gently pat them dry. Handle fresh basil as little as possible, because it bruises easily.

Twenty medium basil leaves will yield about ¼ cup, tightly packed.

Add the sausage and cook thoroughly, about 4 minutes. Pour out any excess fat. Add the garlic and cook for 1 minute longer.

3. Add the tomatoes and the fresh or dried basil, and cook until the sauce begins to bubble. Reduce the heat to *medium low* and cook, stirring often, until the sauce begins to thicken, about 5 minutes. Add salt and pepper to taste. Turn off the heat and let the sauce sit, covered, until the pasta is cooked.

4. Divide the pasta among 4 dinner plates and top with the sauce. Sprinkle with grated Parmesan before serving.

Seafood Linguine

The assortment of seafood makes this an especially tasty and enticing dish.

Ingredients *(serves four)*

12 ounces linguine

2 tablespoons olive oil

½ pound medium shrimp, peeled and deveined (see page 117)

½ pound bay scallops (see Notes)

½ pound bluefish, cut into 1-inch chunks (see Notes)

1 7-ounce can minced clams, drained

3 cups Basic Tomato Sauce (page 182) or your favorite store-bought sauce

1 6-ounce package frozen peas

Grated Parmesan, for serving

Equipment

Pasta pot

Large frying pan with cover

Colander

1. Bring a large pot of water to a boil for the pasta. When the water boils, add the linguine and cook until al dente, about 7 minutes, then drain well in a colander.

2. While the pasta water is coming to a boil and the pasta is cooking, place a large frying pan on *high* heat and let it get hot, about 45 seconds. Add the oil and all the shrimp, scallops, and bluefish. Sauté, stirring and turning often, until the shrimp turns pink, about 4 minutes.

3. Add the clams and tomato sauce, bring to a boil, then reduce the heat to *medium*. Add the peas, cover, and cook for another

Parmesan Cheese

The crème de la crème of Parmesan cheeses is Parmigiano-Reggiano, which is produced exclusively around Parma, Reggio Emilia, and Modena in Northern Italy. It is more expensive than other Parmesan cheese but is well worth the price. Look for pale yellow wedges that are slightly grainy in texture, mellow, rich and both salty and fruity in flavor. To know you're getting the real thing, check the rind: The words Parmigiano-Reggiano are etched around the entire circumference of the 60- to 70-pound wheels, so each wedge should include at least a few letters. To protect your investment, wrap it in aluminum foil and refrigerate for up to several months. Some stores sell their own freshly grated Parmesan, but the truth is that Parmesan loses its flavor very quickly once it is grated. It is always preferable to grate your own just before serving or at the table with a rotary cheese grater.

3 minutes, until the peas are cooked through. Let the sauce sit, covered, until the pasta is done.

4. Divide the pasta among 4 dinner plates, spoon on the sauce, and sprinkle with Parmesan.

Notes

■ If bluefish isn't available, use any fatty fish, such as swordfish, tuna, cod, or mackerel.

■ If bay scallops are unavailable, the larger sea scallops can be used instead. If very large, cut sea scallops in half.

Penne with Tuna, Tomatoes & Roasted Peppers

This is a hearty, rustic sauce that can be put together quickly.

Ingredients *(serves four)*

¾ pound penne

1 7-ounce can solid white tuna in oil

1 4-ounce jar roasted red peppers, drained and thinly sliced

1 6-ounce jar artichoke hearts, drained and quartered

2 tablespoons olive oil, plus additional oil for tossing the pasta

2 shallots, finely chopped

2 cloves garlic, minced

1 28-ounce can whole Italian plum tomatoes, drained

1 cup frozen peas

3 tablespoons fresh parsley, chopped

1 teaspoon salt

Freshly ground pepper

Equipment

Pasta pot

Large frying pan

Small bowl

Serving bowl

Colander

Wooden spoon

1. Bring a large pot of water to a boil for the pasta. When the water boils, add the penne and cook until al dente, about 7–9 minutes. Drain well in a colander and toss with olive oil.

2. While the pasta water is coming to a boil and the pasta is cooking, drain the tuna, transfer it to a small bowl, and coarsely flake with a fork. Add the roasted peppers and artichokes, mix together, and set aside.

3. Place a large frying pan on *medium* heat and let it get hot, about 45 seconds. Add the 2 tablespoons olive oil and the shallots and sauté, stirring frequently, until the shallots are soft, about 3 minutes. Add the garlic and sauté for 1 minute more.

4. Raise the heat to *high* and add the tomatoes, peas, and tuna mixture. Break up the tomatoes with a wooden spoon and cook the sauce until it begins to bubble.

5. Reduce the heat to *medium,* add the parsley, and season with salt and pepper. Continue cooking for 3 more minutes, stirring frequently, until the sauce thickens slightly. Remove the pan from the heat and keep it covered until the pasta is cooked.

6. Transfer the pasta to a serving bowl. Pour the sauce over the pasta, toss, and serve.

Spaghetti Carbonara

Spaghetti carbonara is actually not a traditional Italian dish. It was improvised using the American food supplies—bacon, eggs, and cheese—flown into Italy after World War II.

Ingredients *(serves four)*

12 ounces spaghetti

¼ pound pancetta (Italian bacon),
    slab bacon, or regular sliced bacon

¼ cup white wine (optional)

Yolks of 4 large eggs

⅔ cup grated Parmesan

Equipment

Pasta pot

Large frying pan

Medium bowl

Colander

Whisk

2 large mixing spoons

1. Bring a large pot of water to a boil for the pasta. When the water comes to a boil, cook the pasta until al dente, about 7 minutes, then drain well in a colander.

2. While the pasta water is coming to a boil and the pasta is cooking, cut the pancetta or bacon slices into ½-inch pieces.

3. Place a large frying pan on *medium* heat and let it get hot, about 45 seconds. Add the pancetta or bacon pieces and sauté until cooked through, about 5 minutes. If using wine, drain off the fat, add the wine to the meat, and heat 1 minute longer. If not using wine, turn off the heat, leaving the meat and fat in the pan.

4. Whisk the egg yolks well in a medium bowl. Then stir in half the Parmesan until well combined. Set aside.

5. When the spaghetti is ready, return the frying pan to *medium* heat for 30 seconds, then add the drained spaghetti to the pan. Using 2 large mixing spoons, combine the pasta with the bacon slices.

6. Remove the frying pan from the heat. Immediately pour the egg mixture over the spaghetti and stir quickly until all the strands are coated. (The heat of the pasta will cook the egg and thicken the sauce.)

7. Serve the pasta immediately, topped with the remaining Parmesan.

Empty Cupboard Pasta

The first time you prepare this dish it may be out of desperation, but after that the kids may start requesting it regularly.

Ingredients *(serves four)*

12 ounces spaghetti or macaroni

3 tablespoons butter, cut into small pieces

⅓ cup grated Parmesan

1 teaspoon dried basil, oregano, or parsley

Freshly ground black pepper

Equipment

Pasta pot

Colander

1. Bring a large pot of water to a boil. When the water comes to a boil, cook the pasta until al dente, about 7 minutes for spaghetti, 9 minutes for macaroni. Drain well in a colander and transfer to a serving bowl.

2. Immediately add the butter and Parmesan to the pasta; toss until well coated.

3. Sprinkle on the herbs and freshly ground black pepper. Serve immediately.

PASTA

Cold Tortellini Salad

Most pasta salads leave me cold, but this one, with its earthy flavors and colors, has a lot of punch. It requires a bit of chopping, but the time is well spent.

Ingredients *(serves six)*

1 pint cherry tomatoes, cut in half

3 scallions, coarsely chopped, cut in half

½ cup (4 ounces) sun-dried tomatoes packed in oil, drained and coarsely chopped

1 6-ounce jar artichoke hearts packed in oil, quartered

1 4-ounce jar roasted peppers, drained and coarsely chopped

1 whole clove garlic

½ cup chopped fresh basil, or 1 tablespoon dried

1 teaspoon dried oregano

¼ cup olive oil

1 pound fresh tortellini (see Tip)

¼ pound sliced prosciutto, cut into 2-inch pieces

½ pound mozzarella, coarsely grated

Salt and pepper

Equipment

Pasta pot

Medium bowl

Large bowl

Colander

1. Place the cherry tomatoes, scallions, sun-dried tomatoes, artichokes, roasted peppers, garlic, basil, and oregano in a medium bowl. Add the olive oil and mix gently to coat

Sun-Dried Tomatoes

In Southern Italy, sun-dried tomatoes are still made in the traditional way by salting the tomatoes and leaving them to dry on the roof. After they are dried, they are soaked briefly in water and then covered with olive oil, oregano, and garlic. Gourmet shops and better supermarkets sell them both in olive oil and dried. If using dried tomatoes instead of tomatoes in oil for this pasta salad, first soak them for 15 minutes in warm water, drain, and cover with olive oil. Next add 1 clove garlic and 1 tablespoon oregano, cover, and refrigerate for at least 2 hours. Remove from the refrigerator ½ hour before using. Sun-dried tomatoes are rather expensive, but a few go a long way. Once they are soaked in oil, sun-dried tomatoes will last up to 2 weeks in the refrigerator.

everything with oil. Refrigerate the mixture for 2 hours.

2. Bring a large pot of water to a boil for the pasta. When the water starts to boil, add the tortellini and cook for about 4 minutes, until cooked through. Drain the pasta in a colander, rinse under cold water, then drain again, shaking the colander well to remove all the water. Transfer the pasta to a large bowl.

3. Remove the garlic clove from the tomato mixture, then add the mixture to the pasta along with the prosciutto and mozzarella. Season with salt and pepper, mix well, and serve, or cover the salad tightly and refrigerate. This salad will keep for up to 48 hours. Remove it from the refrigerator ½ hour before serving.

Tip

If you can't find fresh tortellini, use dried fusilli or penne for this dish.

Cold Peanut Noodles

This cool noodle dish makes a perfect warm-weather lunch or dinner.

Ingredients *(serves four)*

6 ounces Chinese ramen noodles or
    8 ounces vermicelli

2 tablespoons vegetable oil

1 cucumber

½ cup smooth, "natural" peanut butter

¼ cup soy sauce

¼ cup white wine

2 tablespoons fresh lemon juice

1 tablespoon honey

1 small clove garlic

1-inch piece fresh ginger or 1 teaspoon
    ground ginger

Chopped scallion, for garnish

Equipment

Pasta pot
Medium bowl
Colander
Blender or food processor

1. Bring a large pot of water to a boil for the pasta. When the water starts to boil, add the pasta and cook the ramen noodles according to the package directions, or the vermicelli until al dente, about 5 minutes. Drain the noodles in a colander and rinse under cold water until cool. Shake the colander well to release as much water as possible, then add the vegetable oil to the noodles and toss gently.

2. While the water is coming to a boil and the pasta is cooking, peel the cucumber

Stir-Frying with a Wok

Stir-frying involves cooking at a very high temperature for a short time, stirring constantly so the ingredients don't burn. You can get good results with either a large, heavy frying pan or a Chinese wok. Do not be afraid to let the pan get very hot before adding the ingredients. Always have your vegetables, meat, and sauce lined up in small bowls ready to be added at the moment the recipe specifies. And don't forget to stir continuously —this is called a stir-fry for a reason.

and cut it in half lengthwise. Scrape out the seeds with the tip of a spoon and cut the cucumber into ½-inch slices. Put the slices in a medium bowl, cover, and refrigerate until ready to use.

3. Blend the peanut butter, soy sauce, white wine, lemon juice, honey, garlic, and ginger in a blender on *medium* speed or in a food processor, until completely smooth. Set the mixture aside.

4. Transfer the noodles to a serving platter. Pour on the peanut sauce and toss gently. Garnish with the cucumber slices and chopped scallion. Serve immediately.

Tip

"Natural" or unhydrogenated peanut butter is available in most supermarkets and all health food stores. It has the proper texture and flavor for this dish. For a more subtle flavor, substitute sesame butter (also known as tahini).

Asian Noodles with Chicken & Ham

This dish requires some serious stir-frying, a technique that is a study in contrasts. First there is the chopping, methodical and neat. Then you heat up the frying pan or wok and start cooking like mad, tossing in ingredients, adding sauces, all the while stirring rapidly. You'll be done with the stir-frying in about 5 minutes, and the results will be better than most dishes you get in a Chinese restaurant.

Ingredients *(serves four)*

¾ pound soba (buckwheat) noodles or thin spaghetti

1 tablespoon olive oil, for tossing the noodles

½ teaspoon curry powder

½ teaspoon Chinese five-spice powder

¼ cup soy sauce

¼ cup white wine or sherry

1 tablespoon honey

1 medium onion, thinly sliced

2 ribs celery, cut diagonally into ¼-inch slices

2 cloves garlic, minced

2 carrots, grated

1 cup frozen peas

2 boneless chicken breasts, cut into thin slices

4 slices cooked ham (about 4 ounces), cut into 2 x ½-inch strips

5 tablespoons corn oil

Equipment

Pasta pot
Colander
4 small bowls
Whisk
Large, heavy frying pan or wok
Large cooking spoon
Medium bowl

1. Bring a large pot of water to boil for the noodles. When the water comes to a boil, cook the noodles until soft, about 4 minutes. Drain in a colander, toss with 1 tablespoon olive oil, and set aside.

2. While the water is coming to a boil and the noodles are cooking, in a small bowl, combine the curry powder, five-spice powder, soy sauce, wine or sherry, and honey. Whisk together and set aside.

3. In another small bowl, combine the sliced onion and celery. In another bowl, combine the garlic, carrots, and peas. Place the sliced chicken and ham in separate bowls.

4. Heat 2 tablespoons of the corn oil in a large frying pan or wok on *high* heat until it just begins to smoke, about 90 seconds.

5. Add the onion and celery, and stir-fry for 2 minutes. Add the garlic, carrot, and peas, and cook 1 minute, continuing to stir constantly. Transfer the vegetables to a medium bowl. Wipe out the pan with paper towels and put it back on the heat.

6. Add the remaining 3 tablespoons oil to the pan and let it get hot, about 15 seconds. Add the chicken slices and stir-fry until opaque, about 2 minutes. Add the ham and cook for 1 minute more. Add the vegetables and noodles to the pan and gently toss them together. Add the sauce, toss again, and turn off the heat.

7. Transfer to a serving bowl and serve immediately.

Soups & Stews

In an old-fashioned country kitchen, you will find a large soup pot simmering on the stove's back burner, ready to receive any of the day's leftover scraps of meat or vegetables. By evening, this potful of stuff has become dinner. Traditional soups in the Béarnaise region of France turn out so thick by day's end that the ladle is known to stand straight up in the pot.

Making a meal in one pot clearly has its advantages: Preparation is relatively simple and there's less to clean up. Soups are also a great way to improvise with the leftovers you have in the fridge.

These dishes generally take an hour or more to cook, so they are not your best bet for a last-minute supper (though a freezer stocked with soup favorites can be your best friend in a pinch). Soups store very well and their flavor actually intensifies after a day in the refrigerator. When freezing soups or stews, use containers that hold enough for one meal so you can defrost exactly what you need.

The Basic Soups

Soups are best when made with homemade stock, so we've provided a couple of recipes. But finding the time to make your own isn't always easy. Fortunately, there are some good canned chicken and beef broths (like those made by College Inn) that can be used instead. Also, bouillon cubes and powders, which are evaporated seasoned meat extracts, can be used to replace stock or enhance the flavor of a soup. Health food stores sell vegetable bouillon cubes for a strictly vegetarian soup.

Once you get the hang of making soup, you'll want to start improvising. The soup pot can accommodate just about anything: almost any vegetable (raw or cooked), most cooked meat, pasta, sausage, and even pieces of cold cuts. If you start with a good stock, you'll find that even the scrappiest scraps can be turned into a hearty, nutritious, and very respectable soup.

The Standard Soup

These clear soups have a broth base to which vegetables and/or pieces of meat, chicken, or fish have been added. Chicken soup falls into this category as does minestrone. To make these soups, the broth is reduced slightly to concentrate its distinctive flavor and then vegetables and additional meat or chicken are added.

The Puréed Soup

Puréed soups are made by simmering stock and vegetables until the vegetables are just cooked, usually about 25 minutes. The vegetables and stock are then puréed until smooth and thickened in a blender or food processor. These are usually light soups, although the addition of potatoes can make them a bit thicker and heavier, and adding milk or cream can make them anything but light.

The Hearty Soup

Minestrone and fish chowder are prime examples of hearty soups, where lots of chopped vegetables and chunks or meat, chicken, or fish come together to produce a filling dish. Pasta, rice, and beans can also be added. These soups are made by first browning the vegetables and meat in the stockpot, then adding the stock and spices and simmering, usually for an hour or so. The soup can be served right from the pot.

A stew is a hearty soup that you can eat with a fork. For the most part, you prepare stew the same way you do soup, only you cut everything up into slightly larger pieces and add less broth. A stew can be a meal in itself or it can be served over rice or broad noodles. No matter how you serve it, you must have some thick slices of bread on the table to sop up what's left in the bottom of the bowl.

Minestrone

Minestrone can accommodate just about any kind of leftover vegetable or meat. Chop it up and throw it in.

Ingredients *(serves six)*

3 slices bacon, cut into 1-inch pieces

1 large onion, coarsely chopped

2 ribs celery, coarsely chopped

2 carrots, coarsely chopped

2 small zucchini, cut into ½-inch pieces

2 cloves garlic, mashed and finely chopped

3 tablespoons tomato paste

2 teaspoons dried basil

1 teaspoon dried oregano

½ teaspoon dried rosemary

1 28-ounce can whole tomatoes,
  with their liquid

8 cups canned beef stock or 4 bouillon
  cubes dissolved in 8 cups boiling water

3 russet or large red potatoes, cut into
  ½-inch cubes

1 cup small elbow macaroni

1 10-ounce can red kidney beans,
  with their liquid

1 cup frozen peas

3 teaspoons chopped fresh parsley or
  1 teaspoon dried

Salt and pepper

Grated Parmesan, for garnish

Equipment

Large stockpot

Medium saucepan

Wooden spoon

Colander

1. Place a large stockpot on *medium-high* heat and let it get hot, about 45 seconds. Add the bacon, onion, celery, carrots, and zucchini, and sauté until the vegetables are soft, about 6 minutes, stirring often. Add the garlic and sauté 1 minute more.

2. Stir in the tomato paste and 3 tablespoons water along with the basil, oregano, and rosemary.

3. Add the canned tomatoes with their liquid, breaking them up with a wooden spoon. Add the beef stock or bouillon and the potatoes. Bring the soup to a boil over *high* heat, then reduce the heat to *low* and simmer, partially covered, for 40 minutes.

4. While the soup is simmering, bring a medium saucepan of water to a boil for the pasta. Cook the macaroni until al dente according to package directions, then drain in a colander.

5. When the soup has simmered for 40 minutes, add the macaroni along with the beans and their liquid, the peas, and parsley. Season with salt and pepper. Simmer for 10 minutes more, until all of the ingredients are heated through. Serve hot in soup bowls and sprinkle with the grated Parmesan.

Note

The not-so-crucial ingredients in minestrone, such as the zucchini, celery, frozen peas, and carrots, can be replaced or combined with other vegetables. Don't be afraid to chop up and add what you have on hand, for example, broccoli, squash or sweet potato, a leek or two, a bit of fennel, baked potato, a piece of cabbage, or some leftover pasta. You can also throw in leftover meat or chicken.

Split Pea Soup

As a kid, my idea of the perfect winter lunch was a bowl of split pea soup and a tuna melt on an English muffin. Of course, I also had to have saltines to break into the soup. I often make this for my own kids and they agree that it's a pretty darn good lunch.

Ingredients *(serves six)*

1 pound split peas

1 ham bone with meat on it, ham hock, or a 1-inch-thick slice baked deli ham

1 medium onion, coarsely chopped

1 rib celery, cut into 1-inch pieces

2 cloves garlic, mashed and coarsely chopped

8 cups canned or homemade chicken stock or 4 bouillon cubes dissolved in 8 cups boiling water

3 carrots, cut into ½-inch slices

½ teaspoon ground cloves

Milk (optional)

Pepper

Saltines, croutons, or thick slices of crusty peasant bread, to serve

Equipment

Medium bowl

Colander

Large stockpot with cover

Food processor or blender (optional)

1. Put the peas in a medium bowl and cover with cold water. Swirl the peas around, pour them into a colander to drain, and return them to the bowl.

Pick through the peas and discard any that are discolored.

2. Put the peas in a large stockpot along with the ham, onion, celery, garlic, and chicken stock or dissolved bouillon. Bring to a boil, cover, and simmer over *low* heat for 1 hour, stirring occasionally. (When stirring, make sure you get right down to the bottom so the peas don't scorch.)

3. Add the carrots, cover and continue simmering and stirring occasionally for another hour.

4. Remove the ham bone from the soup and let it cool a bit; then cut the meat off and chop it into small pieces. If you're using a ham hock, break off any bits of meat you can find. If you're using a thick slice of ham, cut whatever is left into small pieces.

5. Return the bits of ham to the pot along with the ground cloves. Thin the soup, if necessary, with milk or water. Add pepper to taste. (Thanks to the ham you won't need salt.) Serve hot with saltines, croutons, or crusty bread.

Tips

■ Pea soup can be puréed after Step 3. Remove the ham bone, hock, or slice, and run batches of soup through a food processor or blender. Add the bits of ham to the soup after it is puréed. If you decide to purée the soup you can add the carrots with the other vegetables at the very beginning.

■ This soup can also be made without the ham. Just add some extra celery and the white parts of 2 leeks to enhance the flavor.

Dad's Own Chicken Noodle Soup

Years from now your daughter will sit down to a bowl of chicken soup that her new husband has made for her. She'll taste it, and as a tiny tear trickles down her cheek, she'll say "It's good, honey, but not as good as my Dad's."

Ingredients *(serves six)*

1 large leek
1 4–5 pound chicken plus 4 additional
    chicken legs
1 large onion
1 whole turnip
2 whole carrots
1 turnip, cut into ½-inch slices
2 carrots, cut into ½-inch slices

2 tablespoons honey (optional; adds
    interesting flavor)
1½ tablespoons salt
1 teaspoon fresh or dried dill
6 ounces string-shaped egg noodles
1 cup frozen peas
Chopped fresh parsley, for garnish

Equipment

2 large stockpots, or 1 large stockpot
    and 1 very large bowl
Large slotted spoon
Medium bowl
Colander
Cheesecloth
Large spoon

1. Trim the bottom of the leek at the roots and cut the leek in half lengthwise. Separate the layers and rinse them very well on both sides under cold water.

2. Put the leek in a large stockpot along with the whole chicken, chicken legs, onion, turnip, and carrots. Add at least 3 quarts water to cover the chicken and bring it all to a boil over *high* heat. Reduce the heat to *medium low* and simmer for 2 hours 15 minutes, skimming off any scummy foam that collects on the surface as it cooks.

3. Using a large slotted spoon, remove the chicken and chicken parts to a medium bowl and discard the vegetables. When the chicken has cooled, pick off the meat and chop it coarsely. Set it aside (see Tips).

4. Place a clean stockpot or very large bowl in the sink. Line a colander with a double layer of cheesecloth and set it over the stockpot or bowl in the sink. Slowly pour the soup through the cheesecloth so that all the solids are caught in the cheesecloth, being careful not to let it splatter. Discard the solids. If using a bowl, transfer the stock to the stockpot. Using a large spoon, skim and discard the fat floating on top of the stock.

5. Add the sliced turnip and carrots, the honey (if using), salt, and dill to the stock. Bring to a boil over *high* heat, then reduce to *low* and simmer for 30 minutes. Increase the heat to *medium* and add the noodles, frozen peas, and chicken meat (if using). Simmer until the noodles are cooked through, about 8 minutes. Add more salt if necessary. Serve hot, garnished with chopped parsley.

Tips

■ You may find you have more than enough chicken meat for the soup. What's left over makes great chicken salad. See the recipe on page 166.

■ Make the broth (Steps 1–4) the day before you plan to serve the soup. Let the broth cool and refrigerate right in the covered pot. Once the soup is completely cold, skim off the congealed fat.

New England Clam Chowder

Once they taste Dad's homemade chowder, the kids may be asking for it all the time. Fortunately, it's an easy soup to throw together. Serve the chowder with hunks of fresh whole wheat bread to soak up the important stuff that's left in the bottom of the bowl.

Ingredients *(serves six)*

3 slices bacon

1 large onion, coarsely chopped

4 russet or large red potatoes, peeled and dried

1 cup bottled clam juice

2 7-ounce cans minced clams

2 cups milk

2 cups half-and-half

1 tablespoon all-purpose flour

1 tablespoon butter, at room temperature

1 teaspoon salt

Pepper

Chopped fresh parsley, for garnish

Oyster crackers, for garnish

Equipment

Small frying pan

Large stockpot with cover

Small bowl

1. Place a small frying pan on *medium* heat and let it get hot, about 45 seconds. Add the bacon and cook, stirring occasionally, until crisp. Remove the bacon slices to paper towels and pat them dry. Break up the bacon into small pieces and set aside.

2. Pour 1 tablespoon of the bacon fat into a large stockpot. Put the pot on *medium-high* heat and let it get hot, about 45 seconds. Add the chopped onion and sauté, stirring often, until soft, about 6 minutes. Add the potatoes, bacon pieces, clam juice, and 1 cup water, and bring to a boil. Reduce the heat to *low* and simmer, partially covered, for 10 minutes.

3. Increase the heat to *medium high*. Add the clams in their juice, the milk, and half-and-half, and bring to a boil. Reduce the heat to *medium low* and let the soup simmer for 5 minutes.

4. In a small bowl, mix together the flour and butter until completely combined. Break off small pieces of the mixture and add them to the soup one at a time, stirring well to incorporate. Add the salt and pepper to taste. Let the soup come to a boil one last time, then remove it from the heat. Serve the soup hot, topped with a bit of chopped parsley and oyster crackers.

Variation

This recipe can easily be adapted for fish chowder. Simply cut 1 pound skinless and boneless fillets of cod, scrod, red snapper, or any firm fish into 1½-inch pieces. Add these to the pot along with the can of clams and simmer until the fish begins to flake, about 10 minutes. Add the milk and half-and-half and continue as for clam chowder. Alternatively, add 2 pounds of fish and eliminate the clams completely.

Potato & Escarole Soup

This is a thick, hearty soup that can be thrown together in minutes.

Ingredients *(serves six)*

4 russet or large red potatoes
1 large head escarole
1 tablespoon butter or margarine
1 onion, sliced
2 cloves garlic, minced
6 cups chicken stock or 3 bouillon cubes
   dissolved in 6 cups boiling water
Salt and pepper

Equipment

Large bowl
Large stockpot with cover
Colander
Ladle
Blender or food processor (see Tip if using
   the food processor)
Large saucepan

1. Peel the potatoes. Cut them into ½-inch slices and place them in a large bowl of cold water. Set aside.

2. Discard any brown leaves of escarole. Trim the stems and cut the leaves into 2-inch pieces. Thoroughly wash and dry the escarole.

3. Place a large stockpot on *medium-high* heat and let it get hot, about 45 seconds. Add the butter or margarine; when it stops sizzling, add the onion and sauté until soft, about 6 minutes. Add the garlic and sauté for 1 minute more.

4. Add the chicken stock or bouillon and bring to a boil on *high* heat. Drain the potatoes in a colander and add them to the pot. When the soup begins to boil, reduce the heat to *low*, cover, and simmer for 20 minutes, or until the potatoes are soft.

5. Add the escarole to the pot and stir. Cover and simmer for 8 minutes more. Remove from the heat.

6. Using a ladle, fill a blender halfway with soup and purée. Transfer the puréed soup to a large saucepan. Continue blending until all the soup is puréed.

7. Season the puréed soup with salt and pepper. Serve hot, or let it cool, refrigerate for several hours, and serve cold.

Tip

If you want to use a food processor instead of a blender to purée the soup, you will need to strain the soup and separate the solids from the liquid first. Set a colander over a large saucepan and pour the soup through the colander. Then transfer the solids to the bowl of the processor. Add 1 cup of the hot broth to the solids and process until the mixture is smooth.

Stir the puréed mixture back into the soup and stir until combined. If you try to purée the soup in the food processor with too much liquid, the vegetables will remain in little chunks and the liquid may leak.

Carrot & Orange Soup

Here's a simple gem of a recipe that my wife prepares when it's her turn to cook.

Ingredients *(serves six)*

2 tablespoons butter or margarine

1 large onion, coarsely chopped

½-inch piece ginger, peeled and finely chopped

8 carrots (about 1½ pounds), sliced into 1-inch pieces

4 cups chicken stock or 2 bouillon cubes dissolved in 4 cups boiling water

1 cup orange juice, preferably freshly squeezed

Salt and pepper

Chopped fresh mint or parsley

Equipment

Large stockpot with cover

Ladle

Blender or food processor (if using the food processor, see Tip at end of Potato and Escarole Soup, opposite page)

Large saucepan

Adjusting the Seasoning

People have different tastes when it comes to salt and pepper. Most of *Dad's Own* recipes call for a minimal amount of salt. You may find you and your family like more or less salt, so go ahead and adjust the seasoning accordingly. Always add salt or pepper in small amounts, because once a dish is overseasoned, there is little you can do to correct it.

1. Place a large stockpot on *medium-high* heat and let it get hot, about 45 seconds. Add the butter or margarine; when it stops sizzling, add the onion and sauté until soft, about 6 minutes. Add the ginger and sauté for 2 minutes more.

2. Add the carrots and the chicken stock or bouillon to the stockpot and bring to a boil over *high* heat. Reduce the heat to *low* and simmer, covered, until the carrots are tender, about 35 minutes.

3. Remove from the heat. Using a ladle, fill the blender halfway with the soup and purée. Transfer the puréed soup to a large saucepan and continue blending until all the soup is puréed.

4. Return the large saucepan with the soup to *medium high*. Add the orange juice and bring to a boil one more time, then remove from the heat and season with salt and pepper. Serve the soup hot, garnished with chopped mint or parsley. Be sure to let it cool before refrigerating or freezing.

Serving Suggestion

This soup can also be served chilled as part of a refreshing summer meal.

SOUPS & STEWS

Old-Fashioned Beef Stew

Adapted from a recipe by James Beard, the late dean of American cooking, this recipe scores high on the "hearty" scale. Don't worry about making it look pretty. Just get everything into the pot and let it cook. You can serve this over wide noodles or with a thick slice of brown bread.

Ingredients *(serves six)*

2 cups unbleached all-purpose flour

3 pounds beef brisket or chuck, cut into 2-inch cubes (your butcher will cut it for you)

4 tablespoons oil

¼ cup red wine

1 whole medium onion

1 whole carrot

1 turnip

1 teaspoon dried thyme

1 bay leaf

2 cups canned or homemade beef stock or 2 bouillon cubes dissolved in 2 cups boiling water

3 carrots, cut into 1-inch rounds

3 russet or large red potatoes, cut into eighths

2 russet or large red potatoes, peeled and grated

1 large onion, coarsely chopped

3 ribs celery, cut into 1-inch slices

3 cloves garlic, minced

Salt and pepper

½ pound green beans, trimmed and cut in half

10-ounce package frozen peas

Equipment

Large bowl

Large platter or baking sheet

Large frying pan

Large stockpot with cover

1. Measure the flour into a large bowl. Add the cubed meat and toss it in the flour with your hands. Shake off the excess flour and place the meat on a large platter or baking sheet.

2. Place a large frying pan on *high* heat and let it get very hot, about 1 minute. Add 2 tablespoons of the oil and as many pieces of the meat as will fit in a single layer. Brown the meat, turning so the pieces cook on all sides, about 6 minutes.

3. Transfer the browned meat to a large stockpot and finish cooking the rest of beef in the remaining 2 tablespoons oil. Deglaze the frying pan with the red wine and add the liquid and bits of meat to the stockpot along with the whole onion and carrot, turnip, thyme, bay leaf, and beef stock or bouillon. Bring to a boil on *high* heat, then reduce the heat to *low* and simmer, covered, for 1½ hours.

4. Add the sliced carrot, all the potatoes, chopped onion, celery, garlic, and season with salt and pepper. Simmer, covered, until the meat is very tender, about 50 minutes more. Stir the soup occasionally.

5. Adjust the seasoning and add the green beans and frozen peas. Cook for 10 minutes more. Serve hot or let the stew cool a bit before refrigerating or freezing.

Tips

▪ The flavor of the stew is enhanced if it's refrigerated overnight. Reheat the stew in a stockpot over *low* heat, adding a bit more water or beef stock if needed.

▪ An easy way to flour the meat is to use a large plastic container with a tight-fitting lid. Put the flour into the container, add the meat, close the container and shake vigorously, keeping a tight hold on the lid. Lift the meat out with a slotted spoon and shake off the excess flour.

Broccoli & Apple Soup

The subtle sweetness of apples offsets the slight bitterness of the broccoli and gives this soup a refreshing flavor.

Ingredients *(serves six)*

1 large head broccoli

2 large McIntosh or Golden Delicious apples

1 tablespoon butter or margarine

1 medium onion, sliced

6 cups chicken stock or 6 bouillon cubes dissolved in 6 cups boiling water

Salt and pepper

Plain yogurt or sour cream, for garnish

Equipment

Large stockpot with cover

Ladle

Blender or food processor (if using the food processor, see Tip at end of Potato and Escarole Soup, page 202)

Large saucepan

1. Trim and discard about 1 inch from the bottom of the broccoli stalks. Cut the broccoli just below the florets. Set the florets aside and cut the stalks into 1-inch pieces.

2. Peel the apples and cut them into quarters. Trim the core from each quarter and cut into thirds.

3. Place a large stockpot on *medium-high* heat and let it get hot, about 45 seconds. Add the butter or margarine and when it stops sizzling, add the onion and apple slices. Sauté until the onions are soft, about 6 minutes.

4. Add the chicken stock or bouillon and the broccoli stalks. Bring the soup to a boil on *high* heat. Reduce the heat to *low*, cover, and simmer for 20 minutes.

5. Add the broccoli florets to the pot and simmer for 5 minutes more, until the broccoli is heated through. Remove from the heat.

6. Using a ladle, fill the blender halfway with soup and purée. Transfer the puréed soup to a large saucepan and continue blending until all the soup is puréed.

7. Season the puréed soup with salt and pepper and serve hot, garnished with a small dollop of plain yogurt or sour cream, if desired.

Tips

▪ To make handling the soup easier, let it cool a bit before you begin to purée it.

▪ When blending the soup, start on a slow speed and work up to the purée speed in 2 or 3 steps.

Homemade stock: for the truly committed

Beef Stock

Making beef stock is a long process, though once the stock is on the stove it doesn't require much attention. The bones and vegetables need to roast in the oven for an hour, and then simmer for 4–5 hours more. It winds up being a whole day affair, so leave it for a weekend when you're planning to stick around the house. A large pot will yield 4 quarts of stock, allowing you to freeze enough to make a few batches of soup. Roasting the bones and vegetables in a hot oven before simmering helps to intensify their flavor and enhance the color of the stock.

Ingredients

(makes 4 quarts)

  *2 large onions, unpeeled
    and cut into quarters*
  4 cloves garlic
  2 ribs celery
  *2 carrots, unpeeled and
    cut in half lengthwise*
  3 pounds beef bones
  3 pounds veal bones
  1 pound oxtail
  1 bay leaf
  10 peppercorns

Equipment

  Large roasting pan
  *2 large stockpots with
    covers, or 1 large
    stockpot and 1 very
    large bowl*
  Colander
  Cheesecloth

1. Preheat the oven to 500°F.
2. Arrange the onions, garlic, celery, and carrots in a large roasting pan, then layer the bones and oxtail on top of them. Roast in the oven for 1 hour.
3. Transfer the bones and vegetables to a large stockpot. Add 1 quart cold water to the roasting pan and use a large spoon to scrape up any bits of meat or vegetable that have stuck to the bottom. Transfer this to the stockpot along with 5 quarts cold water.
4. Add the bay leaf and peppercorns and bring the liquid to a boil over *high* heat. Once the liquid is boiling, reduce the heat to *low,* cover the pot, and simmer for 5 hours. Remove the pot from the heat and let it cool for $1/2$ hour.
5. Line a colander with cheesecloth and place the colander over another large stockpot or a very large bowl. Very carefully pour the stock through the lined colander so that all of the solids are caught in the cheesecloth. Discard the solids.
6. Let the stock sit for at least 20 minutes to allow the fat to rise to the top. Then use a large serving spoon to degrease the stock. The stock is now ready for use.
7. If you are freezing the stock, let it cool completely before transferring it to well-sealed pint or quart containers.

Chicken Stock

Having a few pints of chicken stock in the freezer can make it a cinch to throw together a tasty soup or to enhance the flavor of a sauce or stew.

Ingredients

makes 3 quarts)

> 1 2–3 pound whole
>   chicken
> 1 pound chicken legs
> 5 peppercorns
> Any or all of the
>   following:
>   1 large onion, 1 carrot,
>   1 rib celery, 1 leek,
>   5 sprigs parsley,
>   4 unpeeled cloves garlic

Equipment

> 2 large stockpots, or
>   1 large stockpot and
>   1 very large bowl
> Colander
> Cheesecloth
> Large bowl

1. Rinse the chicken and the chicken legs. Place them in a large stockpot with enough water to cover them by at least 2 inches. Bring the water to a boil over *high* heat, then skim any scum that has risen to the surface.
2. Add the peppercorns and any or all of the vegetables and herbs to the stock. Return to a boil over *high* heat, then reduce the heat to *medium low* and simmer, uncovered, for 2 hours, skimming occasionally.
3. Remove the chicken to a bowl. (The meat can be removed from the bones and frozen for another use.) Line a colander with cheesecloth and place the colander over another large stockpot or very large bowl. Pour the stock through the lined colander so that all of the solids are caught in the cheesecloth, being careful not to let the stock splatter. Discard the solids. If using a bowl, transfer the stock back into the stockpot.
4. Return the stock to the stovetop and bring to a boil over *high* heat. When it comes to a boil, reduce the heat to *medium low* and simmer, uncovered, for another hour. The stock is now ready for use. When it cools, skim any fat from the surface.
5. If you are freezing the stock, let it cool before transferring to well-sealed pint or quart containers.

Tip

Any bones, skin, or bits of meat you get from boning or trimming chicken for other recipes can be used to enhance the flavor of your stock. Simply freeze the

Degreasing

Degreasing is the process of removing fat from stock or gravy. A large mixing spoon works best for stocks; a soup spoon is best for gravies. There are also special "gravy degreasers" that work well for smaller amounts of liquid. Once a stock or gravy has settled, the fat rises to the surface, forming an even layer across the top or beading up into puddles. The areas of fat glisten slightly. To remove the fat, lower your spoon very slowly into the surface of the liquid, so the edge is dipped just under the fat. This allows the fat to flow into the spoon. Dispose of the fat and repeat the process until all of the fat is gone. Don't worry if some of the broth or gravy mixes into the fat—it can't be helped. Letting the stock cool in the refrigerator will cause the fat to congeal on the surface, making it easy to scrape off. If you have the time, this is the most efficient way to degrease.

scraps in a plastic bag, then when you are making a stock, add them to the pot along with the rest of the chicken and vegetables.

Mexican Chicken Stew

This dish is great whenever you have a hankering for chili but know you should fix something a little lighter. Serve it over brown rice with corn bread for a healthful and tasty dinner.

Ingredients *(serves four)*

1 cup cornmeal

1¼ pounds boneless chicken thighs,
    cut into 2-inch pieces

2 tablespoons corn oil

¼ pound chorizo or hot Italian sausage,
    cut into ½-inch slices

1 green bell pepper, seeded and sliced into
    ½-inch strips

1 red bell pepper, seeded and sliced into
    ½-inch strips

1 large onion, thinly sliced

3 cloves garlic, minced

¼ cup red wine

1 cup canned or homemade chicken stock
    or 1 bouillon cube dissolved in 1 cup
    boiling water

1 28-ounce can whole tomatoes, drained
    and coarsely chopped

1 package chili seasoning mix

2 tablespoons chopped fresh cilantro or
    1 teaspoon dried

Cooked brown rice, for serving

Equipment

2 medium bowls
Large platter or baking sheet
Large frying pan with cover

1. Measure the cornmeal into a medium bowl. Add the chicken pieces and toss them in the cornmeal with your hands. Shake off the excess cornmeal and place the chicken pieces on a large platter or baking sheet.

2. Place a frying pan on *high* heat and let it get very hot, about 1 minute. Add 1 tablespoon of the oil, the sausage, bell peppers, and onion, and sauté for 1 minute more. Transfer the vegetables and sausage to a medium bowl.

3. Add the remaining 1 tablespoon oil to the frying pan and let it get hot, about 30 seconds. Add the chicken pieces and brown, turning so they cook on all sides, about 6 minutes.

4. Return the sausage and pepper mixture to the frying pan. Add the wine and cook until the liquid is reduced by half. Add the chicken stock or bouillon, tomatoes, chili seasoning, and cilantro, and bring to a boil. Reduce the heat to *low*, cover, and simmer for 45 minutes. Serve hot over brown rice.

Variation

If your family's taste will allow it, the flavor of this stew can be enhanced by adding 2 dried ancho peppers. Ancho peppers are mild with a somewhat smoky flavor and are available in many specialty food shops or through one of the mail-order catalogs listed on pages 23–24. To use the peppers, place them in a small bowl and cover with boiling water. Weigh the peppers down with a small bowl or cup and let them soak for 2 hours. When they are soft, cut them open and rinse away the seeds. Chop the ancho peppers coarsely and sauté them with the fresh bell peppers in Step 2. While the ancho peppers are not very hot to the taste, you may want to wear rubber gloves when working with them. And wash your hands well after working with them. The insides of many peppers, and especially the seeds, can sting the skin.

Mediterra-nean Fish & Seafood Stew

This stew is a variation on the traditional bouillabaisse. Though considered a delicacy in fancy American restaurants, in Southern France, where the dish originated, bouillabaisse is standard fare and is often made with whatever wound up in the fisherman's net that morning. Black or French bread, cheese, and a garden salad will turn this into a wonderfully satisfying meal.

Ingredients *(serves six)*

   2 leeks, white part only
   2 tablespoons olive oil
   1 large onion, finely chopped
   2 cloves garlic, minced
   ¼ cup white wine
   1 28-ounce can crushed tomatoes

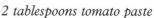

About Cleaning Leeks

For this recipe, cut off and discard (or reserve for another recipe) the green part of the leeks. Trim the roots from the bottoms and cut the white parts in half lengthwise. Separate the layers and rinse them well on both sides under cold water. Grit tends to hide between the layers of the leeks, so they really must be cleaned attentively. Shake the leeks over the sink to release excess water

   2 tablespoons tomato paste
   2 cups bottled clam juice
   1 cup canned or homemade chicken stock
     or 1 bouillon cube dissolved in 1 cup
     boiling water
   ¼ cup chopped fresh parsley
   1 bay leaf
   1 teaspoon dried thyme
   1 teaspoon salt
   2 pounds skinless, boneless firm white fish
     fillets, such as bass, snapper, scrod, cod,
     or haddock, cut into 1½-inch pieces
   ¾ pound shrimp, shelled and deveined
   ¾ pound scallops
   1 7-ounce can whole or minced clams,
     with juice

Equipment

   Large stockpot with cover

SOUPS & STEWS

1. Clean and thinly slice the leeks crosswise (see box on preceding page).

2. Place a large stockpot on *medium* heat and let it get hot, about 45 seconds. Add the olive oil, onion, and leeks, and sauté until soft, about 6 minutes. Add the garlic and sauté for 1 minute more.

3. Increase the heat to *high*. Add the white wine and cook until the liquid is reduced by half. Add the crushed tomatoes and tomato paste and bring to a boil. Add 2 cups water, the clam juice, chicken broth or bouillon, parsley, bay leaf, thyme, and salt, and bring to a boil. Reduce the heat to *low* and simmer, partially covered, for 15 minutes.

4. Increase the heat to *medium*. Add the fish and simmer for 8 minutes. Add the shrimp, scallops, and clams, and simmer for 8 minutes more, until all the seafood is cooked through. Serve hot.

Time-Saver

The tomato broth (Steps 1–3) can be prepared a day ahead. Let it cool before refrigerating in a tightly sealed container. Slowly bring the broth to a boil on *medium low* heat before continuing with Step 4.

Desserts

Let's face it. For most kids (and plenty of grown-ups), dinner is just something to climb over to get to dessert. And to the dismay of child psychologists, desperate parents still use dessert as a bargaining tool: "No dessert unless you finish your vegetables!"

The recipes in this chapter range from brownies and chocolate pudding (sure to inspire your children to finish their broccoli), to American classics like peach cobbler and Key lime pie. By the end of this chapter, Dad's skills will have developed enough for him to attempt a sophisticated tiramisù.

Dad's Own Oatmeal-Raisin Cookies

Most oatmeal-raisin cookies pale next to these extra-special ones made with walnuts and optional butterscotch chips.

Ingredients *(makes two dozen cookies)*

Margarine or cooking spray, for greasing the baking sheets

½ cup (1 stick) butter, at room temperature

6 tablespoons granulated sugar

6 tablespoons light brown sugar

1 large egg, well beaten

¾ cup unbleached all-purpose flour

½ teaspoon baking soda

½ teaspoon salt

3 tablespoons maple syrup

1 cup rolled oats

1 cup raisins or butterscotch chips, or a combination of the two

½ cup chopped walnuts

1 teaspoon vanilla extract

Equipment

2 baking sheets

2 medium bowls

Whisk or hand-held electric mixer

Wire rack

1. Preheat the oven to 375°F. Lightly grease 2 baking sheets with margarine or nonstick cooking spray.

2. In a medium bowl, use the whisk or mixer to cream together the butter and sugars until fluffy. Add the beaten egg and incorporate well.

3. In another medium bowl, whisk together the flour, baking soda, and salt.

4. Add the flour mixture to the butter mixture and stir until well combined. Stir in the maple syrup, oats, raisins and/or butterscotch chips, and walnuts. Stir in the vanilla.

5. One teaspoon at a time, drop the dough onto prepared baking sheets, leaving 1 inch between each cookie. Bake for 8–10 minutes, until the cookies are brown. They should be soft to the bite, so do not overbake.

6. Cool the cookies for 10 minutes, then, using a spatula, transfer the cookies to the wire rack and cool completely.

Chipwiches

Place a dollop of vanilla ice cream between 2 completely cooled cookies. Press together, wrap tightly with plastic wrap, and freeze. You'll be a hero doling out these treats in the summer.

Chocolate Pudding

This is major league chocolate pudding and takes only a few more minutes to prepare than the packaged kind.

Ingredients *(serves four)*

½ cup sugar

2 tablespoons cornstarch

¼ teaspoon salt

2 cups whole milk

*4 ounces bittersweet chocolate pieces
or ⅔ cup chocolate chips*
1½ teaspoons vanilla extract

Equipment

2 medium saucepans
Whisk

1. Combine the sugar, cornstarch, and salt in a medium saucepan.

2. Measure the milk into a second saucepan and scald over *medium* heat (see box below).

3. Remove the milk from the heat and pour it slowly into the dry ingredients, stirring the mixture gently with the whisk so as not to make too many bubbles. Whisk in the chocolate pieces and vanilla.

4. Return the saucepan to *medium-low* heat and bring to a gentle boil, whisking continuously until the pudding thickens. This will take about 90 seconds once the mixture begins simmering.

5. Pour the pudding into a serving bowl or 4 dessert cups. Cool at room temperature, then refrigerate until ready to serve.

Tip

If you don't like skin on the top of your pudding, lay a piece of plastic wrap directly on the pudding as it is cooling.

About Scalding Milk

Measure the milk into a saucepan and bring it to a boil over *medium* heat, stirring occasionally to keep the milk from burning around the edge of the pan. As soon as the surface of the milk begins bubbling, remove the pan from the heat. If the milk boils, it will form a thick scum on top. Remove before using.

Variation

To make chocolate pudding pie, pour the hot pudding mixture into a graham cracker crust. Cool as directed for chocolate pudding. If desired, before serving, cover the pudding or the pie with whipped cream and chocolate sprinkles.

Quick & Decadent Chocolate-Peanut Butter-Granola-Coconut Bars

Every once in a while we all deserve the chance to unashamedly indulge in something gooey, chocolatey, and decadent. These bars are just for that occasion and, fortunately (or unfortunately—you may be tempted to indulge more often than your waistline can withstand), they are incredibly simple to make.

Ingredients *(makes two dozen bars)*

½ cup (1 stick) unsalted butter or margarine
12 4¾ x 2½-inch graham crackers, coarsely crumbled, or 2 cups graham cracker crumbs
1 14-ounce can sweetened condensed milk

½ cup peanut butter

¾ cup granola

½ cup raisins

2 cups (12 ounces) semisweet chocolate chips

1½ cups sweetened flaked coconut

Equipment

9 x 13-inch baking pan

Medium bowl

Metal spatula

1. Preheat the oven to 350°F.

2. Place the butter in a 13 x 9-inch baking pan and place the pan in the oven until the butter melts.

3. Spread the crumbled graham crackers in the baking pan with the melted butter.

4. In a medium bowl, combine the sweetened condensed milk and the peanut butter. Drizzle the peanut butter mixture evenly over the graham cracker crumbs, then sprinkle on the granola, raisins, and chocolate chips. Cover with the coconut and, using the palms of your hands, press down firmly on the mixture.

5. Bake for 25–30 minutes, until light golden brown. Cool completely, then cut into 24 bars and remove from the pan with a metal spatula. Store in the refrigerator in a well-sealed container.

Hermits

This old-fashioned favorite never ceases to please young and old alike.

Ingredients *(makes eighteen hermits)*

½ cup (1 stick) margarine, at room temperature

¾ cup granulated sugar

½ cup light brown sugar

1 large egg

¼ cup molasses

Scant 6 tablespoons water

3 cups unbleached all-purpose flour

1½ teaspoons baking soda

1 teaspoon cinnamon

½ teaspoon cloves

1 teaspoon ginger

½ teaspoon salt

1½ cups raisins

Margarine or cooking spray, for greasing the baking sheets

Equipment

2 baking sheets

2 medium bowls

Whisk or hand-held electric mixer

Wire rack

1. In a medium bowl, use the whisk or mixer to cream together the margarine and sugar until fluffy. Blend in the egg, molasses, and water.

2. In another medium bowl, combine the flour, baking soda, cinnamon, cloves, ginger, and salt. Add to the butter mixture and stir or combine. Stir in the raisins.

3. Chill the dough, covered in plastic, for 2 hours or overnight.

4. Divide the dough into 4 pieces and roll each into a sausage shape.

5. Preheat the oven to 350°F. Grease 2 baking sheets with margarine or cooking spray.

6. Place 2 "sausages" lengthwise on each baking sheet. Bake for 15 minutes. They will come out in 2 flat sheets. Cut into pieces while still warm and remove to the wire rack to cool.

Note

Hermits should be moist and chewy, so don't overcook.

Dave's Key Lime Pie

My brother-in-law makes a dozen of these every morning in his restaurant.

Ingredients *(makes one pie)*

> *Yolks from 4 extra-large eggs*
> *1 14-ounce can sweetened condensed milk*
> *¾ cup Key lime juice (about 6 Key limes; see Note)*
> *1 store-bought graham cracker crust*
> *1 cup whipping cream*
> *¾ cup sugar*

Equipment

> *2 medium bowls*
> *Hand-held electric mixer*

1. Preheat the oven to 325°F.

2. Combine the egg yolks and the condensed milk in a medium bowl. Using a hand-held electric mixer, beat on medium speed until light and fluffy, about 5 minutes.

3. With the beaters on, drizzle in the lime juice and continue beating for 2 minutes more. Quickly pour the filling into the graham cracker crust.

4. Bake on the center rack for 22 minutes or until firm. Do not open the oven door while the pie is baking. If the pie is still a bit loose in the center, bake for 3–5 minutes more.

5. While the pie is baking, thoroughly wash and dry the beaters, then, using a hand-held mixer set at a medium speed, beat the cream in a medium bowl until light and frothy.

6. Add the sugar to the cream 2 tablespoons at a time and beat until the sugar is incorporated and the mixture is stiff, about 5 minutes. Refrigerate until ready to use.

7. When the pie is finished baking, cool for at least 1 hour. Then, using a rubber spatula, very gently spread the whipped cream over the top of the pie.

8. Refrigerate the pie until ready to serve.

Note

If Key limes aren't available, any fresh limes will do. Or use bottled Key lime juice, which is sold in most supermarkets. Check in the produce section or in the frozen foods aisle. The bottle will tell you how much to substitute for fresh juice.

Dad's Own Apple Pie

Baking apple pies is an American pastime and a sure way to earn accolades from your kids. Thanks to ready-made frozen crusts—look for them in the frozen food aisle at the supermarket—making apple pie is a speedy affair. Should you choose to make your own crust, a recipe follows.

Among the best apples for baking are the mild Rome Beauty, the mildly tart McIntosh, and the moderately tart Pippin and Granny Smith apples. Don't hesitate to combine more than one kind in a pie or to experiment with other varieties, but note that the popular Red Delicious apple completely loses its shape when baked. Save it for eating out of hand.

Ingredients
(makes one double-crusted pie)

4 pounds baking apples
  (see above for suggestions)
⅓ cup sugar
2 tablespoons unbleached all-purpose flour
2 tablespoons fresh lemon juice
½ teaspoon cinnamon
¼ teaspoon ground nutmeg (optional)
2 homemade or store-bought pie crusts

Equipment
Large bowl
Wire rack
Rubber spatula (optional)

1. Preheat the oven to 425°F. Position a rack in the lower third of the oven.

2. Peel the apples with a paring knife or vegetable peeler. Cut the apples into quarters, trim off the core, and slice each quarter into thirds lengthwise.

3. Put the apples in a large bowl. Sprinkle on the sugar, flour, lemon juice, cinnamon, and nutmeg, if using. Toss with your hands or a rubber spatula until all the slices are coated with the mixture.

4. Fill the bottom pie crust with the apple mixture, heaping the apples about an inch above the edge of the pie crust.

5. Cover with the top crust and crimp the top and bottom crusts together. Make 3 1-inch slits in the center of the top crust as steam vents.

6. Place the pie in the oven and bake for 10 minutes. Lower the heat to 350°F and bake for 40 minutes longer, until the top crust is golden brown.

7. Let the pie cool for 30 minutes before slicing.

Tips
■ Use unpeeled apples to make this a more rustic pie.
■ Serve with vanilla ice cream or a small wedge of sharp cheddar cheese.

Dad's Own Pie Crust

The trick to making a perfect crust is understanding the process and then moving fast. You may stumble through your first attempt, but after that you'll find it's, well, as easy as pie.

Ingredients *(makes one double crust)*
1½ cups unbleached all-purpose flour
2 tablespoons sugar
½ teaspoon salt
7 tablespoons cold butter
*¼ cup vegetable shortening or
    3 more tablespoons butter*
¼ cup ice water

Equipment
Large bowl
Dinner fork
Rolling pin
9-inch pie plate

1. Measure the flour, sugar, and salt into a large bowl.
2. Cut the butter in half lengthwise, then crosswise into thin slices. Add the butter and shortening to the flour. Working quickly, using just your fingertips, break up the butter and shortening into tiny pieces, about the size of dried split peas. These bits of butter are what make the dough flaky.
3. Add the ice water in a steady stream, stirring with a fork until the water is incorporated into the flour.

4. When all the flour is moist, use your fingertips to form the dough into a ball. Do not handle any more than is necessary. If the dough seems dry or flaky, add more cold water, a tablespoon at a time.
5. Place an 18-inch length of wax paper on your work table. Cut the ball of dough in half and place one half in the center of the wax paper. Cover with another sheet of wax paper.
6. Tap the dough with a rolling pin so it begins to flatten out. Working firmly and quickly with the rolling pin, roll the dough outward from the center in all directions. Continue to roll out the dough until you have a circle that is about 4 inches larger than your pie pan. This will be the bottom crust.
7. Leave the dough between the pieces of wax paper and transfer it to a baking sheet for support. Store in the refrigerator until you're ready to use, up to 12 hours. You must keep the dough cold so the bits of butter don't get mushy.
8. Repeat the rolling process with the second half of the dough, rolling it out into a circle only 1 inch larger than the pie plate. This will be the top crust. Refrigerate until ready to use.
9. When ready to assemble your pie, remove the dough for the pie bottom from the refrigerator. Peel away the top piece of wax paper, carefully flip the crust over into the pie plate, and remove the other piece of wax paper. Gently push the crust into the bottom and around the sides of the pie pan. Trim the crust so it hangs 1 inch over the edge of the pie plate.

10. After the pie is filled, remove the top crust from the refrigerator, and peel away the top piece of wax paper. Carefully flip the crust over the filling and remove the other piece. Crimp the top and bottom crusts together and make 3 1-inch slits in the center of the top crust or as directed in the specific pie recipe.

Oatmeal Chocolate Chip Cookies

These are quite simply the best chocolate chip cookies you can find.

Ingredients *(makes four dozen cookies)*

*Margarine or cooking spray, for greasing
    the baking sheets*
*1 cup (2 sticks) butter or margarine,
    at room temperature*
¾ cup granulated sugar
¾ cup dark brown sugar
2 extra-large eggs
1 teaspoon vanilla extract
1½ cups unbleached all-purpose flour
1 teaspoon baking soda
½ teaspoon salt
2½ cups old-fashioned rolled oats
2 cups (12 ounces) chocolate chips

Equipment

2 11 x 17-inch baking sheets
Large bowl
Wooden spoon
Medium bowl
Spatula
Wire rack

1. Preheat the oven to 375°F. Lightly grease 2 11 x 17-inch baking sheets with margarine or cooking spray.

2. In a large bowl, using a wooden spoon, cream together the butter and sugars until light and fluffy. Stir in the eggs, 1 at a time, until completely incorporated. Stir in the vanilla and set the mixture aside.

3. In a medium bowl, stir together the flour, baking soda, and salt.

4. Stir the flour mixture into the butter mixture and mix until completely incorporated. Stir in the oats. (The batter should be stiff but not sticky.) Add the chocolate chips.

5. Using a tablespoon, drop 2-inch rounds of dough onto a cookie sheet, leaving about 2 inches between each cookie.

6. Bake on the center rack of your oven for 10–12 minutes, until the cookies are light brown on top.

Tip

If you like your cookies chewy, let them cool for a minute on the baking sheet, then remove them with a spatula to a wire rack. If you like crunchy cookies, set the baking sheet on the wire rack and let the cookies cool (and harden). While the first sheet of cookies is baking, prepare the second sheet.

Super-Fast Saucepan Brownies

When you want fudgy brownies in a hurry, these will most certainly do.

Ingredients *(makes sixteen brownies)*

Margarine or cooking spray, for greasing the baking dish
2 extra-large eggs
⅔ cup unbleached all-purpose flour
¼ teaspoon baking soda
¼ teaspoon salt
½ cup sugar
2 tablespoons (¼ stick) butter or margarine
2 tablespoons water
2 cups (12 ounces) chocolate chips
1 teaspoon vanilla extract
½ cup chopped walnuts (optional)

Equipment

9 x 9-inch baking dish
Small bowl
Medium bowl
Medium saucepan
Wooden spoon
Rubber spatula
Wire rack

1. Preheat the oven to 350°F. Line a 9-inch square baking dish with aluminum foil so that the foil extends about 2 inches beyond all 4 sides of the pan, then lightly grease the foil with margarine or cooking spray.

2. Beat the eggs in a small bowl until thoroughly mixed and set aside. Stir together the flour, baking soda, and salt in a medium bowl and set aside.

3. Combine the sugar, butter, and water in a medium saucepan and bring to a boil over *low* heat, stirring constantly. Remove it from the heat and add 1 cup of the chocolate chips. Stir until the chocolate is melted, then stir in the beaten eggs and the vanilla.

4. Add the flour mixture to the chocolate mixture and mix well with a wooden spoon. Stir in the remaining chocolate chips and the walnuts (if using).

Everything Fudge Brownie Sundae

Place a generous brownie square in a dessert plate. Top with an ample scoop of vanilla ice cream. Spoon some chocolate syrup or hot fudge over the ice cream. Finish it off with a dollop of whipped cream and a cherry.

5. Scrape the batter into the baking dish with a rubber spatula and spread it evenly in the pan.

6. Bake on the center rack of your oven for 20–25 minutes, until a toothpick inserted in the center comes out with only a few moist crumbs clinging to it.

7. Transfer the pan to a wire rack and cool completely. Using 2 opposite ends of the foil as handles, life the brownies out of the pan and invert onto a cutting board. Peel away the foil and cut into 16 squares.

Peach-Blueberry Brown Betty

This dessert is a takeoff on the traditional American dessert, apple brown betty. It is simple and delicious, especially when served with vanilla ice cream. It's a foolproof recipe, even for the most inexperienced cook. This dessert can be prepared a day ahead of time and then reheated in the microwave or in a 300°F oven.

Ingredients *(serves four)*

Margarine or cooking spray, for greasing the casserole

4 cups sliced fresh peaches

1 pint fresh or frozen blueberries

½ cup granulated sugar

1¼ cups unbleached all-purpose flour

½ cup dark brown sugar

½ cup (1 stick) butter or margarine, cut into ½-inch slices

Equipment

9 x 14-inch casserole

Large bowl

Medium bowl

1. Preheat the oven to 350°F. Lightly grease a 9 x 14-inch casserole with margarine or cooking spray.

2. Put the peaches and berries in a large bowl, add the granulated sugar and ¼ cup of the flour, and toss gently to coat each piece. Arrange the fruit mixture evenly in the prepared casserole.

3. Combine the remaining flour and the brown sugar in a medium bowl. Add the butter and use the tips of your fingers to incorporate the ingredients and to crumble the mixture into small pieces about the size of dried peas.

4. Spoon the flour mixture on top of the fruit and pat down gently.

5. Bake, uncovered, on the center rack of your oven for 45 minutes, until the top is lightly browned. Let sit for 30 minutes before serving.

Variations

■ To make a traditional apple brown betty, substitute 3 pounds baking apples, cored and cut into slices, for the peaches and blueberries, and replace the ¼ cup flour tossed with the blueberries and sugar with the juice of 1 lemon.

■ To make a pear brown betty, follow the tip above for the apple brown betty but use hard Bosc or Bartlett pears instead of apples. Or make a brown betty with a combination of apples and pears.

Tiramisù

Tiramisù is a swanky Venetian dessert that features alternating layers of coffee-soaked cake, rich, sweet cream, and chocolate. This is a simplified, Americanized version. It will keep for 2 days, but it is best when made in the morning and served that evening.

Ingredients *(serves six)*

> 1 store-bought yellow pound cake or
>   1 box ladyfingers
> 1 16-ounce container ricotta cheese
> ½ cup plus 2 tablespoons sugar
> ½ cup heavy cream
> 8 ounces semisweet chocolate chips
> 1½ cups strong coffee (I use decaffeinated
>   for the kids)
> Unsweetened cocoa powder

Equipment

> 2 medium bowls
> Hand-held electric mixer
> Rubber spatula
> Pastry brush

1. Put a medium bowl in the freezer.

2. Cut the pound cake into ½-inch slices.

3. In a second medium bowl, combine the ricotta with the ½ cup sugar.

4. Remove the bowl from the freezer, add the cream, and beat with a mixer on high speed until it holds stiff peaks.

5. With a rubber spatula, fold the whipped cream into the ricotta mixture. Then fold in the chocolate chips.

6. Line the bottom of a deep glass serving bowl with slices of pound cake, cutting the cake as needed to cover the bottom.

7. Stir the remaining 2 tablespoons sugar into the coffee. Dip a pastry brush in the coffee and dab it on the cake until it is soaked through.

8. Using a rubber spatula, spread ¼ of the ricotta mixture gently over the cake.

9. Arrange another layer of cake on the ricotta mixture and use the pastry brush to soak it with coffee. Cover the cake with another layer of ¼ of the ricotta mixture. Repeat until you have 4 layers of each, ending with a ricotta layer.

10. Cover and refrigerate for at least 4 hours. Sprinkle the cocoa powder on top before serving.

Tip

When serving, scoop all the way down to the bottom of the bowl with your serving spoon so you get to all of the layers. The portions will not be neat, but you'll find that no one will complain once they start eating.

The Simplest & Healthiest Dessert

In the face of more sumptuous desserts, we often forget about the wonderful flavor of a crisp apple or a ripe, juicy peach. Fruit is always best when it is in season locally—that's when you should buy plentifully. But even though more fruits are available year-round in supermarkets, few of us know what to look for when purchasing fruit or what to do when we take them home. You'll need to enlist your senses—eyes, nose, and fingers—when selecting the best fruit.

Apples

Fall apples bought at local stands, with names you don't recognize, are always better than the mass produced varieties available year-round. Flavors vary from sweet (Red Delicious and Golden Delicious) to tart (Granny Smith, Macoun, and Stayman). Choose apples that are smooth, firm, and blemish free. Store them in a plastic bag in the refrigerator.

Bananas

Bananas are fully ripe and sweet when the skins have a few brown speckles. Make sure the skin is unbroken and there are no brown patches. Greenish-yellow bananas will ripen on the countertop away from direct sunlight.

Berries

Buy strawberries and raspberries locally during the months of June and July. Strawberries from California and raspberries from Chile are available at other times of the year. Berries should be firm, plump, and intensely colored (not pale or browned). Store berries covered with plastic wrap in your refrigerator's fruit bin.

Cherries

Cherries are around only for a month or so in early summer, so eat them while you can. Choose plump, bright cherries (with stems) that are slightly tender, but not at all mushy. Store them in a plastic bag in the refrigerator.

Grapefruit

Look for grapefruits that are flat at both ends and heavy for their size and have thin, smooth skin. Store at cool room temperature for up to a week, or longer in the refrigerator.

Grapes

Slightly tart red and green seedless grapes are available year-round. Ripe grapes should be plump and remain firmly attached to their stems when the bunch is gently shaken. Store in a plastic bag in the refrigerator.

Melons

Melons smell fragrant when ripe and their stem ends should yield to gentle pressure. The rind of a cantaloupe should be more beige than green and a honeydew should be cream-colored and waxy. Most melons can do with a day or two at room temperature to increase their sweetness.

Oranges

Since most oranges are dyed a bright orange, do not judge them by color. Look for oranges that are firm and heavy for their size. Florida oranges have thin, smooth skins whereas naval oranges from California have thicker, bumpier skins. Store oranges for a week or more in a plastic bag in the refrigerator.

Peaches

Look for tender peaches with a yellow or cream tinge beneath the blush. Avoid rock-hard peaches as well as soft peaches which are apt to taste woolly. Peaches in supermarkets are often sold before fully ripened and need a day or two on the countertop. Store ripe peaches in a plastic bag in the refrigerator.

Pears

Bosc pears have rough brown skin and are a bit crunchy when ripe. Barletts have smooth green skin, are plump, and have a silken texture. Buy pears when they are still slightly firm and allow them to ripen at home. You'll know a pear is ready to eat when it 'gives' a little at the neck.

Pineapples

The best pineapples come from Hawaii. Look for a plump, bright, sweet-smelling pineapple that yields to slight pressure and has flat, shiny "eyes." A leaf from the center should pull out easily. Store at room temperature away from direct sunlight.

Baked Apples

Ingredients *(serves four)*

> 2 tablespoons butter or margarine, plus
> extra for greasing the baking dish
>
> 4 large cooking apples, such as Winesap
> or Pippin
>
> ¼ cup currants and/or chopped walnuts
>
> ¼ cup apricot, strawberry, or peach jam
>
> ¼ cup real maple syrup or honey

Equipment

> 9-inch square glass baking dish
> Small bowl
> Paring knife

1. Preheat the oven to 375°F and lightly grease a 9-inch square glass baking dish with butter or margarine.

2. Use a paring knife to core the apples ¾ of the way down. Arrange the apples in the baking dish without letting them touch each other. Fill the cores with the currants and/or nuts.

3. Mix the jam and maple syrup or honey in a small bowl and spoon the mixture over the apples. Dot with the 2 tablespoons butter.

4. Bake the apples, uncovered, on the center rack of your oven for 30 minutes. Baste the apples with the pan juice and bake for another 20 minutes.

5. Transfer the baking dish to a wire rack to cool. Serve lukewarm.

Tip

When buying maple syrup, read the labels carefully. Neither maple-flavored syrup (usually a combination of corn syrup and just a tad of real maple syrup) nor pancake syrup (often corn syrup combined with artificial maple flavor) will do for this recipe.

Melon with Honey & Lime

Ingredients *(serves four)*

> 1 large honeydew or cantaloupe
> (or a combination of the two)
>
> ¼ cup honey
>
> 2 limes

Equipment

> Melon baller
> Rubber spatula

1. Cut the melon in half and scoop out the seeds with a spoon.

2. Use a melon baller to scoop out rounds and put the rounds in a serving bowl.

3. Drizzle the honey and squeeze the limes over the melon balls. Toss gently with a rubber spatula. Let the melon sit at room temperature for 30 minutes to intensify the flavor before serving.

Serving Suggestion

Serve on chilled plates as an appetizer or for dessert.

Poached Pears

These are wonderful served with whipped cream or vanilla ice cream.

Ingredients *(serves four)*

5 *hard Bosc or Bartlett pears*
1½ *cups dry red wine (or grape juice)*
½ *cup sugar*
1 *cinnamon stick or ½ teaspoon ground cinnamon*

Equipment

Paring knife or peeler
Medium saucepan with cover
Slotted spoon

1. Using a paring knife or vegetable peeler, peel the skin off the bottom ⅔ of each pear, leaving the upper ⅓ and stem intact. If necessary, trim a bit off the bottom of the pears, so they will sit without falling over.

2. Combine the wine or grape juice, sugar, and cinnamon in a medium saucepan over *medium* heat, stirring to dissolve the sugar. Set the pears in the pan so they're not touching and bring the liquid to a boil.

3. Reduce the heat to *medium low,* cover the pan, and simmer until the pears are soft. Hard pears may take 30 minutes to soften, ripe pears as little as 15 minutes.

4. When the pears are soft, carefully remove them to serving plates with a slotted spoon. Discard the cinnamon stick.

5. Continue simmering the liquid over *medium* heat, uncovered, until thick and syrupy, about 12 minutes.

6. Serve the pears topped with the reduced and thickened syrup.

Sautéed Bananas with Strawberries

Ingredients *(serves three)*

Juice of 1 large orange
2 *teaspoons honey*
1 *teaspoon vanilla extract*
Pinch of cinnamon
3 *medium bananas, peeled and halved lengthwise*
12 *strawberries, hulled and sliced*
Grated orange zest, to taste (see Note)

Equipment

Large frying pan
Grater

1. Place the frying pan over *medium-high* heat until hot. Add the orange juice, honey, vanilla, and cinnamon, and stir to combine. Add the banana halves and sauté about 2 minutes on each side. Remove the bananas from the skillet and put 2 on each dessert plate.

2. Add the strawberry slices to the pan and sauté about 1 minute. Spoon the strawberries over the bananas and drizzle the pan juices on top. Garnish with orange zest and serve.

Note

Orange zest is the orange part of the peel of an orange. When grating, do not include the white part of the peel which is unpleasantly bitter.

Crystallized Orange Sections

When you eat the sliced orange you are served at the end of a meal in a Chinese restaurant, you are participating in a custom that is at least a thousand years old. And there is no reason why you shouldn't adopt this custom in your home. But for those meals when you want the effect to be just a touch more elegant, try this recipe.

Ingredients *(serves four)*

4 oranges, tangerines, or clementines
Whites of 2 large eggs
2 cups sugar
Fresh mint, for garnish

Equipment

11 x 17-inch baking sheet
Pie plate
Medium bowl
Whisk

1. Line an 11 x 17-inch baking sheet with wax paper.

2. Peel and carefully separate the oranges, tangerines, or clementines into sections without breaking the membranes. Remove any of the bitter white pith clinging to the fruit.

3. Beat the egg whites in a medium bowl with a whisk until just frothy. Measure the sugar into the pie plate and shake the plate so that the sugar spreads out and covers the surface.

4. Rest a fruit section on a fork (do not pierce) and dip it into the egg whites, just enough to coat it, then transfer to the pie plate. Repeat. Place about 8 egg-coated pieces of fruit at a time in the sugar and shake the plate so that the sugar coats the fruit.

5. Use a fork to lift the fruit sections from the sugar (do not pierce the fruit), tapping the fork gently on the edge of the pan to release any excess sugar. Transfer the fruit to the wax paper to dry, about 12 minutes.

6. When the fruit sections are completely dry, place a second piece of wax paper on top of them and store in the refrigerator until serving time. Carefully arrange the orange sections on a decorative serving platter and garnish with fresh mint.

Variation

The same process can be used with seedless grapes. Orange sections and grapes together make a colorful presentation.

Making Bread & Pizza with the Kids

Never having tasted homemade bread still warm from the oven is like having watched only black-and-white television—without cable. Baking your own bread is uniquely satisfying: First, there's the tactile sensation of kneading and shaping the loaves; then, as the house fills with the fragrant and comforting aroma, your taste buds begin to anticipate the first bites of warm, sweet, yeasty goodness.

MAKING BREAD & PIZZA WITH THE KIDS

We try to bake bread every Sunday in our house; one loaf goes in the bread drawer, one in the freezer, and we're set for the week. The great thing about baking bread with the kids is that all hands can be involved in the measuring and mixing, and there's always enough kneading and punching to go around. You can incorporate the process into other Sunday afternoon activities. We often assemble the dough before kickoff, let it rise during the first half, punch it down and make the loaves during halftime, and put it in the oven after the third quarter. By the time the teams are heading for the locker room, we're tearing off our first chunks.

Included here are recipes for three basic breads as well as a couple of special breads and a quick pizza primer. Once you master these recipes, you can begin to improvise, and then the sky's the limit. First, though, a few of the ABCs of bread-making.

Bread Basics

To novice breadmakers, the directions for making bread—"punch down," "knead," "double in bulk"—sound more like a physical workout than a recipe. And is yeast really *that* fussy? Dissolve in "warm but not hot liquid." In time you'll learn that yeast, though high spirited, is actually quite resilient. It's the magic that determines all the motions and rhythms of baking bread.

About Yeast

Yeast is a fungus that eats sugar, which results in fermentation. The fermentation creates gas, causing the dough to rise. The yeast feeds first off the sugar added to the dough, and then on the sugar contained in the starch granules of the flour.

Yeast is activated by contact with warm liquid. All recipes specify "lukewarm" liquid (105°–115°F). If it's too hot, it will kill the yeast; if it's too cold, it will slow its action. A good test is to put a few drops on your wrist. If it feels a tad warmer than your body temperature, you'll know, like Goldilocks, it's just right.

Proofing

Proofing enables you to judge if the yeast is active and the liquid is the right temperature (sort of like a pre-game warmup). Combine the yeast, warm liquid, and sugar in a large bowl. After about 5 minutes a distinct odor will develop and a foam of active yeast will appear on the surface of the water. The foam is the proof that the yeast is ready to work.

The Work Surface

A large wooden board is ideal, as the rough surface of the wood helps in the kneading. If necessary, you can use a section of countertop, as long as it is completely dry and there are no appliances around to impede kneading. Keep the surface very lightly floured to prevent the bread from sticking, being careful not to add too much flour. Once the dough stops sticking to your hands and the work surface, do not add any more flour.

Kneading

Kneading helps develop the gluten and the minuscule air pockets in the dough. The process is one of turning, folding, and pressing the dough. First, lightly flour the work surface. Grip the lump of dough in the center with both hands, as if you are

MAKING BREAD & PIZZA WITH THE KIDS

gripping the handlebars of a bicycle. Then dig your palms into the dough as you press down and slightly out, making sure the dough is rubbing hard against the board. Fold the dough over itself and repeat, making sure the new section has contact with the board. This is repeated steadily for 6 to 8 minutes (though it may take up to 10 or 12) until the dough is smooth and satiny.

Lightly pushing the dough against the board is not kneading. You really must put your weight into it. Work on a low table if that gives you better leverage, and provide a stool for the kids if they need it. Above all, kneading requires patience and stamina.

Rising

As the yeast cells multiply, they continue to produce carbon dioxide, which causes the dough to expand and rise. The dough should be in a warm place (though

not in the oven or near a heater) to keep the yeast active. Cover the bowl with a damp dish towel to protect the dough from drafts and contamination. Bread dough usually takes $1\frac{1}{2}$–2 hours to rise until doubled in bulk. Denser doughs, such as pumpernickel, will take a bit longer. Do not let the dough more than double in size. It will lose its chewiness and taste too yeasty.

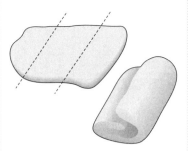

Shaping Loaves

Divide the dough in half. Shape each piece into a rectangle slightly shorter than the length of the loaf pan, then fold up the dough in thirds, the way you would a letter. Gently pinch the seam together and lay the dough in the pan, seam side down.

Testing

When tapped gently on the bottom, a fully baked loaf will sound hollow. Do not judge by the crust, which gets hard before the bread is fully baked and softens as the bread cools. If you don't trust the hollow tapping method, insert a wooden skewer into the middle of the bread. If it comes out clean, the bread is done.

Removing & Slicing

Most breads pull away from the sides of the pan as they bake. Before removing a loaf from its pan, run a butter knife around the edge of the pan to loosen it. Then turn the loaf pan upside down to release the bread. Transfer the loaf to a cooling rack.

You can work all afternoon making some fine bread and then ruin it by slicing it too soon. Be patient and let the loaf cool properly, for at least 20 minutes, before trying to slice it. Still, cutting those first few slices can be tricky. Lay the warm loaf on its side and cut with a serrated bread knife. Use only the lightest possible pressure and cut slowly. If you press down hard you'll wind up crushing the loaf.

Flour

You're at the grocery store ready to buy the all-purpose flour that your recipe calls for and, all of a sudden, you realize that you are being confronted by a myriad of choices. How can this be? All you were looking for was plain old flour. To help you avoid confusion, here is a brief lexicon of the terms you may find on the bags of all-purpose flour in your market.

■ **All-Purpose Flour** *(aka family, plain, white, or general-purpose flour)* This is the most popular kind of flour for home-baking. It is used to make all sorts of breads, cakes, and cookies. I prefer unbleached.

■ **Presifted Flour** Sometimes flour is sifted before it is packaged, ostensibly to save the cook time in the kitchen. Unfortunately, flour settles and becomes more compact in storage, making it advisable to sift flour (if instructed to do so in a recipe) even if the manufacturer claims that the flour was presifted.

■ **Enriched Flour** Because many vitamins as well as valuable dietary fiber are lost in the process used to make white flour, many states require that it be "enriched" with B-complex vitamins (thiamin, riboflavin, and niacin), in addition to iron and sometimes calcium and vitamin D. The "enrichment" does not affect the flour's baking properties.

■ **Bleached Flour** After flour is milled it is either aged naturally—during which time the color of the flour changes from pale yellow to white and the flour's gluten-producing potential develops (gluten is a protein that gives dough its strength and elasticity)—or it is bleached, which speeds up the aging process. If a recipe calls for unbleached flour and all you have in the house is bleached flour, go ahead and use what you have.

■ **Self-Rising Flour** This kind of flour contains salt and a leavening agent, supposedly to save the cook the time it takes to measure and combine these ingredients for an individual recipe. Because the strength of the leavener deteriorates within months, it is not advisable to buy this kind of flour.

Storing & Freezing Bread

Hard-crusted breads should be stored in a paper bag on the countertop or, ideally, in a traditional bread box or drawer. Soft-crusted bread should be stored in a plastic bag on the countertop or, again, in a bread box or drawer. If you plan on keeping a loaf of homemade bread for more than 2 or 3 days (commercial bread will last longer), wrap it in plastic and put it in the freezer. I don't recommend storing homemade bread in the refrigerator as it gets stale more quickly than if left at room temperature. You can freshen stale bread by warming it in a hot oven or toaster for a minute or two.

To freeze loaves of bread, let them cool completely, for at least 2 hours on a cooling rack, before storing in well-sealed plastic bags. If desired, slice the bread before freezing it so that you can take out only what you need.

Country White Bread

This is white bread the way it's supposed to be, thick, chewy, and full flavored. Have some butter and jam ready when it's time for slicing. This bread also makes sublime French toast.

Ingredients *(makes two loaves)*

¼ cup butter or margarine, melted

2 cups milk

2 tablespoons sugar

1 package (1 scant tablespoon) active dry yeast

2 teaspoons salt

5–6 cups unbleached all-purpose flour, plus extra for dusting the work surface

Vegetable oil, for oiling bowl and loaf pans

1 large egg white beaten with 1 tablespoon water (optional)

Equipment

Small saucepan

2 large bowls

Wooden spoon

2 5 x 9-inch loaf pans

Serrated knife

Pastry brush (optional)

Cooling rack

1. Add the milk to the saucepan and heat until just lukewarm. Remove the milk from the heat and let cool slightly.

2. Pour the lukewarm milk into a large bowl. Add the sugar. Sprinkle the yeast evenly on top of the milk. Let the mixture sit in a warm place for 5 minutes until the yeast begins to bubble and foam.

3. Add the melted butter or margarine and the salt to the yeast mixture and stir with a wooden spoon. Add the 5 cups flour, 1 cup at a time, blending well after each addition. Add only enough flour to make a firm but pliable dough that is just slightly sticky.

4. Sprinkle a work surface with a scant ¼ cup flour. Transfer the dough to the work surface and knead the dough for about 7 minutes, until it is smooth and supple. Add more flour, ¼ cup at a time, if the dough is still sticky.

5. Wipe the inside of another large bowl with vegetable oil. Place the dough in the bowl and then turn it over so the top of the dough is coated with a thin layer of oil. Place a slightly damp dish towel over the bowl and put it in a warm, draft-free place until it has doubled in bulk, about 1½–2 hours.

6. Punch down the dough with your fist until all the air pockets burst. Knead the dough a few more times on a lightly floured work surface, then divide the dough in half and shape it into loaves.

7. Wipe the inside of the loaf pans well with oil. Place the dough in the pans, cover with the damp dish towel, and set aside to double in bulk, about 45 minutes.

8. Preheat the oven to 375°F.

9. When the dough has fully risen, use a serrated knife or single-edge razor to make 3 shallow slashes in the top of each loaf. If you want a soft, shiny crust, brush the top of the loaves with the egg white–water mixture. (The crust will be crisp if you don't brush with egg white mixture.) Place the loaf pans on the center rack of the oven and bake about 40–45 minutes, until the loaves sound hollow when tapped in the center.

10. Run a butter knife around the edge of the pan and tip out the loaves. Place them on a cooling rack for at least 20 minutes before slicing.

Whole Wheat Bread

This hearty bread, made slightly sweet with the addition of molasses, could easily become the loaf of preference around your house.

Ingredients *(makes two loaves)*

1 cup milk

¼ cup molasses

2 tablespoons vegetable oil, plus extra for oiling the bowl and loaf pans

2 teaspoons salt

1 teaspoon honey

1 package (1 scant tablespoon) active dry yeast

1–1½ cups unbleached all-purpose flour, plus extra for dusting the work surface

4 cups whole wheat flour

1 large egg white beaten with 1 tablespoon water (optional)

Equipment

Small saucepan

2 large bowls

Small bowl

Wooden spoon

2 5 x 9-inch loaf pans

Cooling rack

1. Heat the milk in a small saucepan over *low* heat until tiny bubbles appear around the edges (this is called scalding). Pour the scalded milk into a large bowl and stir in the molasses, oil, and salt. Cool to lukewarm.

2. Measure 1 cup lukewarm water into a small bowl. Stir in the honey and evenly sprinkle on the yeast. Let sit for 3 minutes, then add this mixture to the cooled milk mixture, stirring with a wooden spoon. Stir in 1 cup all-purpose flour, then add the whole wheat flour, 1 cup at a time, blending well after each addition. Add only enough flour to make a firm but pliable dough that is just slightly sticky.

3. Sprinkle the work surface with a scant ¼ cup all-purpose flour. Transfer the dough to your work surface.

4. Knead the dough for about 9 minutes, until it is smooth and supple, adding more all-purpose flour, ¼ cup at a time, if it is still sticky.

5. Wipe the inside of a large bowl with vegetable oil. Place the dough in the bowl, then turn it over so the top of the dough is coated with a thin layer of oil. Place a slightly damp dish towel over the bowl and set aside in a warm, draft-free place until doubled in bulk, about 1½–2 hours.

6. Punch down the dough with your fist until there are no air bubbles left. Knead the dough a few more times on a lightly floured work surface, then divide the dough in half and shape it into 2 loaves.

7. Wipe the inside of 2 loaf pans well with oil. Place the dough in the pans, cover with the dish towel, and set aside until doubled in bulk, about 45 minutes.

8. Preheat the oven to 425°F.

9. After the dough has risen a second time, use a pastry brush to gently brush the top of the loaves with some water to make a crisper crust. Brush with the egg white–water mixture for a softer, shinier crust.

10. Place the pans on the center rack of the oven and bake for 10 minutes, then lower the heat to 350°F and bake about 45 minutes more, until the loaves sound hollow when tapped and have shrunk slightly from the sides of the pan.

11. Run a butter knife around the edges of the pans and tip out the loaves. Place on a cooling rack for at least another 20 minutes before slicing.

Pumpernickel Raisin Bread

Pumpernickel dough is denser than other dough, so it takes more strength to knead and more time to rise—about 4 hours total as opposed to approximately 2¾ hours for the Country White Bread.

Ingredients *(makes one loaf)*

1¼ cups lukewarm water (105°–115°F)
1 tablespoon sugar
1 package (1 scant tablespoon) active dry yeast
2 tablespoons molasses
2 tablespoons vegetable oil,
*   plus extra for greasing the baking pan*
1 tablespoon salt
1½ cups whole wheat flour
1½ cups rye flour
1 cup unbleached all-purpose flour,
*   plus extra for dusting the work surface*
¼ cup cornmeal
¾ cup raisins

Equipment

2 large bowls
Medium bowl
Wooden spoon
Whisk
11 x 17-inch baking sheet
Cooling rack

1. Measure ¼ cup of the warm water into a large bowl. Stir in the sugar and evenly sprinkle on the yeast. Let the mixture sit for 5 minutes.

2. Stir in the molasses, oil, salt, and the remaining 1 cup warm water. Set aside.

3. In a medium bowl, use a whisk to combine the whole wheat, rye, and all-purpose flours and the cornmeal. Add the flour mixture to the yeast mixture 1 cup at a time, mixing well with a wooden spoon after each addition. The last 2 cups will take a bit more effort to incorporate. Add only enough flour to make a pliable and somewhat sticky dough.

4. Sprinkle a work surface with a scant ¼ cup all-purpose flour. Transfer the dough to the work surface.

5. Knead the dough for at least 10 minutes. It should still be slightly sticky. *Do not try to make the dough completely smooth.* Toward the end of the kneading, spread the raisins, a handful at a time, on the work surface and knead them into the dough.

6. Wipe the inside of another large bowl with vegetable oil. Place the dough in the bowl and then turn it over so the top of the dough is coated with a thin layer of oil. Cover the bowl with a slightly damp dish towel and put it in a warm, draft-free place until doubled in bulk, about 2–2½ hours.

MAKING BREAD & PIZZA WITH THE KIDS

7. Punch down the dough with your fist until there are no air bubbles left. Knead the dough a few more times on a floured work surface, then shape it into a round loaf.

8. Lightly grease an 11 x 17-inch baking sheet. Place the loaf on the baking sheet and cover it with the damp dish towel. Set aside in a warm, draft-free place until doubled in bulk, about 1½–2 hours.

9. Preheat the oven to 375°F.

10. When the dough has fully risen, place the baking pan on the center rack of the oven and bake about 35–40 minutes, until the loaf sounds hollow when tapped.

11. Place the loaf on a rack and cool for at least 20 minutes before slicing.

Corn Bread

This sweet bread can be served with all sorts of meals, most happily with chili. This recipe makes a lot of corn bread, but the kids always seem to gobble it down fast.

Ingredients *(makes twenty pieces)*
*10 tablespoons (1¼ sticks) butter,
    plus extra for greasing the pan*
3 cups unbleached all-purpose flour
2 cups yellow cornmeal
1 cup sugar
1 tablespoon baking powder
1 teaspoon salt
2⅔ cups milk
2 large eggs

Equipment
9½ x 13½-inch baking pan
Small saucepan
Large bowl

Using Stale Bread

While fresh homemade bread tastes so good it's nearly magical, stale bread is sad and unsatisfying. Fortunately, there are ways of salvaging stale bread as long as it is not so old that mold has developed. The easiest thing to do is make toast but there is only so much toast one can eat. Other alternatives including making bread crumbs and croutons.

To make dried bread crumbs, break the bread into manageable pieces and pulverize in a food processor or blender. Alternatively, place the bread in a plastic or paper bag and run over it with a rolling pin. If the bread that you are using is not quite dry, place it in a 250°F oven for a few minutes before turning it into crumbs. If not using immediately, freeze the bread crumbs in an airtight container.

To make your own croutons, see recipe page 168.

Whisk
Medium bowl
Wooden spoon
Rubber spatula
Cooling rack

1. Preheat the oven to 350°F. Grease a 9½ x 13½-inch baking pan with butter.

2. Melt the butter in a small saucepan.

3. Use a whisk to combine the flour, cornmeal, sugar, baking powder, and salt in a large bowl.

4. Whisk together the milk, eggs, and the melted butter in a medium bowl. Pour the liquid mixture into the flour mixture and blend well with a wooden spoon until all the flour mixture is incorporated. The batter should be very moist but not runny.

5. Use a rubber spatula to transfer the batter to the prepared baking pan and spread the batter evenly over the whole pan.

6. Bake the bread on the center rack of the oven about 12 minutes, until it is set (i.e., doesn't wiggle in the middle) and a toothpick inserted in the center comes out clean.

7. Let the bread cool on a rack in the pan for 20 minutes before cutting into squares.

Irish Soda Bread

This bread doesn't use yeast and requires no rising time, so you can throw it together in a jiffy. Keep it in mind when you want to take a gift of food along to a dinner party.

Ingredients *(makes two loaves)*

    4 cups unbleached all-purpose flour
    ¼ cup plus 2 tablespoons sugar
    3 teaspoons baking powder
    1 teaspoon baking soda
    1 teaspoon salt
    1¾ cups buttermilk
    1 large egg
    ½ cup raisins or currants
    *¼ cup vegetable oil, plus extra for
       greasing the baking sheet*

Equipment

    11 x 17-inch baking sheet
    Large bowl
    Whisk
    Medium bowl
    Wooden spoon
    Serrated knife
    Cooling rack

Cake Tester

A cake tester is nothing more than a toothpick or a thin metal skewer. If you have neither of these on hand, use the clean end of a broom bristle. To test breads, cakes, and other baked goods for doneness, simply insert the tester into the thickest part of what you are testing and pull it out. If it comes out clean, or with tiny dry crumbs clinging to it, what you are baking is done. If it is at all damp, then more baking is required.

1. Preheat the oven to 375°F. Lightly grease an 11 x 17-inch baking sheet with vegetable oil.

2. Use a whisk to combine the flour, sugar, baking powder, baking soda, and salt in a large bowl.

3. Whisk together the buttermilk, egg, raisins or currants, and ¼ cup vegetable oil in a medium bowl.

4. Pour the wet ingredients into the flour mixture and mix well with a wooden spoon.

5. Transfer the dough to a lightly floured work surface and knead until smooth, about 2 minutes.

6. Divide the dough in half and shape each half into a round loaf. Place each loaf on the prepared baking sheet, leaving a few inches between them to allow for expansion. Use a serrated knife or a single-edge razor blade to make an "X" in the center of each loaf.

7. Bake the bread on the center rack of the oven about 35–40 minutes, until the top is light brown and a toothpick inserted in the center comes out clean.

8. Let the loaves cool on the baking sheet for 20 minutes. Transfer the loaves to a rack and let them cool for another 20 minutes before slicing.

Dad's Own Pizza

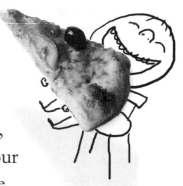

Making pizza at home is a simple operation. It requires few ingredients, little work, and no special equipment. And your pizza will be as good as, if not better than, the pies made in most local pizza shops.

The Dough

Ingredients *(makes two 16-inch pizza crusts)*

2 cups lukewarm water (105°–115°F)

1 teaspoon sugar

2 packages active dry yeast

4½ cups unbleached all-purpose flour

1½ cups whole wheat flour

¼ cup olive oil, plus extra for greasing the baking sheet

1 tablespoon salt

Equipment

11 x 17-inch baking sheet

2 large bowls

Whisk

Wooden spoon

1. Lightly grease an 11 x 17-inch baking sheet with vegetable oil.

2. Measure the lukewarm water into a large bowl. Add the sugar and sprinkle on the yeast in an even layer. Let the mixture sit for 7 minutes.

3. Combine the flours in a large bowl using the whisk.

4. Add the olive oil and salt to the yeast mixture, then the flours, 1 cup at a time, and stir with a wooden spoon until the flour is incorporated. The dough should be slightly sticky.

5. Lightly flour a work surface and knead the dough for 8–10 minutes, until smooth.

6. Divide the dough in half and shape each half into a ball. Place each ball on the prepared baking sheet, leaving about 4 inches between to accommodate expansion.

7. Cover the dough with a damp dish towel and let it rise in a warm, draft-free place for 1 hour.

Freezing Pizza Dough

Pizza dough freezes very well. Follow the recipe for making the dough, but let the dough rise for only 30 minutes (instead of 1 hour). Wrap each half of the dough loosely in 2 layers of plastic wrap and place immediately in the freezer. To use the frozen dough, either transfer it to the refrigerator the night before or leave it on the counter until it thaws, about 4–5 hours, depending on the temperature of the room. If you've thawed the dough in the refrigerator, remove it 1 hour before you bake so it can come to room temperature.

The Pizza

Although pizza can be made on ordinary baking sheets, for a crisper crust it is best to use a round pizza stone or screen. (Both are found in most kitchenware stores.) You can count on using it again and again to make this Friday-night special that kids just scarf up.

Ingredients

(makes two 16-inch pizzas)

Olive oil, if using baking sheets

Flour, for dusting the work surface

1 recipe Pizza Dough or your favorite store-bought dough

2 cups Basic Tomato Sauce (page 182) or your favorite store-bought sauce

1 pound mozzarella cheese, grated

Assorted toppings (see opposite page)

Equipment

Pizza stone, pizza screen, or 2 11 x 17-inch baking sheets

Rolling pin (optional)

Ladle

Large spatula

Pizza cutter

Cutting board

1. Position a rack as low as possible in the oven and preheat to 450°F. If using baking sheets, lightly grease them with the olive oil.

2. Lightly dust a work surface with flour. Punch down 1 ball of dough and use your fingers (or rolling pin) to push it out to half the desired size, roughly 8 inches across.

3. Lightly flour both sides of your hands. Drape the edge of the dough over your fists and use your knuckles to turn and stretch the dough until it is approximately 16 inches across. It should be slightly thicker around the edges.

4. Lay the dough on the pizza stone or screen or fit the dough into the baking sheets.

5. Assemble and bake one pizza at a time, as follows: Ladle 1 cup tomato sauce in the center of the dough and spread evenly to cover.

6. Sprinkle on half the grated mozzarella in an even layer.

7. Arrange your choice of toppings over the cheese.

8. Bake the pizzas, one at a time, on the lowest rack of the oven for about 10 minutes, until the cheese bubbles and the bottom of the crust is crispy.

9. Use a large spatula to slide the pizza from the stone or baking sheet onto a cutting board.

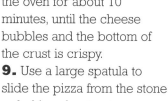

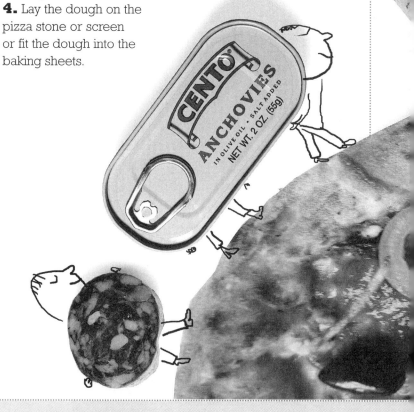

Let the pizza cool for 1 minute before slicing with a pizza cutter or large knife.

10. Assemble the second pizza while the first one is in the oven, then put the second one in the oven as you sit down to eat the first.

Tips

■ Make sure there are no holes in the dough. If any holes appear while you are stretching the dough, patch them up by folding the dough over the hole and stretching again.

■ Stretching the dough over the backs of your hands assures that the crust will be light and crispy, but it takes a little practice. After three or four pizzas, you should get the hang of it. If necessary, roll the dough out fully with a rolling pin.

■ To make a lip around the pizza, fold the dough over itself around the edge.

Topping Suggestions

■ Extra cheese
■ Capers
■ Chile peppers
■ Sun-dried tomatoes
■ Thinly sliced red onion
■ Italian sausage
■ Pine nuts
■ Sautéed spinach
■ Artichoke hearts
■ Anchovies
■ Shrimp
■ Thinly sliced pepperoni
■ Sliced mushrooms
■ Gorgonzola
■ Strips of red, yellow, and green bell peppers
■ Hamburger
■ Sliced olives

Scones

These old-fashioned biscuits are quick and easy to make. Serve with butter, jam, or marmalade.

Ingredients *(makes twelve scones)*

   2 cups unbleached all-purpose flour
   6 tablespoons sugar
   3 teaspoons baking powder
   ½ teaspoon salt
   6 tablespoons (¾ stick) cold butter, plus
      extra for greasing the baking sheet
   1 large egg
   1 cup heavy cream or whole milk
   ½ cup currants, dried cranberries, raisins,
      or chocolate chips (optional)

Equipment

   11 x 17-inch baking sheet
   Large bowl
   Medium bowl
   Whisk
   Wooden spoon
   Pastry brush
   Cake tester

1. Preheat the oven to 375°F. Lightly grease the baking sheet with butter.

2. Using a wooden spoon, mix together the dry ingredients in a large bowl.

3. Cut the cold butter (margarine is not suitable as it changes the consistency of the dough) into small pieces and scatter them into the dry mixture. Working quickly with the tips of your fingers, break the butter into pieces the size of peas.

4. Beat the egg with a whisk in a medium bowl, then add the cream or milk. Set aside 2 tablespoons of the egg mixture to use later for brushing on top of the scones. Add the currants, cranberries, raisins, or chocolate chips to the egg mixture.

5. Pour the wet ingredients into the flour mixture. Stir with the wooden spoon until the liquid is just incorporated. The dough should be soft and slightly sticky. If the dough sticks to your fingers, add more flour 1 tablespoon at a time. If the dough is stiff and doesn't hold together, add more cream or milk 1 tablespoon at a time.

6. Divide the dough in half and shape into 2 balls. Place each ball on either end of the prepared baking sheet and press down to form 2 circles, each about 6 inches across and 1 inch thick.

7. Cut each circle of dough into 6 wedges, then pull the wedges away from each other slightly so they are barely touching. Lightly brush the tops of the wedges with the reserved egg mixture.

8. Bake on the center oven rack for 12 minutes, or until the tops are lightly browned and a cake tester inserted in the thickest part comes out clean.

Time-Saver

Steps 2, 3, and 4 can be done in advance. Just cover the separate bowls with plastic wrap and refrigerate the liquids.

Cooking in the Great Outdoors

In other times and other cultures women tended to the fire, but today in suburban America, Dad is often in charge of the charcoal. This chapter will expand your repertoire beyond hamburgers, hot dogs, and steak— to impressive fare like chicken saté and Asian swordfish.

The Basic Grill

You don't need to spend a lot of money on a deluxe grill with fancy gadgets. A good, sturdy grill with a cover and rack that can be adjusted toward or away from the flame will do. It should be made of heat-resistant material that won't rust if left in the rain (such as enameled steel, stainless steel, or treated cast-iron). Brands to look for are Weber, Sunbeam, and Kingsbord.

Consider your needs and the size of a grill: A small hibachi is fine for grilling a couple of pieces of chicken or a single steak. But if you've got a family of four or more, or plan on hosting outdoor functions, think about investing in a medium-sized or large grill.

Grill aficionados regularly debate the merits of charcoal vs. gas. The advantage of a gas grill that runs on bottled propane: it has an instant flame (though you have to wait for coals to heat), and you can control the strength of the flame during cooking. Though more convenient, a gas grill is a greater initial expense. Charcoal grills, on the other hand, have tradition as well as taste on their side, the charcoal imparting a slightly smoky flavor to the food. And with charcoal, there's more hands-on connection to the process.

Getting the Coals Ready

Though convenient, chemical starters are damaging to the environment and not recommended. Instead, use either an electric starter or a chimney. This cylinder of perforated metal makes lighting charcoal simple and fast. Place a loosely-crumpled sheet of newspaper in the bottom of the chimney and pile the coals into the top. Light the paper. In about ten minutes the coals on top will be gray. Dump them into the grill.

If you really must use charcoal starter, first cover the bottom of the grill with a dense single layer of coals. Then arrange the briquets in a tight pyramid in the center of the grill. Squirt about $1/3$ cup of fluid on the coals and let them soak for 2 minutes. Give one more quick squirt, then light the coals—from both sides so they'll burn evenly.

Whichever method you use, you'll know that the charcoals are lit when the edges of the individual briquets start turning gray. Let them heat in the pyramid for 30 minutes, then spread them out over the grill floor with a grilling fork or spatula.

After spreading the coals, set the grilling rack in place and wait about 5 more minutes until the coals are about half gray. A single layer of briquets will give you 40–50 minutes of optimum heat.

Grilling Technique

Grilling is an inexact science, requiring ingenuity and improvisation. Fires invariably reach different temperatures, altering cooking times. In other words, you don't just leave the chicken or burgers alone while you sip mint juleps with the guests. You have to be a "nudge" at the grill, regularly checking, turning, rotating, monitoring flareups, and basting. Because the heat is not uniform and certain areas of the grill are hotter than others, grilling requires constant adjustment. Even short distraction can mean the difference between succulent medium rare and dried out. Here are some tips to help with your grilling technique:

■ Trim excess fat from all cuts of meat to reduce flareups.

■ Have a table nearby to hold your spray bottle, platters, utensils, and a cold beer, so you'll never have to leave the grill for any period of time.

■ Make sure the coals are hot enough before you begin to barbecue. You shouldn't be able to hold your hand 5 inches over the grill for more than 3 seconds.

■ Determine your grill's hot spots—for example, the center is usually hotter than the edges. Rotate the food around the grill so that the pieces cook evenly, which may mean moving each piece of food every few minutes.

■ When you grill chicken, keep the dark meat around the hottest part of the grill and the white meat where it is less hot. This will help all of the chicken cook at the same rate.

■ Always begin cooking bone-in chicken with the bone side down to keep the skin from burning.

■ Designate one of the kids as chief assistant, responsible for all emergency runs into the house.

Grill Maintenance

Always keep your grill in good working order. For gas grills, refer to the manufacturer's instructions for cleaning and maintenance. For charcoal grills, refer to the following tips:

COOKING IN THE GREAT OUTDOORS

■ Clean out the ashes after every use. Make sure ashes have cooled completely, then tip the grill and pour the ashes into a garbage bag.

■ Scrape the grill rack with a wire brush before and after each use to keep the grease from building up. If desired, clean the outside with warm, sudsy water. If you need to clean the inside, brush it down with the same brush you used to clean the grill.

■ Always cover your grill when you're finished using it. Top-grade grills won't be bothered by a little rain, but it's best to store your grill in the garage, or under a protected awning or grill tarp.

■ Store the grill in the garage for the winter. If you must leave it outside, cover it with plastic. A painter's plastic drop cloth does the trick nicely.

About Marinades

The flavor and tenderness of some cuts of beef, lamb, and poultry can be enhanced by letting them sit in a marinade for several hours in the refrigerator. Turn the meat 3 to 4 times so that all sides can absorb the marinade. If you are pressed for time, you can marinate at room temperature, which speeds up the process, but do not leave meat or fish out for more than 1 hour before you begin cooking it. Better cuts of meat, such as porterhouse and sirloin don't need marinating. Chicken and pork can always do with a marinade to keep them from drying out. Fish or seafood should not be marinated for more than 2 hours as the flesh begins to break down. Thin fillets, such as sole and flounder, should not be marinated at all. Do not reuse the marinade the raw meat or fish was in—if you want to baste while grilling, set aside some marinade before you marinate the meat or fish.

Marinating Technique

1. Place the meat, chicken, or fish in a large plastic container or sealable plastic bag.

2. If you want to baste while cooking, set aside about ½ cup of the marinade. Pour the rest over the meat, chicken, or fish, turn it once so both sides are covered, cover the container, and refrigerate, turning occasionally.

3. After marinating, remove the meat, chicken, or fish from the marinade and place on the hot grill. Discard the marinade. About 5 minutes before the end of the cooking, brush the top of the meat, chicken, or fish with the reserved marinade and turn over. Cook for 1 minute, brush the other side, and turn over again. Continue cooking and turning every minute or so until the meat, chicken or fish is nicely glazed.

Cooking Times

It would be nice if there were exact cooking times for the barbecue, but unfortunately, too many variables are involved in grilling. Besides, one person's medium rare is another person's "on the hoof." Only you can cook your idea of the perfect steak. Nevertheless, keep these general hints in mind when you're tending the grill:

■ Keep a close eye on the food for doneness. An extra-hot fire can turn a medium-rare steak into a medium-well steak in an instant. It is best to use the professional chef's method— pressing a finger into the meat—to gauge doneness. Remember that meat begins to get more taut as it cooks. Uncooked meat is soft and flabby while overdone meat is stiff and tough. In between, it has a kind of tight springiness. Poke a steak

Steaks

	Rare	Medium-rare	Medium
1 inch	4–5 minutes a side	5–6 minutes a side	6–7 minutes a side
1¹/₂ inches	5–6 minutes a side	6–8 minutes a side	7–9 minutes a side
2 inches	8–10 minutes a side	9–12 minutes a side	10–13 minutes a side

Hamburgers

	Rare	Medium-rare	Medium
1 inch	3–4 minutes a side	4–5 minutes a side	5–6 minutes a side
1¹/₂ inches	4–5 minutes a side	5–7 minutes a side	6–8 minutes a side
2 inches	5–7 minutes a side	6–8 minutes a side	7–9 minutes a side

Lamb Chops (Loin)

	Rare	Medium-rare	Medium
1 inch	3–4 minutes a side	4–6 minutes a side	6–8 minutes a side
1¹/₂ inches	3–5 minutes a side	5–7 minutes a side	7–9 minutes a side
2 inches	4–6 minutes a side	6–9 minutes a side	9–11 minutes a side

Pork Chops (Loin) *Cook with the grill partially covered.*

1 inch	6–7 minutes a side
1¹/₂ inches	7–8 minutes a side
2 inches	8–9 minutes a side

Chicken *Cook 5–6 inches from coals (medium-high setting).*

Half	20–25 minutes a side
Breasts (bone in)	15–18 minutes a side
Boneless breasts	6–8 minutes a side
Dark meat	20–25 minutes a side

Fish *Use a hinged wire grill basket for best results.*

	Steaks	Fillets	Whole fish
1 inch	5–6 minutes a side	4–5 minutes a side	5–6 minutes a side per inch at thickest point
1¹/₂ inches	6–7 minutes a side	6–8 minutes a side	

COOKING IN THE GREAT OUTDOORS

you've cooked to your liking to get a sense of how it feels for future reference. If absolutely necessary you can cut into a piece of meat to see if it is cooked, but remember that you will release some of the meat's flavorful juices.

■ When you're figuring your cooking times, remember that meat and poultry continue to cook after they're removed from the grill. A medium-rare steak will become almost medium by the time it reaches the table, so remove it from the grill accordingly.

■ Do not judge whether your meat is cooked by how it looks on the outside. Meat and poultry can quickly char on the outside and remain uncooked on the inside. If necessary, douse the coals slightly to cool them down.

■ The cooking times on the previous page are educated ballpark figures. Your best gauge of doneness is an attentive eye and experience. If you like your meat more well-done than "medium," just leave it on the grill a few minutes longer. Unless otherwise noted, times are given according to the thickness of the cut. The fire should be at its peak heat with the grill rack set 4–5 inches from the coals.

Equipping the Grill

■ **Long Spatula** for flipping burgers and fish.

■ **Long Tongs** for turning and rearranging food on the grill. Never use a fork, as piercing the meat will cause it to lose flavorful juices.

■ **Spray Bottle or Squirt Gun** filled with water to spritz coals flaming from dripping grease.

■ **Basting Brush** for spreading on sauce or marinade during the last moments of grilling.

■ **Flame-Resistant Cooking Gloves,** preferably the longer variety, to protect your hands and arms.

■ **Wire Brush** for scraping the grill before and after each use.

■ **Hinged Wire Grill Basket** for grilling fish fillets and vegetables.

■ **Skewers** for all kinds of kebabs. Use thick metal skewers for meat and thin skewers for vegetables. Bamboo skewers are excellent for foods that have short cooking times. Soak the bamboo skewers in warm water for 1 hour before using in order to keep them from burning. Bamboo skewers won't get hot like the metal ones, so you can transfer them directly from the grill to the dinner plates. Food cooked on metal skewers should be removed from the skewers before serving.

■ **Charcoal** Regular charcoal briquets work very well, but "natural" untreated charcoal further enhances the flavor of whatever you're grilling. You should, however, avoid the presoaked briquets as they have a tendency to impart a vaguely chemical taste to the food.

If your rack is not adjustable, partially or fully cover the grill to slow cooking down.

Basting

Basting sauces should be applied only during the last stages of grilling. The sauce does not actually add flavor to the meat itself, but forms a tasty coating over the meat. Sauces, especially those that contain sugar or honey, will burn if applied too early, diminishing the flavor of both the sauce and the meat.

Dad's Own Barbecue Sauce

This sauce is best for chicken, flank steak, ribs, or pork chops.

Ingredients *(makes enough for 1 cut-up chicken or 2 pounds meat)*

1 tablespoon vegetable oil
1 medium onion, finely chopped
3 cloves garlic, minced
1 cup ketchup
2 tablespoons Dijon mustard
2 tablespoons honey
2 tablespoons Worcestershire sauce
1 tablespoon malt or cider vinegar
1 tablespoon molasses (or honey)
¼ teaspoon ground cinnamon
1 teaspoon salt
Dash of cayenne pepper

Equipment

Medium saucepan
Medium bowl

1. Place a saucepan on *medium high* until it gets hot, about 45 seconds. Add the oil and the onion and sauté until soft, about 5 minutes. Add the garlic and sauté for a minute more.

2. Transfer the onion and garlic to a medium bowl. Add the ketchup, mustard, honey, Worcestershire sauce, vinegar, molasses, cinnamon, salt, and cayenne pepper, and mix well.

3. Pour over the meat.

Wine-&-Herb Marinade

This marinade is best for chicken and fish.

Ingredients *(makes enough for 1 cut-up chicken or 2 pounds chicken or fish)*

2 cups white wine
1 medium onion, thinly sliced
3 whole cloves garlic
2 tablespoons chopped fresh parsley
2 tablespoons chopped fresh oregano or
   2 teaspoons dried oregano
2 tablespoons chopped fresh basil or
   2 teaspoons dried basil
½ teaspoon chopped fresh or dried
   rosemary

Equipment

Medium bowl

In a medium bowl, combine all the ingredients. Pour over the meat.

COOKING IN THE GREAT OUTDOORS

Asian Marinade

This marinade is suitable for chicken, fatty fish, flank steak, ribs, or pork chops.

Ingredients *(makes enough for 1 cut-up chicken or 2 pounds meat or fish)*

> ¾ cup soy sauce
> ¾ cup white wine
> ¼ cup lemon juice
> 3 scallions, chopped
> 3 tablespoons dark brown sugar
> 1 teaspoon garlic powder
> ½ teaspoon ground ginger

Equipment

> *Medium bowl*

Combine all the ingredients in a medium bowl. Pour over the meat.

Barbecued Chicken

As far as I'm concerned, grills were made for barbecuing chicken. This recipe will probably leave you with some leftovers to serve for lunch the next day.

Ingredients *(serves four)*

> *Dad's Own Barbecue Sauce (page 247), for basting the chicken*
> *2¾-pound chicken, cut into quarters*

Equipment

> *Tongs*
> *Barbecue brush*

1. Light the charcoal. When the briquets are hot, place the chicken pieces on the grill, skin side up. Grill the chicken for 25 minutes, then turn and grill for 15 minutes more.

2. Baste the chicken with the barbecue sauce, turn, and grill for 3 minutes more, until the chicken begins to get dark brown. Baste again, turn, and grill for 3 minutes more. The skin should start getting very dark, but don't let it burn.

Serving Suggestion

Serve with corn, coleslaw, thick crusty bread, and lots of extra sauce on the side (see Tips).

Tips

■ Because the dark meat legs take longer to cook than the white meat breasts, arrange the legs in the center of the grill, where it is hotter, and place the breasts around them. If the breasts still finish cooking sooner than the legs, move them to the outer edge of the grill or transfer them to a platter and cover with foil.

■ Larger chickens may need longer cooking times. To check for doneness, press down on the breast. If it is firm but springy, it is done. If it is very firm, it is overdone. If you're not sure, cut into 1 of the breasts to see if the meat is white. To check the legs for doneness, prick the thigh area. If the juices run clear (not pink), they are done.

■ After you have finished basting the chicken with the barbecue sauce, transfer the sauce to a small saucepan and simmer for several minutes. This is to kill any bacteria that may have been transferred while basting from the not-yet-fully-cooked chicken. Alternatively, make extra barbecue sauce for serving and discard the sauce used for basting.

Barbecued Spareribs

Ribs are surprisingly easy to make; just remember to get them started early in the day so they have time to marinate. They take up a lot of room on the grill, so if you don't have a large grill, be prepared to cook them in shifts.

Ingredients *(serves four)*

4 pounds country-style or baby-back
    pork ribs
1 large onion
3 whole cloves garlic
2 bay leaves
Double batch (about 3½ cups) Dad's Own
    Barbecue Sauce (page 247) or favorite
    store-bought sauce

Equipment

Large pot
Colander
1 or more large plastic containers or
    stainless-steel bowls
Spray bottle or squirt gun
Barbecue brush

1. Trim away any excess fat from the ribs.

2. Because the ribs would burn and dry out if cooked solely on the grill, you want to parboil them first. Put the ribs in a large pot and add enough water to cover. Add the onion, whole cloves of garlic, and bay leaves, and bring to a boil over *high* heat. Reduce the heat to *medium low* and simmer, uncovered, for 1 hour.

3. When the ribs are done simmering, drain them in a colander and place them in a large plastic container or stainless steel bowl. You may have to use more than 1 bowl or pan. Set aside ¾ cup of the barbecue sauce for basting. Pour the rest over the ribs, cover, and refrigerate for at least 2 hours.

4. Light the charcoal. When the briquets are hot, place the ribs on the grill. Cook for 20 minutes, turning frequently. Keep your spray bottle or squirt gun handy as fat dripping from the ribs can cause small flareups. To control larger flareups, cover the grill for about 30 seconds.

5. Baste the ribs and continue cooking for 10 more minutes, turning and basting every couple of minutes.

Serving Suggestion

Serve hot with coleslaw, potato salad, corn bread, and lots of napkins.

Variation

Instead of parboiling the ribs before grilling them, you can bake them. Preheat the oven to 350°F. Arrange the ribs on a lightly oiled baking pan, cover the pan with foil, and bake them on the center rack of the oven—1 hour for country-style ribs, 45 minutes for baby backs.

Lamb Shish Kebab

Grilling on skewers is one of the oldest ways to cook and still one of the best. Here is a basic recipe, but feel free to improvise. Just about any meat or vegetable that fits on a skewer can be grilled.

Ingredients *(serves four)*

½ cup olive oil
¼ cup red wine or dry sherry
¼ cup fresh lemon juice
2 tablespoons soy sauce
1 medium onion, thinly sliced
2 cloves garlic, minced
1 teaspoon dried cumin
1 teaspoon dried rosemary
Freshly ground black pepper
*1½ pounds lamb for shoulder or leg,
    cut into 1½-inch cubes*
2 medium onions, cut into eighths
*2 red or green bell peppers, seeded and
    cut into 1½-inch squares*

Equipment

*Large plastic container, stainless-steel bowl,
    or glass or enamel baking dish*
Medium bowl
4 metal skewers

1. In a medium bowl, combine the olive oil, red wine or sherry, lemon juice, soy sauce, onion, garlic, cumin, rosemary, and pepper.

2. Arrange the cubed lamb in a large plastic container, stainless-steel bowl, or glass or enamel baking dish.

Kebab-O-Rama

In addition to lamb, many other kinds of meat, poultry, and fish can be used to make great kebabs. Here are a couple of ideas to get you started.

■ 1½-inch pieces of boneless chicken thighs marinated in either the Asian or Wine-&-Herb marinade. Look for "roaster" thighs, which are bigger and meatier and hold up better on the grill. Grill for 7–8 minutes on each side.

■ 1½-inch chunks of swordfish or tuna, marinated in the Asian marinade. Grill for 6–7 minutes on each side.

■ 1½-inch pieces of sirloin or round steak, marinated in the Asian marinade. Grill for 7–8 minutes on each side.

3. Set aside ½ cup of the marinade for basting. Pour the rest over the lamb, mix well, cover, and refrigerate for at least 4 hours. Do not marinate the vegetables.

4. When the meat is ready, light the charcoal. While the coals are heating, assemble the skewers, alternating pieces of lamb with the onion and bell pepper.

5. When the coals are hot, cook the shish kebabs for 12–18 minutes, turning once after 7 minutes, until the meat is cooked through. During the last 5 minutes of cooking, baste the shish kebabs with the reserved marinade and turn the skewers frequently.

Serving Suggestion

Serve with rice pilaf and green salad.

Grilled Vegetables

Grilled vegetables make a colorful centerpiece when served on a platter or over rice. Many vegetables can be cooked on the grill right along with the main course. Others need to be skewered or cooked in a hinged grill. Vegetables must be cut specially to fit the skewers. The grill basket accommodates various sizes of vegetables, conveniently rests right on the barbecue grill, and can be turned easily for even cooking.

■ **Carrots** Cut into 2-inch pieces for skewers, in half lengthwise for the grill basket. Blanch in a large pot of boiling water for 5 minutes and then refresh with cold water. Brush lightly with oil before grilling for 6–8 minutes, turning once.

■ **Cherry Tomatoes** Marinate whole in vegetable oil along with ½ teaspoon each dried basil and dried rosemary. Place on a thin skewer and grill for 5 minutes, turning often.

■ **Corn** To roast with foil, husk the ears and wrap them in foil. Place on the grill for 12 minutes, turning 3 or 4 times. To roast without foil, husk the ears and rub lightly with butter. Grill for 8–10 minutes, turning often until they begin to brown.

■ **Mushrooms** Leave them whole, trimming only the bottom of the stem. Skewer through the stem with a thin metal or bamboo skewer, working slowly to keep the mushrooms from splitting, or place them in a hinged grill. Brush lightly with oil before grilling for 6–8 minutes, turning 3 or 4 times.

■ **Onions** Peel a medium onion and cut it into quarters, then cut each quarter in half crosswise. Skewer across the grain or place in a grill basket. Brush lightly with oil before grilling for 10–12 minutes, turning 2 or 3 times.

■ **Bell Peppers** Seed and cut into 2-inch squares for skewers, quarters for the grill basket. Brush lightly with oil before grilling for 8–10 minutes, turning 2 or 3 times.

■ **Potatoes** Use small new potatoes whole or cut large potatoes into 1½-inch cubes. Put the potatoes in a pot and cover them with cold water. Bring to a boil, reduce the heat, and let simmer until just barely cooked through, about 12 minutes. Immediately drain the potatoes and when they are cool enough to handle, place them on thin skewers or in a grill basket. Brush them lightly with oil before grilling for 10–12 minutes, turning 3 or 4 times.

■ **Summer Squash and Zucchini** Cut into 1-inch rounds for skewers, halve lengthwise for a grill basket. Brush lightly with oil or Italian salad dressing before grilling for 6–8 minutes, turning 3 or 4 times. (Skewer the rounds through the skin and grill them with the cut sides on the rack.)

Tip

Vegetables that take approximately the same amount of time to cook can be skewered or arranged in a grill basket together.

Asian Grilled Swordfish

Swordfish holds up well on the grill and is a nice change of pace from the usual barbecue fare. Marinate the steaks for no more than 2 hours and remove them from the grill when they are just cooked through and begin to flake.

Ingredients *(serves four)*

¼ cup soy sauce

2 tablespoons lemon juice

2 tablespoons sherry or sake

1 teaspoon sesame oil

1 clove garlic, mashed and chopped

1 teaspoon sugar

4 8-ounce swordfish steaks,
    1–1½ inches thick

Vegetable oil, for brushing on the grill rack

Equipment

Large plastic container or glass baking dish

Medium bowl

Barbecue brush

Large spatula

1. In a medium bowl, combine the soy sauce, lemon juice, sherry or sake, sesame oil, garlic, and sugar, then pour it over the fish. Cover the fish with plastic wrap and marinate for at least 30 minutes and no more than 2 hours, turning once.

2. Lay the fish in a large plastic container or glass baking dish.

3. Brush the grill rack with vegetable oil, and light the coals. When the fire is very

hot, lay the fish on the grill. Cook for about 5 minutes for 1-inch steaks, 6 minutes for 1½-inch steaks. Turn the fish carefully with a large spatula and grill until it begins to flake, about 5 minutes more.

Serving Suggestion

Serve with corn on the cob and rice.

Pork or Chicken Saté

An Indonesian specialty, these skewers of meat can be served as appetizers or a main course. The meat is cut into small pieces so it grills very quickly.

Ingredients *(serves six as an appetizer, four as a main course)*

½ medium onion, quartered

3 cloves garlic

1-inch piece lemon zest (yellow part of
    skin), finely chopped

1 tablespoon brown sugar

2 tablespoons fresh lemon juice

¼ cup soy sauce

1 tablespoon curry powder

1 pound boneless pork, cut into 1-inch
    cubes

OR

¾ pound skinless, boneless chicken breasts,
    cut into 2 x ½-inch strips

Peanut Dipping Sauce (recipe follows),
    for serving

Equipment

Medium bowl
Blender or food processor
*Approximately 24 bamboo or thin metal
  skewers*

1. Put all the ingredients (through curry powder) in a blender or food processor and purée. Transfer to a medium bowl.

2. Add the pieces of pork or chicken to the marinade and stir to coat the meat uniformly. Marinate at room temperature for 1 hour or in the refrigerator for at least 2 hours.

3. If using bamboo skewers, soak them in warm water for 1 hour before grilling.

4. Light the charcoal. While the coals are heating, place 1 chicken strip or 2 pork cubes on each skewer (the skewer should be inserted through the chicken lengthwise).

5. When the coals are ready, place the meat on the grill for 6–8 minutes for chicken, 10–12 minutes for pork, turning once. Serve hot with peanut dipping sauce.

Note

To make beef saté, cut a ½-inch-thick piece of sirloin into 4- or 5-inch strips. Marinate and place on skewers. Grill for 8–10 minutes, turning once.

Serving Suggestion

Accompany with rice pilaf and a few skewers of grilled vegetables.

Peanut Dipping Sauce

Ingredients

½ cup smooth "natural" peanut butter
¼ cup fresh lime juice
¼ cup water
2 tablespoons soy sauce
1 tablespoon honey
½ teaspoon sesame oil
1 whole clove garlic
½ teaspoon ground coriander

Equipment

Food processor or blender

Place all the ingredients in a food processor or blender and process until smooth. Serve at room temperature in individual dipping bowls.

Mary Cleaver's Boneless Chicken Breasts with Balsamic Vinegar & Rosemary

The New York caterer Mary Cleaver is a wonderful chef who makes light and intensely flavored food. Here is one of her favorite dishes for marinated, grilled chicken. The marriage of a few simple yet bold flavors is typical of Mary's food. I prepared this dish many times working in the Cleaver Co. kitchen and now make it for my family on our patio grill.

Ingredients *(serves four)*

¼ cup extra-virgin olive oil

¼ cup balsamic vinegar

4 cloves garlic, peeled and mashed

2 sprigs fresh rosemary or
    1 teaspoon dried

Freshly ground black pepper

2 whole boneless, skinless chicken breasts,
    cut in half

Equipment

Small bowl

*Plastic container or stainless steel or
    ceramic bowl*

Grill

1. Combine the oil, vinegar, garlic, rosemary, and pepper in a small bowl.

2. Rinse the chicken breasts in cold water and pat them dry. Place the chicken in a plastic container or stainless steel or ceramic bowl just large enough to hold them and pour on the marinade. Turn the chicken breasts to coat both sides with marinade. Cover and refrigerate for at least 6 hours and up to 24 hours.

3. Light the coals in the grill. When they are hot, place the chicken breasts on the rack and grill for 4–5 minutes. Turn the chicken, basting it with the marinade, and grill for 4–5 minutes more, until cooked through.

Serving Suggestion

Boneless breasts don't take up much room on the grill, so plan on grilling an assortment of skewered vegetables, such as bell peppers, tomatoes, and onions right alongside.

Cooking for a Crowd

Making dinner for 12 people is not much more work than making dinner for four. It's simplye a matter of roasting an 18-pound turkey instead of a 4-pound chicken, or putting 12 potatoes in the oven instead of four. Coming up with the extra seating might be more of a problem than preparing the extra food.

Cooking for a crowd does, however, require extra planning. It means leaving more time for preparation, choosing dishes that lend themselves to feeding larger numbers, and making sure you have large enough pans and serving platters for the quantity of food you're cooking and serving. The recipes included in this section will allow you to cook for eight to twelve guests without too much fuss. These entrées were chosen so that Dad can enjoy the company and not spend the whole night in the kitchen.

Baked Smoked Ham

There are a lot of advantages to serving a baked ham at a dinner party: It's easy to prepare, it goes a long way, and you can serve it either hot or at room temperature. And when you're done, you'll have the bone to make a great soup. Smoked hams are available in most supermarkets or at your local butcher. Even though these hams are smoked, they still need to be cooked through.

Ingredients *(serves twelve to sixteen)*

1 smoked ham, bone in, about 10 pounds
About 8 cups apple cider
1 cup brown sugar
2 tablespoons Dijon mustard
1½ cups bread crumbs

Equipment

Large roasting pan
Medium bowl

1. Preheat the oven to 350°F and position a rack in the lower third of the oven.
2. Place the ham, fat side down, in a large roasting pan and fill the pan halfway with apple cider. Place the pan on the lower rack of the oven and bake for 18 minutes per pound (3 hours for a 10-pound ham).
3. Meanwhile, combine the brown sugar, mustard, and bread crumbs in a medium bowl. Set aside.
4. When the ham is cooked, remove it from the oven (leave the oven on) and use a knife to trim off the skin and fat. Spread the bread crumb mixture on the surface of

Country Hams

Dry-cured country hams, like Smithfield hams, are available through the mail and come with specific cooking instructions. These hams have a somewhat sharper and more distinct flavor than smoked hams. Dry-cured hams need to be soaked in water for 12–24 hours to remove the curing salt, so be sure to leave yourself enough time.

the ham and bake for 30 minutes more, until the glaze is crusty. Let the ham sit for 10 minutes before slicing.
5. Slice the ham across the grain and straight down toward the bone. Serve topped with some of the pan juices.

Serving Suggestions

Serve the ham with mashed potatoes, baked sweet potatoes, or hash browns. (If you have a double oven you can make oven-fried potatoes.) Irish soda bread is also a great companion for ham. For vegetable accompaniments, consider corn on the cob, string beans, or carrots.

Dad's Own Chili

A great pot of chili with hot corn bread is always a crowd pleaser. Save yourself a bit of trouble and make it a day in advance. The extra time in the refrigerator will enhance its flavor.

Ingredients *(serves twelve)*

3 tablespoons corn or vegetable oil
1 large onion, diced
1 green bell pepper, diced

2 cloves garlic, chopped

2 pounds ground beef

*2 cups beef broth or 2 bouillon cubes
   dissolved in 2 cups water*

1 35-ounce can crushed tomatoes

3 tablespoons tomato paste

¼ cup chili powder (see Note)

2 teaspoons ground cumin

1 teaspoon dried oregano

1 teaspoon salt

¼ teaspoon cayenne pepper

1 16-ounce can red kidney beans, drained

Equipment

Large frying pan

Large soup pot

Colander

1. Place a large frying pan on *medium-high* heat and let it get hot, about 45 seconds. Add 1 tablespoon of the oil, then the onion and peppers, and sauté until soft, about 6 minutes. Add the garlic and sauté for 2 minutes more. Transfer the mixture to a large soup pot.

2. Increase the heat under the frying pan to *high* and let the pan get very hot, about 90 seconds. Add 1 tablespoon of the remaining oil and 1 pound of the ground beef. Brown the meat for about 6 minutes, then transfer it to a colander to let the fat drip off. Repeat with the remaining oil and beef. Transfer the meat to the soup pot.

3. Add the beef broth, crushed tomatoes, tomato paste, and all of the spices to the soup pot. Bring the mixture to a boil over *medium-high* heat, then reduce the heat to *low* and simmer for 45 minutes, stirring occasionally.

4. Add the beans and simmer for 15 minutes more, until the beans are heated through.

Note

The flavor and spiciness of standard supermarket-brand chili powders are usually much less robust than the flavor and spiciness of specialty chili powders, such as those from New Mexico.

Serving Suggestions

■ Prepare bowls of sour cream, grated Monterey Jack or cheddar, chopped bell pepper, crumbled cooked bacon, and chopped red onion, and let people add their own toppings.

■ Serve with corn bread (recipe on page 235) and a mixed green salad, or with fresh corn and French bread.

Variations

■ You can substitute ground turkey for any or all of the ground beef and end up with a tasty pot of reduced-fat chili.

■ Some chili aficionados assert that real chili features small chunks of beef instead of ground meat. If you're so inclined, cut 2 pounds chuck steak or round steak into small cubes and use in place of the ground beef.

Red Snapper Vera Cruz

The slightly sweet taste of red snapper combines wonderfully with the piquant tomato sauce in this effortless dish. Buy the freshest fillets you can lay your hands on.

Ingredients *(serves eight)*

2½ pounds red snapper fillets

*2½ tablespoons butter, melted, plus extra
   butter for greasing the baking dish*

Salt and pepper

2½ tablespoons olive oil

1¼ cups chopped onion

*1⅓ cans (28 ounces) of solid pack
tomatoes, with water*

6-ounce can tomato paste

1¼ tablespoons hot green chiles, chopped

1 tablespoon capers

1 teaspoon salt

⅛ teaspoon black pepper

½ cup Spanish green olives, for garnish

Sprigs of watercress, for garnish

Equipment

Shallow 10 x 13-inch baking pan
Basting brush
Large sauté pan

1. Preheat the oven to 350°F. Butter a shallow 10 x 13-inch baking pan.

2. Place the snapper fillets in a single layer in the pan, brush the fillets with the melted butter, and season with salt and pepper.

3. Bake for about 18–20 minutes or until the fish flakes easily when tested with a fork.

4. While the fish is baking, add the olive oil to a large sauté pan. Place the pan on *high* about 45 seconds. Add the chopped onion and sauté over *medium-high* heat until tender, about 5 minutes. Add the canned tomatoes, tomato paste, chiles, capers, salt and pepper. Simmer uncovered over *medium* heat for about 15 minutes.

5. When the fish is done, transfer it to a large serving dish. Pour the tomato sauce over the snapper, then garnish with olives and watercress.

Serving Suggestions

To complement this robust dish, serve mildly flavored side dishes, such as green beans, rice, or boiled new potatoes. Serve with salad.

Chicken Breasts with Prosciutto & Mozzarella

These luscious chicken bundles are first sautéed and then quickly finished in the oven. This recipe calls for a little too much cheese in the stuffing, which means it usually leaks out when it's baking—but I wouldn't have it any other way.

Ingredients *(serves eight)*

*4 large whole, skinless, boneless chicken
breasts, cut in half*

Salt and pepper

2 tablespoons dried basil

8 ounces mozzarella, grated

8 slices prosciutto or smoked ham

2 large eggs

2 cups Italian-style bread crumbs

2 tablespoons olive oil

1 tablespoon butter

*1 cup Basic Tomato Sauce (page 182) or
your favorite store-bought sauce*

2 tablespoons chopped fresh parsley

Equipment

Meat pounder
Platter
Medium bowl

Pie plate
Large frying pan
11 x 17-inch baking pan
Small saucepan

1. Preheat the oven to 350°F.

2. Using a meat pounder, flatten each chicken breast to a thickness of ¼ inch and arrange them on your worktable with the smooth outer side down. Season each breast lightly with salt and pepper and a pinch of the basil.

3. Place about 2 tablespoons of the grated mozzarella in the center of each breast, leaving a ½-inch margin all around. Lay a slice of prosciutto over the cheese.

4. Fold the breasts lengthwise, place on a platter, and set aside.

5. Beat the eggs in a medium bowl. Put the bread crumbs in a pie plate.

6. Dip each chicken bundle in the egg and then dredge it in the bread crumbs, holding it carefully to keep it from unfolding. Gently shake the bundle to release excess bread crumbs, then place it back on the platter, seam side down.

7. Place a large frying pan on *medium-high* heat and let it get hot, about 45 seconds. Add 1 tablespoon of the olive oil to the center of the pan and place ½ table-spoon of the butter in the pool of oil. When the butter stops sizzling, spread it around the pan and add 4 of the breasts, seam side down. Cook until the bottoms are lightly browned, about 2 minutes. Turn and cook 2 minutes more.

8. Transfer these bundles to the baking pan. Wipe out the frying pan with a paper towel and repeat with the remaining oil, butter, and breasts.

9. Place the chicken in the oven and bake until firm and springy to the touch, about 8 minutes.

10. While the chicken is baking, heat the tomato sauce in a small saucepan. Wash and dry the platter and arrange the cooked breasts on it. Top each one with a bit of tomato sauce and a sprinkling of parsley. Serve immediately.

Tip

The chicken breasts can be prepared through Step 4 up to a day ahead of time. Refrigerate, tightly covered, until ready to use.

Serving Suggestion

Serve with a simple pasta or rice pilaf and a vegetable, such as green beans, zucchini and tomatoes, or broccoli.

Jambalaya with Shrimp & Chicken

There are as many ways to make jambalaya as there are cooks in New Orleans. Start with this version and then create your own. There are lots of ingredients here, but there's not a lot of work.

Ingredients *(serves eight)*

> *1½ pounds boneless chicken thighs*
> *½ pound andouille or chorizo sausage (see Note) or smoked ham*
> *2 teaspoons salt*
> *2 teaspoons chili powder*
> *1 tablespoon dried oregano*

1 teaspoon garlic powder

1 teaspoon dried thyme

1 teaspoon paprika

1 teaspoon onion powder

½ teaspoon cayenne pepper

3 bay leaves

2 tablespoons corn oil

1 large onion, chopped

4 ribs celery, finely chopped

2 large green bell peppers, chopped

4 cloves garlic, minced

2 cups canned crushed tomatoes

1 cup Basic Tomato Sauce (page 182) or your favorite store-bought sauce

4 scallions, chopped

3 cups chicken broth or 3 bouillon cubes dissolved in 3 cups boiling water

3 cups white rice, uncooked

1 pound shrimp, peeled and deveined (see page 117)

Equipment

Small bowl

Large frying pan, preferably cast-iron

11 x 17-inch baking pan

1. Preheat the oven to 350°F.

2. Cut the chicken into ½-inch pieces. Cut the sausage or ham into ½-inch slices. Set aside.

3. Mix together all the spices through the cayenne pepper in a small bowl, add the bay leaves, and set aside.

4. Place a large frying pan, preferably cast-iron, over *high* heat and let it get very hot, about 1 minute. Add 1 tablespoon of the oil and the sausage pieces, and brown on all sides, about 3 minutes. Add the chicken pieces and cook until the chicken is brown, about 4 minutes. Transfer the

chicken and sausage, including any crunchy bits stuck to the bottom, to an 11 x 17-inch baking pan.

5. Put the frying pan back on *high* heat, add the remaining tablespoon of oil, and let it get hot, about 15 seconds. Add the onion, celery, and bell pepper, and cook, stirring often, until the vegetables just begin to brown, about 6 minutes. Add the garlic and cook for 1 minute more.

6. Reduce the heat to *medium* and add all the spices and the bay leaves. Cook for 3 minutes more, stirring continuously to keep the spices from sticking to the pan.

7. Add the tomatoes, tomato sauce, and scallions, and simmer for 8 minutes.

8. Add the broth or bouillon and increase the heat to *high*. Bring the liquid to a boil, then turn off the heat. Carefully transfer the contents of the frying pan to the baking pan.

9. Stir the rice and shrimp into the mixture in the baking pan. Cover the pan well with aluminum foil and bake until the rice is cooked through, about 25 minutes.

Note

Andouille and chorizo are both highly seasoned pork sausages. Andouille, French in origin, is a Cajun specialty. Chorizo is a specialty of Spain and Latin America. Both are usually sold at specialty food shops.

Tips

■ Jambalaya can be prepared through Step 8 the night before you plan to serve it. Let it cool. Cover and refrigerate. When you're ready to resume cooking, add an extra ½ cup broth to the mixture, bring to a boil, and continue with the recipe at Step 9.

■ If you don't feel like peeling and deveining the shrimp, buy them precleaned or substitute ½ pound smoked ham cut into chunks.

Serving Suggestion

Serve the jambalaya with a mixed green salad, lots of corn bread, cold lemonade, and beer.

Whole Roast Beef Tenderloin

Beef tenderloin is a pricey but easy entrée to cook for a crowd. Roasted to medium-rare perfection, it will instantly turn any gathering into a special occasion.

Ingredients *(serves twelve)*

1 beef tenderloin (3½–5 pounds), trimmed of fat and tied by the butcher
¼ cup Dijon mustard
3 cloves garlic, minced
1 2-inch piece fresh ginger, finely chopped
2 tablespoons soy sauce
Vegetable oil, for oiling the roasting rack
1 bunch watercress, for garnish
Chopped parsley, for garnish

Equipment

Small bowl
Roasting pan with rack

1. Preheat the oven to 500°F for ½ hour. Remove the meat from the refrigerator while the oven is preheating.

2. In a small bowl, combine the mustard, garlic, ginger, and soy sauce and set aside.

3. Line a roasting pan with a double layer of aluminum foil. Lightly oil a roasting rack and set it inside the roasting pan.

4. Place the meat on the rack and cover it with a thick coating of the mustard mixture.

5. Transfer the meat to the oven and roast to medium rare: 35 minutes for a 4-pound piece of meat; 42 minutes for a 5-pound piece of meat. Do not open the oven door while the meat is roasting.

6. Remove the meat from the oven and let it rest for 10 minutes before slicing. To serve, remove the strings and cut the meat across the grain into ¾-inch slices. Arrange the slices on a serving platter and top with some of the pan juices. Garnish with the watercress on the sides and a sprinkling of chopped parsley down the center of the meat.

Moroccan Veal, Sausage & Chicken with Couscous

This mild and delicious curry, sweetened with raisins, spooned over a bed of couscous, is an excellent introduction to Middle Eastern cuisine. A staple of North Africa, couscous is gaining popularity in the States. These grains of pasta take just a few minutes to prepare. Do not be intimidated by the list of ingredients. They all wind up in one big pot.

COOKING FOR A CROWD

Ingredients *(serves twelve)*

5 tablespoons vegetable oil

¾ pound Merguez sausages, cut into
1-inch pieces

1½ pounds veal shoulder or leg, cut into
1½-inch cubes

1½ pounds boneless, skinless chicken
thighs, cut into 1-inch pieces

1 large onion, halved and thinly sliced

4 cloves garlic, coarsely chopped

2 28-ounce cans crushed tomatoes

9 cups canned chicken broth or 9 bouillon
cubes dissolved in 9 cups of water

2 tablespoons mild curry powder

1 teaspoon ground cumin

1 teaspoon ground cinnamon

1 teaspoon salt

2 9-ounce packages frozen artichoke hearts

1 cup raisins

4 cups couscous

Equipment

Large frying pan
Slotted spoon
2 large casseroles with covers

1. Place a large frying pan on *high* heat and let it get very hot, about 90 seconds. Add 1 tablespoon of the oil and the sausage pieces and cook, stirring often, until they are browned on all sides, about 4 minutes. Using a slotted spoon, transfer the sausage to a large casserole.

2. Return the frying pan to *high* heat and add 1 tablespoon of the remaining oil and the veal. Cook, stirring often, until browned on all sides, about 4 minutes. Use the slotted spoon to transfer the veal to the casserole with the sausage.

3. Return the frying pan to *high* heat and add another tablespoon of the oil. Add the chicken and onion and cook, stirring often, until the chicken is browned on all sides, about 4 minutes. Add the garlic and cook 1 minute more.

4. Transfer the chicken mixture to the casserole and add the crushed tomatoes, 4 cups of the chicken broth or bouillon, the curry powder, cumin, cinnamon, and salt and stir well. Bring the mixture to a boil over *high* heat, then reduce the heat to *medium* and simmer, uncovered, for 20 minutes, stirring occasionally. Add the artichoke hearts and raisins and cook 10 minutes more. Turn off the heat and cover the casserole.

5. Make the couscous in another large casserole. Bring the remaining 5 cups chicken broth or bouillon and the remaining 2 tablespoons oil to a boil. Stir in the couscous, turn off the heat, cover the pot, and let the couscous sit for 5 minutes. Immediately fluff the couscous with a fork to help separate the grains.

6. To serve, transfer the couscous to a large platter and spoon on the curry, being sure that the sauce covers all the couscous.

Time-Saver

The veal, sausage, and chicken curry can be made up to 2 days in advance. Let the mixture cool before refrigerating. Reheat the casserole over *medium* heat for 10 minutes before making the couscous.

Note

Merguez is the traditional sausage of Morocco and gives this dish its distinctive flavor. You can find it at many specialty food stores.

Thanksgiving Dinner for Twelve

Holidays are an excuse for bringing this traditional fare to table. But the obligatory Thanksgiving bird can make a lot of people thankful any time of year. A turkey dinner requires advance planning, but your oven actually does most of the work. Make the stuffing and Dad's Own Apple Pie (page 216) the night before.

MENU

Roast turkey with Dad's own apple sausage Stuffing

Quick cranberry chutney

Candied sweet potatoes

Breads

Dad's own apple pie

COOKING FOR A CROWD

Roast Turkey

A bird this large is as simple to prepare as a small one, but it does take a long time to cook—about 4½ to 6 hours—so plan ahead. If you buy a frozen bird, you also need to allow time for it to defrost: about 3 to 4 hours per pound. Leave the turkey in its original wrapping and defrost on a tray in the refrigerator.

Ingredients *(serves sixteen)*

1 16–20 pound turkey

½ cup (1 stick) butter or margarine

2 oranges

Dad's Own Apple Sausage Stuffing (recipe follows), optional

1 large onion, peeled (if not stuffing turkey)

Rosemary sprigs (if not stuffing turkey)

Salt and pepper

Equipment

Small saucepan

Thin metal skewer or toothpicks

Large roasting pan

Cheesecloth

Bulb baster

1. Preheat the oven to 325°F.

2. Remove the giblets from the front and back cavities of the turkey. Rinse the inside and outside of the turkey thoroughly with cold water and pat dry with paper towels.

3. Melt the butter or margarine in a small saucepan and set aside.

4. Cut the oranges in half. Squeeze the juice of 1 orange into the large cavity and rub it around. Squeeze the juice of the second orange over the outside of the bird.

5. Fill the cavity loosely with the stuffing, if using and secure the opening with a thin metal skewer or toothpicks. If you're not stuffing the bird, leave the orange halves inside the cavity, along with a peeled onion and a couple of sprigs of rosemary. Salt and pepper the outside of the turkey.

6. Place the turkey, breast side up, in a large roasting pan. Cut a double layer of cheesecloth to cover the top and sides of the turkey. Dip the cheesecloth in the melted butter, and then drape it over the turkey. Drizzle on the remaining butter.

7. Roast the turkey for about 18 minutes per pound—basting with pan juices every 30 minutes after the first hour of cooking. The bird is done when a meat thermometer inserted in the thickest part of the thigh registers 180°F and the stuffing, if used, registers 165°F (A stuffed turkey may take longer to cook.) Remove the cheesecloth for the last ½ hour of cooking to allow the skin to crisp.

8. Remove the turkey from the oven and let it sit for 20 minutes before slicing. Remove all of the stuffing from the bird and serve it in a separate dish.

Note

To determine when the turkey is done without a meat thermometer, try moving the leg. If it feels loose and moves easily in the joint, the turkey is ready. Another way to tell is to prick the skin at the thigh. If the juices run clear, not pink, the turkey is done. Begin checking the turkey for doneness about 20 minutes before its allotted time.

Serving Suggestion

For a vegetable accompaniment, try cooked hubbard squash, string beans, cauliflower, or peas with cream and almonds.

Dad's Own Apple Sausage Stuffing

To save time on the day you are cooking the turkey, prepare the stuffing a day ahead and store it in an airtight container in the refrigerator. Do not stuff the bird until you are ready to put it in the oven.

Ingredients

(enough to stuff a 16- to 20-pound turkey)

3 large, tart apples, such as McIntosh or Macoun

1 pound sweet Italian sausage meat, crumbled

¼ cup (½ stick) butter

1 large onion, diced

1 small fennel bulb, diced (optional)

½ cup marsala or sherry

1 chicken bouillon cube

3 cups (about 5 slices)diced whole wheat bread

3 cups (about 5 slices) diced white bread

¼ cup chopped fresh parsley

1 teaspoon dried thyme

Salt and pepper

Equipment

Large frying pan
Colander
Large bowl

1. Core and coarsely chop the apples and set aside.

2. Place a large frying pan on *medium-high* heat and let it get hot, about 45 seconds. Add the sausage meat and cook, stirring constantly, until browned, about 4–5 minutes. Transfer the meat to a colander, let the fat drain off, then transfer it to a large bowl.

3. Wipe out the frying pan with a paper towel, return it to *high* heat, and add the butter. When the butter has melted, add the diced onions, chopped apples, and fennel, if using. Cook, stirring frequently, until soft, about 12 minutes. Add the marsala or sherry and the bouillon cube and cook until the bouillon is dissolved and the liquid is reduced by half, about 3 minutes. Transfer to the bowl with the sausage.

4. Add the diced bread, parsley, thyme, and salt and pepper to the bowl, and stir gently to combine. Let the mixture cool before stuffing the bird, or cover and refrigerate until ready to use.

Variations

■ Substitute 3 cups cooked white, brown, or wild rice for 3 cups of the diced bread.

■ Substitute 3 cups crumbled corn bread for 3 cups of the diced bread.

■ Substitute 1 cup chopped walnuts or pecans and ½ cup raisins for the sausage.

Time-Saver

If you don't have time to make your own stuffing from scratch, you can purchase bags of preseasoned bread crumbs, intended for stuffing making, in the grocery store. Follow the instructions on the bag but feel free to improvise a bit with your favorite ingredients. For example, if you like chestnuts or raisins in your stuffing, go ahead and add some.

Quick Cranberry Chutney

Fresh oranges and strawberry vinegar help to refine a Thanksgiving classic.

Ingredients *(serves twelve)*

1 seedless orange, cut into eighths
1 12-ounce package fresh cranberries
1 16-ounce can whole berry cranberry sauce
¼ cup dried currants
1 tablespoon strawberry or red wine vinegar

Equipment

Food processor
Baking pan
Medium bowl

1. Put the orange sections (with the skin) in the food processor fitted with the steel blade. Pulse a few times until the orange sections are very coarsely chopped.

2. Wash and drain the fresh cranberries, then dump them in the baking pan and sort through them, discarding any that are mushy.

3. Transfer the cranberries to the processor bowl along with the orange. Pulse until the cranberries are very coarsely chopped (roughly cut into thirds). Transfer the chopped cranberries and orange to a medium bowl.

4. Add the can of cranberry sauce, the currants, and vinegar, and mix together well. Refrigerate until ready to serve.

Candied Sweet Potatoes

Kids especially like this Thanksgiving treat topped with tiny marshmallows.

Ingredients *(serves twelve)*

3 tablespoons butter
10 medium-large sweet potatoes
1 cup brown sugar or 1⅓ cups real maple syrup
24 tiny marshmallows (optional)

Equipment

12 x 18-inch baking dish
Large bowl
Vegetable peeler

1. Preheat the oven to 375°F. Grease a 12 x 18-inch baking dish with 1 tablespoon of the butter.

2. Peel the sweet potatoes and cut them in half lengthwise. Cut each half into 1-inch pieces. Put the cut pieces in a bowl of cold water to keep them from turning brown as you finish cutting the rest.

3. Arrange the sweet potatoes in the prepared baking dish and top with the brown sugar or syrup. Cut the remaining 2 tablespoons butter into little pieces and dot the top of the potatoes with them.

4. Bake the sweet potatoes on the center rack of the oven for 1¼ hours or until the top is nicely browned and glazed. If using marshmallows, add them during the last 10 minutes of cooking.

How to Throw Your Own Cocktail Party

Cocktail parties are best attended, not hosted. But if you're feeling adventurous, filling your living room with friends can be a lot of fun. The food at a cocktail party should be simple, flavorful, and not too messy. Your memories of the party should be in your heart, not smeared into your upholstery.

Start the party early, about 6:30 or 7:00 PM, and figure it will last about two hours. Make it clear on the invitation that the guests are joining you for cocktails. This way they won't be expecting dinner. Plan to serve about six or seven appetizers, some to be passed, others to be set out in baskets or on platters.

You will need to set aside a couple of hours the day before to plan what you're serving, shop, and do some preliminary set up.

Here are some party tips from a pro:

Pace the food. The first 10 guests can wolf down all the shrimp, leaving none for those arriving fashionably late. Set the food out slowly, but be prepared for a rush around 30 minutes after the party starts. Hold one dish back until the second half of the party. This will keep the surprises coming.

Keep the bar simple. It's better to invest in a few high-quality wines and liquors than in lots of cheaper stuff.

Don't feel you have to serve your guests mountains of food. They'll probably be going out for dinner afterward. Rather, present them with a few distinct and interesting dishes. For a rough idea of the amount of food you will need, figure 1½ portions of each appetizer per person.

The Drinks

The caterer's rule of thumb for the bar is one drink per person per hour. What you stock the bar with depends on who's coming. A younger crowd will favor vodka, wine, beer, and sparkling water. Old groups savor their Scotch and martinis. If your guests are mostly friends, then you probably know what they like most.

The Basic Bar for 25 Guests

5 bottles white wine
(chilled)
5 bottles red wine
1 fifth Scotch
1 fifth vodka
1 fifth gin
8 ounces vermouth
2 liters tonic water
5 liters sparkling water
2 quarts orange juice
2 quarts grapefruit
juice
2 quarts cranberry
juice

Equipment for the Bar

Corkscrew
Pitchers for water and juice
Ice bucket and tongs
3 limes, cut into wedges
2 lemons, half cut
into wedges, half
cut into twists
10 pounds ice
Beer opener
Bucket for slop
(remnants of drinks)
Tub to keep back-up
ice and wine in
Stirrer
Cocktail napkins
50 glasses

Tips

You'll need a 4-foot table for the bar.

■ Most guests leave their glasses somewhere and then go back to the bar for a new one. For this reason, stock the bar with at least 2 glasses per person.

■ Open 2 bottles of white wine to start and the rest as you need it. Don't open any red wine until someone asks. There is a chance no one will. Here are a few wine suggestions:

■ **White wines** Robert Mondavi "Woodbridge" Sauvignon Blanc, Georges Duboeuf Chardonnay, and Fontana Candida Frascati

■ **Red wines** Sebastiani Zinfandel, Georges Duboeuf Beaujolais, and Lindemans "Bin 99" Pinot Noir

Simple Nibbles & Ethnic Edibles

Here's the easy way to lay out a great cocktail party spread with little fuss and only about an hour of shopping. Investigate your local gourmet shops, bakeries, restaurants, and ethnic food stores to see what they have in the way of dips and finger foods. Then assemble an assortment of international taste treats along with some American standbys. You will have little more to do than assemble what you bought on platters, and your guests will appreciate the variety of flavors. Quantities given assume you will be serving at least six appetizers.

Spring Rolls & Dim Sum

Order a variety of spring rolls and dim sum (Chinese appetizers) from your favorite Chinese restaurant. Reheat them in a 300°F oven and serve them with duck sauce and Chinese mustard. Also look for small steamed or baked buns, dumplings, or chunks of beef or chicken steeped in various spicy sauces (these can be served with toothpicks). Order 30 spring rolls for a party with 25 guests.

Guacamole

A good local Mexican restaurant might sell you some great guacamole. But it's also a cinch to make yourself. Cut open 3 very ripe California avocados, scoop out the flesh into a medium (preferably wooden) bowl, and mash it with a potato masher or large fork. Stir in 1 cup chopped tomatoes, ½ cup chopped red onion, 3 tablespoons chopped fresh cilantro, the juice of 2 limes, and salt and pepper to taste. Serve with 2 pounds of corn tortilla chips.

Miniature Quiches

Many gourmet shops, pastry shops, and local caterers sell a variety of mini quiches, such as onion, ham, broccoli, and mushroom, that are perfect for parties.

Just heat them on a baking sheet according to the shop's instructions and let them cool before serving, so they can be handled comfortably. Buy 30 mini quiches for 25 guests.

Pâté

Vegetable, liver, and other pâtés are readily available, both in supermarkets and gourmet shops, but the quality and taste vary widely. Be sure to sample before you buy. One and a half pounds will serve 25 guests. Serve the pâté on a small wooden cutting board with a sharp paring knife. Guests will cut what they want. Accompany with a basket of sliced French bread and/or pita triangles and a bowl of grainy Dijon mustard.

Dolmas & Spanakopita

Dolmas are savory stuffed foods and among the most common are little grape leaf packets stuffed with rice, spices, and sometimes ground lamb. They are available in better supermarkets and at shops featuring Middle Eastern specialties. Spanakopita (spinach pies) are available in Greek bakeries. Cut them in half or quarters, depending on the size. Buy 40 dolmas and 12 spanakopita.

Tapenade & Pesto

Tapenade is a dip made from puréed olives, capers, anchovies, olive oil, and fresh basil and other seasonings. Pesto is a mixture of fresh basil, Parmesan, olive oil, and pine nuts. Both dips go well with crudités and small rounds of French bread. One and a half pounds will be enough for 25.

Pizza Rotolo

Available in some pizza shops and Italian specialty stores, this is a hearty and filling appetizer. It's basically pizza crust rolled around spicy ham, salami, provolone, and roasted peppers. Cut into ¼-inch slices and arrange on a platter. About two pounds will serve 25 guests.

Salmon Caviar

Cheap caviar *tastes* like cheap caviar. But fresh salmon roe is very palatable and not too pricey. Look for bright, glistening orange eggs that are round and full with no shriveling. Serve in a small ceramic bowl set in a larger bowl of ice. Accompany with melba toast and a small bowl of sour cream. Three-quarters of a pound will suffice.

Goat Cheese Pita Pizza

Crumble goat cheese on pita rounds and heat them in a 325°F oven just until the cheese melts, about 10 minutes. Let them cool slightly before serving. Goat cheese works well because it doesn't run and it tastes good warm.

Barbecued Chicken Wings

Buy the best quality barbecue sauce you can find and marinate the wings for 4 hours in the refrigerator. Cook as described in the recipe for Jerk Chicken Wings on page 277. Serve at room temperature.

Hummus or Baba Ghanoush with Pita Triangles

Find a local gourmet shop that makes really great dips. Buy about 2 pounds of hummus or baba ghanoush and set it in a bowl next to a basket of pita bread cut into cracker-size triangles.

Shrimp & Cocktail Sauce

Spring for 2 pounds of cleaned and cooked shrimp from your local fish store. It'll save a lot of time. Accompany with homemade cocktail sauce (page 282).

Cheese & Crackers

Set out a selection of 1-pound chunks of 3 or 4 different cheeses and a basket of assorted crackers. Remember that some guests will go for the soft and semisoft cheeses while others will stick to hard cheese. For many suggestions on what cheese to serve consult the Cheese Primer on page 280.

A Menu for a Fancy Cocktail Party for 25

If you're up for it, you may want to prepare some of these more elegant appetizers, which are sure to impress even the most jaded party goer. Be forewarned: This fancy party menu takes time. You'll need a few hours the day before to do the shopping, and plan to spend most of the day of the party preparing the food. You'll also need some help in the kitchen and one waiter to replenish the hors d'oeuvres. Usually kids love to be part of the action, so enlist their help in passing the trays of hors d'oeuvres. The shopping list and the timetable are to help keep you on track.

MENU

Fresh salsa & chips

Sopressata or dried salami with French bread

Crudités with sun-dried tomato & roasted red pepper dip

Jerk chicken wings

Shrimp & cocktail sauce

Melon & prosciutto

Salmon hash in endive

HOW TO THROW YOUR OWN COCKTAIL PARTY

The Timetable

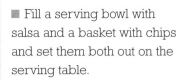

A Few Days Before the Party
■ Purchase the liquor, wine, mixers, juices, lemons, limes, plastic glasses, and cocktail napkins for the bar.
■ Make sure you have the necessary platters on hand. If not, borrow some.
■ If you're not using plastic cups, make sure you have enough glasses for the bar.

The Day Before the Party
■ Do all your shopping.
■ Marinate the chicken wings.

The Morning of the Party
■ Make the crudité dip and refrigerate.
■ Make the salmon hash and refrigerate.
■ Shell and devein the shrimp. This takes a lot of time; try to find someone to help you.
■ Cook the shrimp and refresh them under cold water. Drain well, cover tightly, and refrigerate.
■ Make the cocktail sauce.

■ Blanch, then refrigerate any crudité vegetables that require it.
■ Make the salsa and refrigerate.

3 Hours Before the Party
■ Slice the sopressata or salami and the French bread. Arrange the salami on one side of the basket and the bread on the other. Cover everything with a lightly damp paper towel.
■ Bake the chicken wings.
■ Cut the melon into chunks.
■ Set up the bar.

2 Hours Before the Party
■ Arrange the crudités on a platter, cover it with a damp paper towel, and leave it at room temperature.
■ Put toothpicks in about 15 shrimp and arrange them on a lettuce-lined platter with a bowl of cocktail sauce. Cover the shrimp with a slightly damp paper towel.
■ Fill a small bowl with dip and set the crudité platter on the serving table.

■ Fill a serving bowl with salsa and a basket with chips and set them both out on the serving table.
■ Finish cooking the chicken wings under the broiler. Arrange a dozen or so on a platter lined with lettuce. Set the rest aside at room temperature, uncovered.
■ Assemble the melon and prosciutto.
■ Assemble the salmon hash and endive.

During the Party
■ Replenish the trays as needed.

1. Soak the sun-dried tomatoes in hot water in a small bowl for 2 hours or until soft.

2. Remove the tomatoes from the liquid, reserving the liquid, and place them in a blender or the bowl of a food processor fitted with the steel blade. (The processor works best for this.)

3. Add the rest of the ingredients and process until the mixture is smooth, 1–2 minutes. Add a bit of the liquid from the tomatoes if the dip seems too thick.

4. Transfer the dip to a decorative serving bowl and serve with crudités.

Fresh Salsa & Chips

Ingredients *(serves twenty-five)*

2 pounds plum tomatoes, quartered

1 large red onion, quartered

1 green bell pepper, seeded and quartered

2 cloves garlic, mashed

Juice of 2 limes

4 tablespoons finely chopped fresh cilantro, or 1 tablespoon dried

1 tablespoon chili powder

1 teaspoon salt

½ teaspoon cayenne pepper

2 pounds tortilla chips

Equipment

Food processor or blender

Medium bowl

1. Put the tomatoes, onion, bell pepper, and garlic in the bowl of your food processor fitted with the steel blade. (The vegetables will process evenly if they are all cut into approximately the same size pieces.) Pulse about 4 times until the vegetables are coarsely chopped.

2. Transfer the vegetables to a medium bowl. Stir in the lime juice, cilantro, chili powder, salt, and cayenne pepper.

3. Transfer the salsa to a decorative serving bowl. Serve with a large bowl of tortilla chips.

Jerk Chicken Wings

These wings have a real Jamaican flavor. The list of ingredients is long, but the cooking is easy.

Ingredients *(serves twenty-five)*

1 cup water

½ cup ketchup

½ cup malt vinegar

¼ cup white wine vinegar

¼ cup vegetable oil

4 tablespoons Pickapeppa or Worcestershire sauce

¼ cup tomato paste

¼ cup sugar

3 tablespoons salt

1 tablespoon garlic powder

1 tablespoon onion powder

2 teaspoons ground allspice

1 teaspoon cinnamon

1 teaspoon freshly ground black pepper
½ teaspoon Tabasco sauce
Dash of cayenne pepper

4 pounds chicken wings
Margarine or cooking spray, for greasing the pan
Lettuce leaves, for lining the serving platter

Equipment
Medium bowl
Large plastic container
11 x 17-inch baking pan

1. Mix together all the ingredients (except the chicken wings and lettuce) in a medium bowl.

2. Put the chicken wings in a large plastic container and cover with the marinade. Stir so that all the wings are coated. Refrigerate, well covered, for 24 hours.

3. Preheat the oven to 375°F. Line an 11 x 17-inch baking pan with aluminum foil and lightly grease the foil with margarine or cooking spray.

4. Arrange as many wings as will fit in the pan in 1 layer. Bake for 20 minutes.

5. Remove the wings from the oven and turn on the broiler.

6. Broil the wings 5 inches from the flame until they brown, about 5 minutes. Turn and broil for 3 minutes more. Repeat with the remaining wings.

7. To serve, line a platter with lettuce and arrange the wings on top.

Note
Have plenty of cocktail napkins on hand.

Salmon Hash in Endive

A variation of the exquisite snapper hash served at Zarela, my favorite Mexican restaurant in New York.

Ingredients *(serves twenty-five)*
15 ounces high-quality canned Sockeye or red salmon
1 small red onion, finely chopped
½ green bell pepper, finely chopped
2 scallion greens, finely chopped
¼ cup of your favorite bottled salsa
1 clove garlic, minced
1 teaspoon chili powder
Salt
Dash of cayenne pepper
1 lime, halved
6 medium Belgian endive

Equipment
2 medium bowls

1. Drain the salmon and place it in a medium bowl. Carefully pull the meat apart to expose the backbone. Remove this, along with any other bones or pieces of skin. Working with a little at a time, flake the salmon into a second medium bowl, removing any remaining bits of bone or skin.

2. Add the onion, bell pepper, scallion greens, salsa, garlic, chili powder, salt to taste, and cayenne pepper, and mix together. Squeeze on the lime juice and mix well.

Refrigerate the mixture until ready to fill the endive spears.

3. Trim about ½ inch off the base of each head of endive and separate the spears. Use only the first few layers, those that are about 4 inches long. The smaller, inner leaves should be saved for salad.

4. Place a scant teaspoon of salmon hash in each endive spear, about a third of the way up from the bottom. Arrange the spears on a platter and serve. If desired, place a fresh flower, such as a lily or rose, in the center of the platter for decoration.

Melon & Prosciutto

This version of the traditional Italian appetizer, which appears on page 156, is easy to adapt for a crowd. Serving it on bamboo skewers makes an attractive hors d'oeuvre that doesn't require a plate.

Ingredients *(serves twenty-five)*

2 large cantaloupes or 1 large honeydew
½ pound prosciutto or Black Forest ham, thinly sliced
2 limes, halved

Equipment

6-inch bamboo skewers or frilled toothpicks
Large plastic container

1. Cut the melons in half, scoop out the seeds, and cut each half lengthwise into 3 sections.

2. With a paring knife, cut the flesh from the rinds and slice each section into 1-inch pieces.

3. Wrap each piece of melon with ½ slice of prosciutto. Pin the prosciutto in place with a skewer or toothpick.

4. Refrigerate the melon and prosciutto in a large covered plastic container until ready to serve. Squeeze lime juice over the melon before arranging on a platter.

HOW TO THROW YOUR OWN COCKTAIL PARTY

Cheese Primer

Most cheese is made by heating milk to separate the curd from the whey. Enzymes or acids are added to the curd, which is then shaped and allowed to harden. This can take a couple of hours, a few months, or a year or more, depending on the type of cheese. The flavor of cheese depends on the kind of milk used (cow, goat, or sheep), the different cultures that are added, and how it is aged. At right is a chart showing some of the more common cheeses. A store with a large cheese department will surely let you taste a number of different kinds so you can widen your appreciation.

Cheese Wisdom

■ **Storing:** Cheese should be stored well wrapped in plastic in the refrigerator. The exception is feta cheese, which should be stored covered in water. Softer cheeses generally last 3–5 days if they are properly stored. Harder cheeses can be stored much longer. Discard any moldy sections of a piece of cheese about $1/2$ inch beyond the point where the mold ends. Discard the entire piece of cheese if it tastes distinctly bitter.

■ **Freezing:** Cheese can be frozen, but it loses some of its flavor and texture so once frozen it is best used for cooking or melting. Cut it into pieces of one pound or less and wrap each piece in aluminum foil.

■ **Buying:** Look for cheese with a smooth, even texture. There should be no evidence of hard, dry spots or cracking or green mold. Packaged cheese in the supermarket should have no liquid inside. Check the expiration date.

■ **Grating:** Hard cheeses grate easily. If you need to grate a soft cheese, put it in the freezer for a few hours before grating. It is best to grate cheese or slice it thinly before melting.

HOW TO THROW YOUR OWN COCKTAIL PARTY

	Flavor	Color	Texture	Uses	Melts
American	Mild	Usually yellow, sometimes white	Semisoft slices	Sandwiches, cubed, or sliced for salads	Yes
Blue	Very sharp, pungent, and tangy	White with blue or green streaks	Firm and crumbly	Crumble in salads and egg dishes	No
Brie	Mild, with a bit of tanginess	White	Soft and creamy with firm, edible rind	Snacking, melted on fancy hors d'oeuvres, sandwiches	Yes
Camembert	Mild, with subtle pungency	White	Very soft and creamy with gray-ish edible rind	Snacking, cooking, sandwiches	No
Cheddar	Mild to extra sharp, depending on style	Yellow or white	Firm	Snacking, cooking, sandwiches, salads	Yes
Colby	Moderately tangy	Yellow	Firm	Snacking, cooking	Yes
Cottswold	Sharp and tangy, enhanced with herbs	Deep yellow with flecks of chives	Hard	Elegant snacking, cooking	Yes
Edam	Mild, slightly tangy	Pale yellow	Firm	Snacking, cooking, sandwiches	Yes
Feta	Sharp, pungent, domestic is milder	White	Firm and crumbly	Salads, omelets	Yes
Gouda	Mild, slightly nutty flavor	Pale yellow	Firm	Snacking, cooking, sandwiches	Yes
Goat	Earthy, smoky, pungent	White	Semisoft	Cooking, snacking, salads	Yes
Gruyère	Strong, pungent	Cream	Firm	Cooking, snacking, sandwiches	Yes
Jarlsberg	Mildly tangy	Pale yellow	Firm	Sandwiches, snacking	Yes
Monterey Jack	Medium sharp	White	Firm	Cooking, snacking, sandwiches	Yes
Mozzarella	Mild	White	Semisoft	Sandwiches, pizza, salads, pasta	Yes
Meunster	Bland to sharp	Pale yellow	Semisoft	Sandwiches, snacking	Yes
Romano	Strong, pungent	Light yellow	Hard, crumbly	Grating, cooking	No
Parmesan	Strong, earthy	Light yellow	Hard, crumbly	Grating, cooking	No
Saga Blue	Sharp, slightly sweet	White with green/blue streaks	Semisoft	Snacking	No
St. André	Rich, mildly tangy	White	Semisoft, creamy	Elegant snacking	No
Swiss	Medium-sharp	Light yellow	Firm	Sandwiches, snacking, cooking	Yes
Talleggio	Mild, tangy	White	Semisoft	Snacking	No

Shrimp & Cocktail Sauce

Cocktail parties and shrimp seem to be synonymous. Upon arrival, after hitting the bar, most guests start scoping out the shrimp. Why disappoint them? Buy large or jumbo shrimp. To save time, buy shrimp shelled and deveined at your local fishmonger.

Ingredients *(serves twenty-five)*

2½ pounds large shrimp (31–35 per pound)
1½ cups ketchup
2 tablespoons bottled red horseradish, or more to taste
1 small red onion, grated
Juice of 1 lemon
Dash of Tabasco sauce, or more to taste
1 teaspoon garlic powder
½ teaspoon paprika
Lettuce leaves, for lining the serving platter

Equipment

Paring knife
1 or 2 plastic containers
Large pot
Colander

1. Clean and devein the shrimp as described on page 117, making sure to keep the shrimp cold while you're cleaning them. After they're cleaned, refrigerate immediately in a well-sealed plastic bag or container.

2. Mix together the ketchup, horseradish, onion, lemon juice, Tabasco, garlic powder, and paprika in a small serving bowl. Refrigerate until ready to serve.

3. Bring 6 quarts water to a boil in a large pot.

4. Add the shrimp all at once to the boiling water and stir briefly to separate. Cook for 3 minutes, then remove one shrimp from the water and cut it in half. If it is opaque in the center it is done. If it's not cooked through, check the shrimp again in 20 seconds.

5. When the shrimp are done, drain immediately in a colander, then rinse briefly under cold water to stop the cooking process. Transfer the shrimp to a clean plastic container, cover, and refrigerate until ready to serve.

6. To serve, line a serving platter with large leaves of clean lettuce. Put the serving bowl of sauce in the center of the platter. Put toothpicks in the shrimp and arrange them on the platter.

Throwing a Birthday Party for Your Child

This year *you* are going to throw your child a birthday party—cake, decorations, games— the works. And as your child throws her arms around you at the news, for a moment, you are truly tops.

From planning the theme and games together to decorating the house and cake, you and your birthday girl (or boy) share the anticipation and excitement. Even the big day goes smoothly because you planned out everything in advance (*Dad's Timetable*) and kept the party short (*Party Tips*). And the smile on her face when you bring out the "cake that Dad made" makes it all worthwhile.

Party Themes

A theme for a party can be just about anything, including favorite superheroes, characters from a well-loved book, animals, or a favorite sport. Let the theme influence all aspects of the party. If it's a dinosaur party, for example, play Pin the Tail on the Dinosaur and get some dinosaur cookie cutters and cut cookies or sandwiches into dinosaur shapes. You can even put little dinosaurs on the birthday cake. If it's an alphabet party (a good idea for very young kids), make letter-shaped cookies and let each child try to spell his or her name. Have extra cookies on hand so kids with short names don't feel cheated.

Activity Ideas

Create a large mural

Get some plain brown wrapping paper and tape a long sheet of it to the floor. Give each kid an assigned space on the paper and some colored pencils, crayons, stickers, or stencils.

Musical chairs

You need space for this. Make a circle of chairs with the seats facing out, one for each kid, less one. Play the piano or put some fun music on the stereo and have the kids walk around the chairs until you stop the music suddenly. The child who's left without a chair is out. The rounds continue until only one child is left sitting. Have a prize ready for the winner.

Make a large collage

Buy a roll of transparent contact paper. Remove the backing, lay the paper, sticky side up on the floor, and tape it down at the edges. Get out the big bag of stuff you've collected over the past few weeks—bits of yarn, bottle caps, string, small pieces of colored paper, foreign coins, and pictures from magazines. Have the kids sit along the length of the contact paper and stick on their items of choice.

For Older Children

If your child is older (6–10) you might consider taking her or him with invited friends to a roller-skating rink, a bowling alley, an ice skating rink, or a local museum or sports event. Then return home for cake, ice cream, and presents. Be sure to have at least one other adult with you to help drive and to keep the high spirits from getting out of control.

Party Bags

However you do it, all the kids who come to the party should go home with a little present. It's called a "party bag." It can be filled with lots of little trinkets and candy, a small toy, or a book. Hand these to the kids as they are on their way out the door.

Make your own music videos

(You'll need a video camera for this one.) On the invitation, ask each child to bring a cassette of a favorite song (s)he knows very well. Provide a box full of costume pieces—old clothes, hats, and accessories—for the kids to put on, and find a neutral background. Set up the camera and cassette player and let the kids sing along or lip-sync the songs as they move to the music.

Hold backyard races

If you have a backyard, set up lots of relay races, two-legged races, potato sack races, and obstacle courses.

Set up a treasure hunt

Kids love treasure hunts with lots of clues—enlist a few neighbors to have clues hidden on their porches or in their yards.

Pass the parcel

Get a small gift for each child, for example, a box of decorated Band-Aids, a Matchbox car, magnets, crayons, flip books, or playing cards. Wrap 1 item, then wrap the second item with the first, then the third with the first 2, and continue until all presents are wrapped in 1 large package. The kids sit in a circle and unwrap the parcel 1 layer at a time and keep the toy they unwrap. The last toy should be special as the last kid has to wait the longest.

Make body puzzles

Get a few rolls of brown wrapping paper and spread out kid-sized sheets of it on the floor. Have the kids lie on the paper on their backs and ask an adult to trace their outlines with a crayon. Have the kids color their own figures. Then have the adults cut out the figures and then cut the figures into 6 or 7 large sections. The kids now have puzzles of their bodies. Mix up the pieces and have a race to see who can reassemble themselves the fastest.

Birthday Party Tips

■ Keep the food simple. The kids are usually too excited to eat much and the majority of molecules in their bodies are focused on the cake and ice cream anyway.

■ Keep the party short: $2^1/2$ hours maximum. After that the kids start getting cranky.

■ Come up with a theme for the party; it makes decorating easier and allows you to be inventive about coordinating the games and food with the décor.

■ If you are serving ice cream (and what birthday party would be complete without it?), save a lot of aggravation by preparing it ahead of time in the following manner. Put a scoop of ice cream in a muffin tin liner (one per child) and lay the muffin liners on a cookie sheet. Refreeze quickly, then cover the entire sheet with plastic wrap. When it's dessert time, empty 1 scoop on each plate with the cake or in a bowl for sundaes.

THROWING A BIRTHDAY PARTY FOR YOUR CHILD

Timetable for a One O'Clock Party

4–5 Weeks Before the Party

Decide on the location and theme for the party. Send out invitations.

2 Weeks Before the Party

Get all the paper plates, tablecloths, candles, and plasticware you need. Decide on what activities and games you want to play and buy any supplies you need. This is also a good time to enlist a neighborhood teenager or favorite babysitter to help out at the party.

2 Days Before the Party

Prepare your shopping list and shop for the food and party favors. Remember all of the ingredients necessary for cake, frosting, and toppings.

1 Day Before

Bake the cake and frost.

The Day of the Party

9:00 Make the food. Do all the chopping and crumbling, and make the ice cream scoops. Be sure anything that needs defrosting has been attended to.

11:00 Decorate the space, setting new trends in your work with balloons and rolls of crepe paper. Set the lunch table. Make sure your table is well protected with a tablecloth.

1:00 The guests start arriving. Collect the gifts, making sure cards are firmly attached so you can help your child write thank-yous. Put the gifts out of the way until later.

1:15 Get the activities started. If you are having entertainment of any kind— a clown, a pony, a video— this is when it should happen.

2:00 Serve lunch.

2:30 Serve dessert and the birthday cake. The party photographer (maybe Mom will volunteer for this job) should get in position for the blowing-out of the candles.

3:00 Open gifts and hand out the party bags.

3:30 Make sure each of your child's friends leaves with his or her parent or other responsible adult.

3:45 Pop a video in the VCR for your child to watch. Give yourself a pat on the back and collapse.

Party Food

The highlight of a birthday party is always the cake. However, if you want to feed the kids a little something before dessert, here are ideas for the munchies and the main course.

Munchies

Try to keep the chips to a minimum; instead, serve bowls of air-popped popcorn and low-salt pretzels as well as fun-to-eat fruits like grapes, bananas, and berries.

Pizza

The most popular party food to serve both the kids and their parents. You can make the pies yourself (see page 237) or order in. Be sure you have plenty of plain slices for the kids who don't like extra toppings. Figure on 1½ slices per child.

Turkey Tacos

Follow the directions on the back of the taco seasoning packet but use ground turkey instead of ground beef. Put out bowls of shredded lettuce, chopped tomato, shredded cheese, and mild salsa, and let the kids build their own tacos. This can get messy, but it's also a lot of fun.

Design Your Own Cupcakes

Make a batch of cupcakes using the birthday cake batter as explained on pages 289–90 and vanilla frosting, page 291. Set out bowls of toppings—chocolate chips, M&Ms, nuts, and sprinkles—and let the kids decorate their own cakes.

Sandwiches

Get some brown lunch bags and write the kids' names on them. Fill each bag with a peanut butter-and-jelly, tuna salad, turkey, or cheese sandwich (preferably on whole wheat bread), a small bag of trail mix, and an apple. Put a little toy in the bag, like they do at the fast-food chains, and the kids will be thrilled.

Barbecued Hamburgers & Hot Dogs

An outdoor barbecue is a great idea provided, of course, your child was born in the spring of summer. If your grill station

THROWING A BIRTHDAY PARTY FOR YOUR CHILD

Make your Own Sundaes

The sundae bar is always a favorite at parties. Put a paper cloth down on the table and set up little bowls full of sundae toppings: sprinkles, chocolate syrup, broken-up Oreos, chopped Reese's peanut butter cups, M&Ms, nuts, raisins, sliced strawberries, whipped cream, cherries, etc. Drop a scoop of ice cream into each bowl and let the kids proceed down the table concocting their own monstrosities. Plan to do this right before the end of the party so the kids are already heading home when the sugar starts pulsing through their veins.

isn't protected from the rain, have a back-up plan ready (for instance, the telephone number of the nearest pizza parlor).

Lasagna

This is a great party food because it can be made weeks ahead of time and frozen until the day of the party. See page 184 for the recipe.

Beverages

If you can get away with it, skip the soda; instead, have plenty of milk (regular and chocolate) and all-natural fruit juice on hand. And don't forget the straws!

The Birthday Cake

You don't have to make a cake from scratch to make your child's birthday party terrific (with all the excitement, the kids won't know the difference). Buy a cake mix (one box will yield two layers), and take the extra five minutes to make your own frosting (recipe follows). But there is a certain pride in making your *own* cake. Bake it the night before the party so you have energy for the sugar highs of the next day.

Primo Birthday Cake

This is the perfect birthday cake because it's foolproof and can be decorated just about any way imaginable. With the same batter you can also make cupcakes or a sheet cake. Directions for the variations are given at the end of the recipe.

Ingredients *(makes one 3-layer cake)*

4 large eggs

1¼ cups (2½ sticks) butter or margarine, at room temperature, plus extra for greasing the cake pans

2 cups sugar

2 teaspoons vanilla extract

3 cups cake flour

3 teaspoons baking powder

1 teaspoon salt

1 cup milk

Equipment

3 9-inch round cake pans (disposable aluminum pans are fine)

2 medium bowls
Small bowl
Large bowl
Hand-held electric mixer
Whisk
Large rubber spatula
Cake tester or toothpick
Cooling racks

1. Preheat the oven to 350°F.

2. Place a 9-inch round cake pan on a piece of wax paper and trace around the bottom with a pencil. Cut out the circle, then repeat 2 more times for a total of 3 circles. Butter 3 9-inch round cake pans. Lay the wax paper circles in the cake pans, and lightly butter them.

3. Separate the eggs, putting the whites in a medium bowl and the yolks in a small bowl.

4. In a large bowl, using a hand-held electric mixer on medium-low speed, cream the butter, 1½ cups of the sugar, and the vanilla until light and fluffy, about 4 minutes. Add the egg yolks in 2 additions, beating well after each addition. Rinse and dry the beaters.

THROWING A BIRTHDAY PARTY FOR YOUR CHILD

About Separating Eggs

Have two bowls, one for the whites and one for the yolks. Crack the egg neatly in the center and hold it over a bowl to receive the whites. The yolk should rest in the bottom half of the shell. Gently roll the yolk from the bottom shell to the empty top half, letting the white spill off into the bowl. Pass the yolk from shell to shell, until all the white has dropped off. Put the yolk in another bowl. Be careful not to break the yolk. Even a drop of egg yolk mixed with the whites will keep the whites from beating up properly.

5. In a second medium bowl, whisk together the cake flour, baking powder, and salt.

6. Using a hand-held electric mixer on low speed, beat the egg whites until foamy and opaque, about 30 seconds. Raise the speed to medium and continue beating until very soft peaks begin to form. In a slow, steady stream, add the remaining ½ cup sugar and continue beating until firm (but not stiff) peaks form.

7. Using a large rubber spatula, alternately fold the flour mixture and the milk into the butter mixture in 3 additions each. Do not mix the batter vigorously.

8. When the flour and milk have been incorporated, use a rubber spatula to gently fold in the beaten egg whites in 3 additions (see Note).

9. Divide the batter among the 3 prepared cake pans and bake on the center rack of the oven for about 25 minutes, until a toothpick or cake tester inserted in the center comes out clean. If the cakes don't all fit on one oven rack, the cake on the top rack may take a bit longer.

10. Let the cakes cool on racks for 1 hour before removing them from the pans. Let the cakes cool another 30 minutes before frosting.

Variations

■ To make cupcakes, lightly grease a cupcake tin and insert paper liners. Fill the liners ⅔ of the way to the top with batter and bake for 21 minutes. Let the cupcakes cool completely before frosting. This recipe makes 24 cupcakes.

■ To feed a larger group, this batter can easily be turned into a sheet cake. *First, increase all the ingredients 1½ times.* Instead of using 3 round cake pans, use an 11 x 17-inch baking pan. Prepare the baking pan in the same way, by greasing the pan with butter or margarine, laying on a sheet of wax paper cut to fit inside, and lightly greasing the wax paper. Bake for the same amount of time, 25 minutes. Test for doneness with a toothpick or cake tester. Let the cake cool completely, at least 1 hour. Then run a butter knife around the edge of the cake, loosening it from the pan. Lay the bottom of a second baking pan of equal size over the cake and then invert. Cut a piece of cardboard the same size as the cake and place it over the cake. Invert the cake onto the cardboard. It's now ready for frosting. This rectangular cake can be easily decorated to look like a football field, basketball or volleyball court, or dinosaur play area.

Note

After you whip the egg whites, it is important to incorporate them into the batter without causing them to lose all the air you have beaten into them. You must add them slowly, or "fold" them in, using a large rubber spatula. As you add the egg whites to the batter, move the spatula continuously in a slow, steady motion down the edge of the bowl and up through the center, until the egg whites are completely incorporated.

Luscious Chocolate Frosting

Ingredients *(enough for a 3-layer cake)*
   5 ounces semisweet chocolate
   ½ cup (1 stick) butter, at room temperature
   4 cups confectioners' sugar, sifted
   ½ teaspoon salt
   6 tablespoons heavy cream
   2 teaspoons vanilla extract

Equipment
   Double boiler or saucepan and stainless-steel bowl to fit on top
   Medium bowl
   Hand-held electric mixer
   Sifter

1. Melt the chocolate in the top of a double boiler or in a stainless-steel bowl set in a saucepan filled with 3 inches of very gently simmering water, stirring the chocolate frequently as it melts. Remove the chocolate from the heat and set aside.

2. In a medium bowl, using a hand-held electric mixer on medium speed, beat the butter until light and fluffy. Add the melted chocolate. Gradually beat the sifted sugar into the butter mixture until fully incorporated. Beat in the salt, heavy cream, and vanilla.

3. Gradually beat in the remaining 1 cup sugar until the frosting is smooth and spreadable.

Quick Vanilla Frosting

Young kids tend to like their frosting in different colors, for example, lime green and pale pink. All it takes is a few drops of food coloring, so go ahead and indulge your child's fancy.

Ingredients *(enough for a 3-layer cake)*
   14 tablespoons (1¾ sticks) butter, at room temperature
   5 cups confectioners' sugar, sifted
   ½ teaspoon salt
   5 tablespoons heavy cream or whole milk
   1 tablespoon vanilla extract

Equipment
   Medium bowl
   Sifter
   Hand-held electric mixer

1. In a medium bowl, using a hand-held electric mixer set at high speed, beat the butter until light and fluffy, about 2 to 3 minutes. With the mixer running, gradually add 4 cups of the sifted sugar, ½ cup at a time, until it is fully incorporated. Add the salt, cream or milk, and vanilla, and continue beating until well combined.

2. Gradually beat in the remaining 1 cup sugar a few tablespoons at a time, until the frosting is smooth and spreadable. (You may not need to use all the sugar.)

Frosting the Cake

1. Cut a circle slightly smaller than the cake out of heavy cardboard. Place the circle on a cake stand or a flat surface.

2. If your cake layers are rounded on top, cut off the rounded portion by holding a serrated knife parallel to the work surface and gently sawing through the cake to make it flat.

3. Place 1 of the cake layers on the cardboard. Spread the frosting over the top of the first layer with a rubber spatula or a long-bladed metal spatula.

4. Place the second layer on top of the frosting and press down very gently so that the cakes are as even as possible. Frost the top of the second cake.

5. Place the third layer neatly on top of the second layer, then frost the top. Once the top is frosted, begin working around the sides, applying the frosting in short, circular strokes. Always be gentle with the cake, especially around the sides.

6. After the cake is frosted, it should be refrigerated. Use a cake box from your local bakery or a plastic cake saver. Or make a tent out of aluminum foil using toothpicks; insert them into the cake to keep the foil from touching the top or sides of the cake. You may have to touch up the frosting in some places before serving.

INDEX